AWAKENING
MEET THE WOMEN BIRTHING A NEW EARTH

PUBLISHING

Copyright © 2020 AMA Publishing

All Rights Reserved. Apart from any fair dealing for the purposes of research or private study, or criticism or review, as permitted under the Copyright, Designs and Patents Act 1988, this publication may only be reproduced, stored or transmitted, in any form or by any means, with the prior permission in writing of the copyright owner, or in the case of the reprographic reproduction in accordance with the terms of licensees issued by the Copyright Licensing Agency. Enquiries concerning reproduction outside those terms should be sent to the publisher.

CONTENTS

Introduction	vii
1. Abigail Mensah-Bonsu *DNA Activation: Divine Technology for Humanity's Awakening*	1
About the Author	12
2. Bridget Aileen Sicsko *Sovereignty - Reclaiming Your Personal Power*	13
About the Author	20
3. Cenly Wong *Preparing Students for the New Earth*	21
About the Author	28
4. Chanel Morales *Starting Your Own Online Business*	29
About the Author	41
5. Charlotte Björndotter *Sacred Connections with Nature & Animals*	43
About the Author	51
6. Diana Beaulieu *Awaken Your Womb Wisdom*	53
About the Author	61
7. Dominique Oyston *Connecting to Your Goddess Voice*	63
About the Author	73
8. Eleonor Amora Marklund *The New Generation of Children: Their Frequencies, Traits, & How to Avoid Toxins*	75
About the Author	83
9. Ellen Sirena *Money, A Divine Spiritual Blessing*	85
About the Author	92
10. Emma Turton *Heal from Within: How to Hear the Whispers of Your Soul & Become Your Own Medical Intuitive*	93
About the Author	102
11. Gabriela Brunner *Shifting Out of "Hustle" into Allowing & Flow Through Conscious Connection*	103

About the Author	111
12. Helen Martineau	113
Mary Magdalene: The Female Christ Initiate	
About the Author	122
13. Hollis Citron	123
Creativity & Empowering Experiences	
About the Author	131
14. Jacqstar Davies	133
The Art of Sacred Success	
About the Author	143
15. Jem Minor	145
Daoist Sacred Embodiment Practices to Heal the Nervous System	
About the Author	156
16. Julia Chai	157
How Qigong & Interdimensional Work Can Help Us Move Forward	
About the Author	165
17. Kavita Arora	167
Quantum Prosperity & Productivity During Tough Times	
About the Author	178
18. Kayleigh O'Keefe	179
Soul Excellence Leadership - A New Paradigm for High-Performing Female Leaders	
About the Author	187
19. Krystal Alexander-Hille	189
Expanding into Galactic Embodiment	
About the Author	199
20. LaChelle Amos	201
Journey to the Heart Wisdom Leader: Conflict Resolution in a New World	
About the Author	210
21. Leigh Jane Woodgate	211
The Rise of Divine Feminine Leadership & Sustainable Business Growth	
About the Author	220
22. Leonie Laukkanen	221
Overcoming Fear & Returning to Wholeness	
About the Author	230
23. Lindsay Crowther	231
The Chakra System: Your Energetic Roadmap to Worth & Wellness	
About the Author	240
24. Lisa Farrington	241
Pinterest Marketing	
About the Author	249

25. Mary Gooden — 251
Discovering Your Soul's Purpose Through Yoga, Meditation & Reiki

About the Author — 260

26. Michelle Aspinwall — 261
Fasting Over 40 for Beauty, Vitality & Longevity

About the Author — 268

27. Natalie Anne Murray — 269
Creating Authentic, Deep & Meaningful Relationships

About the Author — 277

28. Peta Panos — 279
The Art of Ascension Alchemy – Finding Your Way Back into the Light of Love

About the Author — 288

29. Rache Moore — 289
Elemental Alchemy & Intuitive Wisdom

About the Author — 299

30. Sandra Suarez Dominguez — 301
Soul Journeys: Deepen the Connection to Your Luminous Inner Wisdom

About the Author — 308

31. Sarah-Jane Perman — 309
Reclaiming Your Sovereign Feminine Power

About the Author — 317

32. Sasha Moss — 319
The Invitation: to Reconnect, Remember & Shine

About the Author — 326

33. Saskia Esslinger — 327
Grow Your Own Food

About the Author — 335

34. Sierra Melcher — 337
Conscious Parenting: Profound Implications from Micro-shifts & Micro-adjustments

About the Author — 346

35. Tamala Ridge — 347
The Sacred Art of Detoxing

About the Author — 355

36. Tarsh Ashwin — 357
Selling Your Soul Work In The New Earth Economy

About the Author — 364

37. About AMA Publishing — 365
& Adriana Monique Alvarez

INTRODUCTION

This book called to me in the early morning and when I heard the title I felt nervous to put the word out. I didn't know if we were ready.

The world had changed and no one knew what was around the corner. Then a couple days later I remembered that the outer world can rule the inner world or the inner world can inform the outer.

I was unwilling to sit on guidance because of what was happening in the world. I was ready to recognize that beyond change, chaos, and fear, was the shift that we had yearned for.

The Great Awakening was upon us.

The word 'awakened' has made its way into the urban dictionary and it's defined as "spiritually aware of the universe and its direct metaphysical connection to one's own being and the connection it has to all life forces."

What exactly is a spiritual awakening?

Some say it's when we can both maintain separation and connection to all that is. Becoming the observer is one thing, asking who is observing is another.

It's a time for us all to re-evaluate, re-invent, and re-assess what our truest expression is now.

The skills that were most valued in the past are fading away and we are seeing a return to the Mother, the Earth, to our roots and our hearts.

INTRODUCTION

Humanity is evolving before our eyes. May the words in this book ignite your gifts and speak to your soul.

The old is falling away, the new is rising.

What are you ready to give birth to?

* * *

While most feel lost and afraid, there are some who thrive in the dark.

The deep end and the mysteries intrigue visionaries, often described as ahead of their time. They can see in the dark and navigate deep waters.

Able, ready and willing to release the old, the past, that which no longer serves us to take a hold of what's on the leading edge -- that's a VISIONARY!

* * *

Everything in our lives has prepared us for this moment.
- Adriana Monique Alvarez

ABIGAIL MENSAH-BONSU

DNA ACTIVATION: DIVINE TECHNOLOGY FOR HUMANITY'S AWAKENING

Humanity is Divinity. Being human is divine. Through our incarnation, we forgot this sacred truth. It is now time to remember.

A long time ago, there were those chosen to receive light activations that awakened their dormant, divine genome. These chosen ones came from wealth and power. They were the sons of kings, high priests, and leaders.

Few women were chosen to study in the mystery schools. The mystery school is an ancient school where those chosen get initiated in the gnostic and esoteric teachings. They studied and got initiated in topics such as Alchemy, Sacred Geometry, Kabbalah, sacred rituals, energy healing and so much more. The most important of all the initiations was the DNA Activations.

This was because DNA activation awoke and activated one's divine blueprint and heightened their connection with their Higher Self and divinity. It was important for each student or initiate to get as many Activations as possible because it helped them to receive, implement, and embody these higher-level teachings. DNA Activations were not accessible to the public.

Now, because humanity and the earth are rising in frequency and light and awakening at an increasing speed, this powerful technique is now accessible to each person on this earth who is ready to awaken to their magnificence and their multidimensionality, and embody the highest versions of themselves. This is what I'm here to talk to you about. But first, a little about myself and my journey.

WHO AM I?

For the longest time, I walked on this earth without being fully in my physical body. The truth was that I didn't want to be here. I was so angry at the divine for letting me incarnate into this life, as if the divine made me. Born as a spirit child, I was deeply connected to the spirit realm and barely rooted in the physical realm. Growing up, my world consisted of angels, archangels, the goddesses, divine mothers, and ascended masters. All my clairvoyant senses were activated; my intuition was on point, but I had no one to guide me. I felt for the longest time that I was a grown woman in a little girl's body. It was no surprise that my friends were much older than me.

I had this deep grief within me such that, regardless of what joy surrounded me, I felt cold and alone inside. People loved to be around me and they would tell me that it was because of my smile and how great they felt in my presence. On the outside, it looked like I was the happiest person on earth and everything was going well for me. On the inside, I was alone and lost, and didn't want to be on earth.

The deep grief and loneliness got so bad that after a car accident and a concussion, in which the doctor told my boyfriend at that time to wake me up every couple of hours, I felt myself sinking deep, as if I was leaving my body. I hoped my boyfriend would forget to wake me up so I could just leave. Of course, he woke me up just in time for me to return to my body. This was not the first time I tried to leave. I remember at a young age, probably around 11 or 12 years of age, I had these concurrent dreams where it was judgment day and the heavens opened up. There was a long line to the gates of heaven.

Standing at the gate was Jesus and the Angels. I was so excited to finally get to go home that I ran past everyone to the entrance. There, I was stopped by the Ascended master, Jesus, who said to me, "It's not your time yet. You got a lot to do." I was so upset I couldn't go in. He then said, "You've got work to do. Go back." One of the Angels escorted me back and I woke up. That wasn't the only time I have had this dream. I had it two more times before it stopped, each time being turned away. Through soul work, I remembered and came to understand why I didn't want to be here on this planet.

My awakening journey began when I noticed my outside world did not reflect my inner world. I was tired of not being able to enjoy my life. I decided if I couldn't go back home, then I wanted to LIVE. I wanted to Live my best life ever. From that moment onward, I began to draw in spiritual teachers and mentors who mentored me to heal, awaken, and remember who I am and what I'm here to do.

MY SPIRITUAL AND PHYSICAL TRAINING

I studied in a modern-day mystery school, where I walked the spiritual paths and was initiated into the Spiritual Alchemy, Kabbala, Ritual Mastery, Shamanism and High Priestesshood. On top of that, I was also initiated as a Healer and Teacher. One of the main requirements for these initiations was to get regular DNA Activations.

The more we were activated, the more light we embodied and the easier it was for us to receive the sacred teachings and use it to transform ourselves and our lives. Being an initiate at the mystery school opened me up to the truth of who I am. I went there to remember the truth of who I am, which is a spiritual, multidimensional being of Love always connected to the divine.

In College, I studied Psychology and Pre-Medicine. I always dreamt of becoming a doctor. I was fascinated, and still am, with the human mind and body. I then got my Masters of Science in Acupuncture and Chinese Herbal medicine. I wanted a path that gave me the freedom to channel and use my divine gifts to guide others. I knew deep down that my path would require me to combine all the tools, initiations, and soul gifts from the many past lives I've lived to serve humanity in a big way.

Now here I am, a Divine Embodiment Coach, a Leader, a Divine Feminine Activator and a Multidimensional Healer, creatrix of the Moon Goddess Circles and Moon Goddess Academy, helping women and sometimes men cultivate their inner world so they can create their soul-aligned life with ease through coaching, quantum energy healing, DNA Activations, clearing, meditations, etc.

I combine all the teachings, initiations, and degrees I have received to help you return to your wholeness by bridging the physical, mental, emotional, and spiritual gap, bringing your physicality back to its original balance and divine radiance and reconnecting you to your higher Selves and expression.

I now Awaken and Empower my clients to their power center, their womb, and teach them how to live a passionate, empowered, juicy life. I help facilitate powerful transformations in my clients by helping them move from fear, disempowerment, disconnection, and confusion so they can experience clarity of vision and mission, motivated, empowered, and living a life where they really can have it ALL. I inspire, activate, and empower my clients to step into their power to create the life they desire with ease and grace.

I am a woman of many tools and this gives me the ability to Activate, Awaken, Uplift, Heal, and Empower you on all levels of wholeness: physically, emotionally, mentally, and spiritually. I absolutely love what I do and how I serve. It is literally out of this world.

* * *

Getting a DNA Activation is like turning the lights on in a dark, forgotten room.

* * *

WHAT IS DNA ACTIVATION?

A DNA Activation is a light Activation. It is the process of channeling the highest frequency of divine light to awaken the dormant divine strand of your DNA. We begin with a 2 DNA helixes and each strand has 12 codons. As we evolve and get activated, more strands show up. Your highest potential lies in the activation of the 12 codons of your DNA. It is said that we have only tapped into a small portion of our potential because most of the codons of our DNA are still dormant.

We know of the two strands, the physical and the spiritual strands, As Above, So Below.

Scientists have discovered what the physical DNA strand is comprised of and what each codon represents, but they are still discovering what the spiritual strand, also known as junk DNA, is all about. Scientists now know that what they thought was junk, is actually not junk at all, and much more than they can comprehend.

In the physical strand, there are codons expressed as our hair color, eye color, how tall we are, the shape of our face, etc. Your physical DNA strand tells you what makes you unique, physically.

The same goes for our spiritual DNA. Each codon also has an expression. Your spiritual DNA strand tells you what makes you unique, spiritually and divinely.

THE 12 CODONS OF OUR SPIRITUAL DNA STRAND AND WHAT THEY ARE EXPRESSED AS

Have you ever heard someone say that they are connected to a certain Archangel or ascended master?

Have you ever wondered where your soul came from?

Have you wondered what your service to humanity is and what you are here on this planet to do?

Within these 12 codons lies the answers to the above questions and so much more. You were created to be extraordinary and nothing less and I'm going to show you just how extraordinary you are. There is so much more to you than you realize and let's see exactly how much.

The 12th codon of your Spiritual DNA represents *your Oneness with God/Divine.* When this codon is activated, you can truly understand what it means to be one with everything. You come to realize that you were never separated from the divine. You are always connected.

The 11th codon represents your *Archangelic lineage.* Yes, we are connected to an Archangel. This is where we get our Angelic wings. When this codon is activated, you open up the gateway to your angelic gifts and powers, which we use to serve humanity.

Our Archangelic Lineage is about our Service to humanity.

The 10th codon represents your connection to a *Master of Light.* A master of light or an Ascended Master is a spiritual mentor who has chosen to mentor you in this lifetime. When this codon is activated, you open up to receive the guidance and wisdom from your Master Mentor, whether it is Mother Mary, Mary Magdalene, Master Jesus, St. Germain of the violet flame, etc.

You were never meant to walk this path and try to figure this life out by yourself. We always had divine intervention, if we only know to ask and connect.

The 9th codon represents your connection to your *Group Soul or Soul Family.* For those of you looking for your soul family, this is it. When this codon is activated, you begin to draw to you your soul family, not just physically but also spiritually.

The 8th codon represents your *Individual Soul Expression.* This is how your soul wants to think and feel as well as your financial independence.

THERE ARE 4 main soul types:

The Om Souls - These are the Earth Souls types and they represent the physical embodiment of God/Divine.

The Andromeda Souls - These are the Water souls and they represent the heart and Love of God/Divine.

The Zephyrs - These are the Air Souls and they represent the Mind of God/Divine.

And the Ras - These are the Fire souls and they represent the Spirit of God/Divine.

Knowing your soul type tells you how you *Create* and how you *Connect* to God/Divine.

Your 7th codon represents your connection to your *Spiritual monads.* Are you an Earth seed or Star seed? Which star is your soul from? The answers come from this codon activated.

The 6th codon represents your connection to your *Higher Self.* I cannot stress enough how important this codon is, especially at the time of great awakening and transformation. Anything that comes down from the spiritual realm comes through your Higher Self.

When you channel, you channel through your Higher Self. Everything from the spiritual realm, filters through your Higher Self. Your Higher Self connects straight into the Divine/Source light. And the Higher Self has its own technology that empowers, uplifts, and protects you.

These technologies are especially for these times we are in. These technologies include your *Light Body, Your Angelic Wings* and your *Golden Dragon Body.* Your Higher Self oversees the activation of these three powerful layers of your consciousness. If you've had a hard time connecting to your Higher Self or the spiritual realm, it's time for an activation.

The 5th codon activates the wisdom of your *Archetypes and your Wheel of Life.* We all have 12 main archetypes that represent who we are on all levels. I know there are so many archetype systems out there. In this case, I'm talking about the soul archetypes. Imagine a golden wheel spinning around you and within this wheel are the 12 aspects of you. Want to know who you truly are expressed in this physicality? This codon needs to be activated.

The 4th through the 1st codons are connected to your elemental bodies.

The 4th codon activates the element of *Fire*, representing our spirit and connection to the divine.

The 3rd codon activates the element of *Air*, representing our higher minds and thoughts.

The 2nd codon activates the element of *Water*, representing our emotions.

The 1st codon activates the element of *Earth*, representing our bodies, physical reality, and roots.

Did you notice how I began from the 12th codon instead of the 1st? That is because the 12th codon is the highest in energy and frequency and the closest to your divine self. Light flows down from the 12th codon to the 1st.

The 1st codon is usually deactivated or barely has any light within it and that's because it is the densest and closest to the physical plane. Activating your DNA brings light into all 12 codons of your spiritual DNA strand, which then pours into your physical DNA and finally activates a 3rd strand of your DNA.

We are Multidimensional beings after all.

I remember my first DNA activation; it was like I could breathe again. That night, I had the best sleep ever. My dreams were so vivid and clear, as were my meditations. It was as if the whole world lit up. Everything was physically brighter. I felt a deep sense of peace and connected to something bigger.

The second DNA activation, I felt a deep sense of clarity in all my senses. It was like I was experiencing everything for the first time. The third Activation left me buzzing. I felt like I was hovering above the ground. I felt uplifted and looked at things from a higher perspective. By the 12th activation, everything changed. I felt like a new person. I lost weight with ease. I felt grounded in my body and my connection with the divine strengthened, clarified, and blossomed.

New soul gifts opened up and I was blown away. My connection with the Angels got stronger. My connection with my beloved twin flame became clear and stronger. I stepped into my power and was no longer afraid of my power. This was about 7 years ago, and since then, I've had many activations to support me in my life, business, and my service to humanity.

SO WHY DO I BELIEVE EVERYONE SHOULD GET THEIR DNA ACTIVATED?

I believe there is so much more to you than you realize. I believe we are all multidimensional beings, spirit in physical bodies here to have certain experiences and have the best life. I believe we all came in with certain gifts and super powers to help us create the life we desire and be of service to humanity and the planet. I believe we also called in amazing spiritual teachers and mentors to guide us through our lives and help us remember what we have forgotten. A DNA Activation gives you access to all of that wisdom and divine connections that you are meant to have.

Most people who've never had their DNA activated usually think of it as a spiritual, woo-woo stuff that has no physical proof. Then they get activated and everything shifts and aligns within them, in their lives and in their businesses. Everyone experiences something different after getting activated, but here are some common benefits:

- Discovering your latent talents and soul gifts.
- Detoxing your mind, body, and emotions.
- Gaining clarity in your life.
- Discovering your purpose, soul mission, and why you are here.
- Activating your psychic powers.
- Increasing self-confidence and feeling empowered.
- Reducing stress and anxiety.
- Healing old emotional wounds.
- Moving through blocks and resistance easily.

Think of a DNA Activation as getting a huge dose of light in your body, mind, heart, and spirit that spreads through all areas of your life. It is powerful, potent, transformative, and life changing. One of the cool things I ask my clients to do before they receive an activation is to take a before pic and then afterwards take another pic. There is a physical radiance that shows up. That's one of the first physical results. DNA activation is an epic modality to share with humanity to aid in its awakening, ascension, and empowerment.

A LIGHT ACTIVATION EXPERIENCE

I would like to take you through an experience of a light blessing and activation. It is not a full DNA activation, but it will certainly get things moving in the right direction. To experience a full DNA activation, check out my Ignite Your Cosmos program on my website.

Find a comfortable space where you will not be disturbed.

Close your eyes and take in a deep breath.

As you inhale, imagine a pillar of light coming down from above. Allow this light to enter through your crown and down through your head, neck, arms, and chest. When it reaches your heart, see the light anchor there, igniting your heart's threefold flame. Allow the light to continue down to your stomach, infusing every organ and cell within you with divine light. It now continues down your legs and out through your feet, entering into mother earth, going deep to the center of the earth as it roots down securely.

Now bring your awareness to your head, see, sense or feel a ball of light representing your mind. Allow this ball of light to drop down into your heart space.

Inhale!

And Exhale!

Now repeat after me:

I now call upon my Higher Self and my holy spirit self within me.

I call upon the divine light to flow through every part of my mind, body, and spirit to lift me up.

I now call upon my Divine Christ light to surround me in all directions.

I call upon the gatekeepers of the North, South, East, and West to create a sacred circle around me.

I welcome the central sun of my own divine consciousness, radiating out from the center of my being, growing and expanding within and all around me.

Inhale and exhale.

I now call upon my Angels, Archangels, guides, and Ascended masters of light to join me as I prepare to receive an influx of divine source light from the 7th dimension to raise and upgrade my consciousness, my energy field, my body, and my life.

I now call upon Archangel Metatron to clean, clear, and Align all 7 of my chakras so I may receive as much light from this activation.

Imagine, see, sense, or feel a huge ball of golden light right above your head. This is pure divine source light. See this ball begin to open up and pour down upon you. Open up completely and receive this light. See this light flow down your spine, igniting your spinal cord and nerves and flowing outward. Every cell within you opens up to drink up this divine light. Light flowing into your body filling every part of it.

This divine light now fills up your heart until your light grows and expands, radiating in every direction around you.

Imagine, see, sense, or feel that you are now standing in a bubble of golden light, glowing in this divine light that is radiating from within and out. This bubble surrounding you is programmed to magnetize to you all that is for your highest good while repelling anything that is not in this high frequency of divine love.

Breathe!
Inhaling and exhaling.

Now repeat after me:
    I now call upon my highest potential and greatest success to unfold in my life.
    I bless my life, my body, my mind, and my heart.
    With divine light, I cast out all darkness.
    May I be invisible to my enemies.
    I welcome all divine interventions and blessings that I am here to receive.
    I trust and know that my divinity is always guiding me in all ways.
    I surrender into divine will.
    Good always finds me with ease and grace.
    I am always in the right place at the right time.
    So be it and so it is.
    It is done.

May this light activation light you up to receive even more light. This is just a little taste of what it's like to work with the light. A DNA activation takes it to a whole different level. If you are ready to transform your life, your mind, and your body, then a DNA activation is for you.

I've always believed that there is so much more to you and it is in times like this that brings out the truth of who you really are. There is a power within you, a presence that wants to come out and play. This part of yourself is limitless.

It is time to connect and step into your Sovereign Divinity and service to humanity.

Your magic is needed.

It is time to rise up and embody your divine radiance.

You are magic.

You are Divinity in a human body.

You are magnificent.

You are Amazing!

We are all cheering for you.

ABOUT THE AUTHOR

Abigail Mensah-Bonsu is a Divine Embodiment Coach, a Leader, a Divine Feminine Activator, and a Multidimensional Healer. She is the creatrix of the Moon Goddess Circles and Moon Goddess Academy and a #1 International Bestseller for her co-authored books Empire Moms and Voices of the Avalonian Priestesses.

Abigail helps women, and sometimes men, cultivate their inner world so they can create their soul-aligned life with ease through coaching, quantum energy healing, DNA Activations, clearing, meditations, etc.

She helps facilitate powerful transformation in her clients by helping them move from fear, disempowerment, disconnection, and confusion to experiencing clarity of vision and mission, motivated, empowered, and living a life where they really can have it ALL. She inspires, activates, and empowers you to step into your power to create the life you desire with ease and grace.

> **Website:** www.moongoddessacademy.com
> **Youtube:** www.youtube.com/user/amensahb01
> **Instagram:** www.instagram.com/intuitivegoddesscoach
> **Facebook:** www.facebook.com/groups/1891328034484414
> and www.facebook.com/ShaktiMoonGoddess
> **Books:** https://www.amazon.com/dp/1734973005
> and https://kdp.amazon.com/amazon-dp-action/us/dualbookshelf.marketplacelink/B087C9L27Y
> **Subscribe:** www.anchor.fm/s/1dea2fb4/podcast/rss

BRIDGET AILEEN SICSKO

SOVEREIGNTY - RECLAIMING YOUR PERSONAL POWER

My intention for this journey together is to provide an experience of remembrance, to create a deep sense of purpose, to let you know you are loved, and to give you the permission to be yourself.

These words will serve as the reminder you need, the nudge you've been ignoring, and the deepest soul reconnection experience. These words are beyond words - they are infused with love to activate the dormant potential within you.

I invite you to sink into deep inner awareness. Allow the words to be more of a transmission than something you need to logically wrap your head around.

Deep breath in.
Deep breath out.
Deep breath in.
Deep breath out.
Deep breath in.
Deep breath out.

YOU ARE a vessel of light and love.
You deserve to feel good.
You are worthy of living a life of your dreams.

You are capable of creating a life that honors the true you.

Welcome home.

I'm Bridget, your guide for this journey over the next few pages. For most of my years, the aforementioned words didn't always feel like "truth" to me.

I lived most of my life trying to impress other people, not sure of my connection to any Divine source, and I never fully felt my ability to step into something great.

After a deep awakening experience prompted by an illness at a young age, I began to question my existence and ask the deeper questions like "Why are we here?", "What am I here to do?", and most importantly "Who am I"?

Those answers didn't come in a quick flash of light. The more I deepened my spiritual practices, the more portals opened up. I began to feel the deepest sense of innate self- worth. I started connecting to my intuitive abilities by realizing I am powerful and that happiness + freedom are my birthright.

I'm not here to tell you what to do or how to live; I'm here to provide you with an experience that you can't deny. I want you to feel your innate *worth*, your inborn *sovereignty*, and give you the tools to step up into the person you have the right to be. The person who feels strong, powerful, heart-centered, driven, and knows they are here to make an impact on humanity.

As I mentioned before, I intend for these words to feel far greater and more meaningful than just words. I work as a channel and a messenger for the divine.

So to be transparent and help you feel into this experience, I will ask for guidance.

* * *

"Masters, teachers, and loved ones of the highest realms and all else who help me on the Earthly Journey, I call upon you now. Please speak through me. Please use my hands and fingers as instruments for change. Please allow my words to serve as the most beautiful transmission and remembrance for all who read these pages. Thank you. And so it is."

* * *

SOVEREIGNTY

"The privilege of a lifetime is being who you are" - Joseph Campbell.

WHAT A GIFT. You get to be yourself here. Let's remember the beginning.

When you came onto Earth, you were born in wholeness, as a spark of the Divine. You were deeply connected to your spiritual gifts and you only knew love. But as the journey of life continued, fear, judgement, worry, and anger, started to replace your inborn state of love. Societal pressures, educational demands, and ancestral narratives replaced the remembrance of your wholeness, your inborn sovereignty.

In this human experience we have the ability to feel the entire spectrum of human emotions, thoughts, and feelings. So to feel "frustrated" or "angry" isn't bad or good, it's simply just an experience.

However, many times we forget the truth of who we really are. We allow life to get in the way of our remembering experience. I want to remind you that it is SAFE to be yourself, it is safe to feel your emotions and journey back to love.

"Love is what we are born with. Fear is what we learn. The spiritual journey is the unlearning of fear and prejudices and the acceptance of love back in our hearts. Love is the essential reality and our purpose on earth. To be consciously aware of it, to experience love in ourselves and others, is the meaning of life. Meaning does not lie in things. Meaning lies in us." - Marianne Williamson

SOVEREIGNTY IS DEFINED AS: *supreme power or authority* and for the intention of this chapter, we will look at sovereignty as connecting with your personal power. You are reading these words for a reason, because you are ready to enter the portal of deeper connectedness to yourself and your purpose here on Earth.

RADICAL RESPONSIBILITY

"If you can take radical responsibility for one thing this year, let it be your vibration, your alignment, your energy. You cannot out do, out work or out skill the instruction your energy is giving to your life." - Peta Kelly, Earth is Hiring

THE RESPONSIBILITY we are talking about here is more than the chores you were encouraged to do as a child. This type of responsibility is radical, meaning it will change your life. When you begin to take radical responsibility for your life, you step into the driver's seat — hands on the wheel, wind blowing through your hair. You are the navigator. You decide the path.

This type of responsibility for your thought loops, words, and actions actually gets to feel good because you know that it is all for the purpose of your own sovereignty. This type of responsibility says, *"I cannot control the weather, but I sure can control my reactions to the weather."*

AND THEREIN LIES POWER.

IF YOU ARE READING this now, you are making a conscious decision to remember your inherent worth; the power that has always been there.

In taking radical responsibility for your life, you are choosing to consciously release the blame game for once and for all. You are choosing to not be victimized by your environment because you are here to reclaim your life and step into an energy of living at your highest potential.

You might have experienced moments in your life where you "gave away your power," maybe in a conversation, at a job, or in your relationships. You might have allowed someone else's view of reality to become your truth. You lost your course and moved away from your own values and needs. You might have seen fear-based thought patterns creep in or feelings of judgement, anger, worry, and frustration surface.

Elizabeth Gilbert's book, *Big Magic*, talks beautifully about this concept and its relation to fear. She invites us to place fear in the passenger's seat and place our hands on the wheel. That way, we can tune into our sovereignty, knowing fear will probably peek its head in from time to time but that, at the end of the day, we have our hands on the wheel.

Now, if you are feeling that your hands aren't on the wheel, do not fret.

I INVITE you to ask yourself:

- Who have I given my power to? (Is it a relationship, a job, a role?)
- Why do I want to reclaim my power and step into the driver's seat of my life?
- How can I realign with the sovereign being I am?

SIT WITH THOSE ANSWERS. This is a place to simply be curious and inquisitive about how you have been living your life.

Step back to a place of alignment; that is where true sovereignty lies. Release all the narratives that have held you back from the truest expression of you and embrace the infinite expanse of your true vibration, the vibration in alignment with your soul.

STAY TRUE TO YOU

As a sovereign leader of your own life, it is imperative that you stay true to yourself. As my teacher Guru Jagat says, "Hold the nucleus of your mission." Respect others' opinions and how they see the world, but don't let others sway your nucleus; aka stay centered, grounded in your truth.

A leader believes whole-heartedly in their mission. Think of this like your foundation. When you build a rock-solid foundation, you're going to need a lot more than just the wind to blow you off course.

Build your home or your life from the ground up. A sovereign leader knows that their life requires a foundation that is steady, stable, and unwavering. From that foundation, this leader builds their life to reflect the values that are deeply rooted in the foundation. Stay true to your values. Identify what matters to you in this Earthly journey and remain steady. Hold your ground.

Along the journey, you will come across people who don't share your beliefs, your values, and possibly even your morals. The beauty in this world is that we all have different opinions and different ways of seeing our lives.

The intention is to honor all the opinions as you do not need to spend your time or energy convincing others to believe your core truths. Instead, allow yourself to see others as simply other souls navigating through their life as best as they can. Honor their opinions and just stay true to your own values.

When you are stepping up into your personal power and becoming a sovereign leader, you are able to see others from a soul perspective. You know that this is all a part of their journey and you are able to see them in their innocence. Remember your true North, stay rooted in your foundation, and honor all those along your journey.

THE TIME IS NOW

It is time. It is time. It is time.

THESE TIMES CALL for more leaders. Not just the presidents, the CEOs, the diplomats, but everyday leaders who are ready to reclaim their sovereignty and live a life of authenticity and full-body alignment.

You are a leader. We are all leaders. You get to be the leader of your own life if you choose to do so. The times are opening a portal for this to be even more possible than ever. You are here for a very important reason and it is time for you to step into your personal power, to be the leader of your life and live a life of soul sovereignty - where you are free to be yourself and you feel empowered through your words, actions, choices, and relationships. This is the time to step up.

Get clear on who you are. Get clear on your values. Get clear on the risks of NOT stepping up into the person you were born to be. You are a leader and the time is now.

I invite you to use this mantra, *"I choose to be the person I was born to be."* A mantra is a tool or a vehicle for the mind to aid in concentration or meditation. All of our words are truly mantras. Mantras have the ability to reprogram the subconscious mind through the use of *jappa*, or repetition. Choose your words.

The time is now. It is time. Who are you? Who are you choosing to be? What are you choosing to do with your life? You are a leader. You are the dreamer of your dream as Gabby Bernstein likes to say.

SOVEREIGNTY IS YOUR BIRTHRIGHT.

EMERGE

I invite you to remember how we began this journey. We began with remembering your truest essence.

Remember, these words weren't all about the words. They were about the intention behind them and the message, feeling, and experience beyond the words. Even if you feel that you don't have all your i's dotted and your t's crossed, these words were able to leave an imprint on our soul. You were ready to receive them.

I invite you to place your hands on your heart and simply be with yourself for the next few moments. Remember the simplicity of your human experience. Remember what sovereignty means to you. Remember your truest essence. Get ready to DECLARE your existence and who you are becoming.

Breathe in, breathe out.
And so it is.
With love,
Bridget Aileen

ABOUT THE AUTHOR

Bridget Aileen Sicsko is a visionary, multi-dimensional leader, yoga teacher and creator of The Soulful Essence Experience, her heart-centered coaching program. She activates women to reclaim their power and remember the potential within. Her magic is in breaking down spiritual, mystical and energetic principles into bite size nuggets of wisdom.

She weaves energetic mastery, yogic practices + teachings, mindset tools and quantum mechanics to create epic soul transformations. Bridget has studied at the Lilypod School for Yoga and Ayurveda in Ibiza, Spain, the Institute of Integrative Nutrition and is certified in Kundalini, Restorative & Yin Yoga as well as Sound Healing + Metaphysics. In her spare time, she enjoys gardening, hiking, doing obstacle course races with her husband, Eric, and spending time with her dog, Finn.

Take a peek into her world: www.bridgetaileen.com
Join her luminary leadership society sisterhood: www.facebook.com/groups/LuminaryLS
Email her: Iamblissfulbridget@gmail.com

CENLY WONG

PREPARING STUDENTS FOR THE NEW EARTH

Greetings! This is coming from the perspective of a registered school teacher in Queensland, Australia with a fair amount of experience in all kinds of different schools in the state, ranging from private to public to special schools.

Due to my background in Medical Science and having worked in the biochemistry and endocrinology areas of pathology laboratories, I am trained as a chemistry teacher, although I am also qualified to teach Humanities such as geography and history. Being a science teacher is a give-in to also teach mathematics. Having high hopes upon graduation, ready to go out and feel "the world is my oyster," my bubble was crushed by utter disappointment.

My whole journey to become a teacher in the first place was challenging for me. Inspired to start my new life as a single mum of two young boys back in 2009, I thought having a career change would be good for me, plus it is more kid-friendly, as I could leave the shift work behind and have access to a childcare centre's hours of care. I did not want to burden my ageing parents with looking after my boys.

Another reason I choose education is that I have been tutoring on and off since I was 14 and I thought that I would make a good teacher. Being a teacher would enable me to work closely with children. I do not think I have a strong enough heart to be a paediatrician. To tell the parents of a child that we did our best but we could not help their child…I do not think I would be able to do that.

Growing up, I wanted to be a doctor. I love helping and I love children. I wanted to make them better. I had not thought of the other side of the occupation. Thinking back, not having high enough marks to make it into medicine was a blessing in disguise. Even though, at that time, I was devastated because I thought it was the only path for me. I came second in my high school and, when my Dad told me to repeat Form 7 again, I said no. There was no way I was going back. I do have my pride and, very soon after, I was offered a place studying Medical Science at Queensland University of Technology.

At the time, I had no idea what medical science was, but it sounded good. I longed to move away from the nest. I am so glad I did, which in turn opened a whole wide world for me, not only the new country I moved to alone, but the world of medicine, sciences, and research.

I am very grateful for my life journey and that I didn't go down the medicine path as I watched my medical friends burning the midnight oil, working in hospitals 16-17 hours at times, sleeping in the hospitals during their internships, and now during this COVID-19 pandemic working around the clock even more so. I know that if I continue working in the medical/pathology testing industry, I would not have my four beautiful boys now. I went through SARS and the bird flu H1N5. That was enough.

My first year of relief teaching upon graduation was the toughest in my teaching career. Ask any teacher and he/she will tell you the same. It was such a learning curve for me. Relief teaching in public schools at low socio-economic regions was so different from my practicums at private schools.

There were a few schools where the teachers themselves did not treat me like their own, but rather as competition. There were schools where the teachers did acknowledge me and were fully supportive, but they were limited because they themselves were struggling with behaviour issues from their students and getting little support from school management. And my, I can tell you that what you've heard about 80% behaviour management and 20% teaching content is very true.

How schooling, culture mentality, and children rights have evolved over time.

I went to primary schooled in Malaysia (Standard 1-6) in a prestigious public school in Damansara Heights, Kuala Lumpur, where most government officials lived in the late 1980s. I remember being embarrassed by my Dad's yellow old Renault and asking him to drop me off further from the school gates, where all these Mercedes, BMW, Rolls Royce, Volvo etc. with chauffeurs dropped off students.

I did not know at the time that it was all superficial and did not matter. Society back then was very materialistic. Had I not been brought up and raised in Auckland, New Zealand where I did my secondary schooling, my mindset would possibly still be the same as others. In New Zealand, we were taught to think outside the box, that rote-learning and memorising no longer serves as much.

Then I did tertiary studies in Brisbane. Three different countries, three different schooling systems. I love learning so much that I have also studied the art of learning and retaining information. Jim Kwik is the pioneer in this field, along with Adam Khoo and his first book, *I Am Gifted, So Are You!* where he teaches you how to mind map and presents practical strategies and practices on how to study effectively. The key is not to study hard; it is to study smart.

In Asia, teachers are highly respected and are considered guardians while students are at school. Students were indoctrinated from a young age to sit down and shut up. They are expected to just absorb all the teachings. Those who are outside the norms are often made examples of.

Puan Juliah was notorious. Both my younger brother and I had her. Back then, I had an Indian friend who was constantly being hit by Puan Juliah, who used the wooden ruler and "rotan" (rooster feathers duster). Not only because she was not academically sound, but also because of her poor family background and her race.

I remember Puan Juliah calling us Chinese "Babi Hutan" (Wild Pigs) – a derogatory term used to address Chinese because Chinese people eat pork and Muslims do not. I remembered I was talking in class one minute and the next minute, I had a duster being thrown into my mouth.

My brother had it bad with her. If you did not do homework (we were expected to complete 40 maths questions every night, along with other subjects' homework) or got some wrong, you got punished in front of your classmates. Students were queued to get whacked by the wooden ruler/rotan on the hand.

The rotan was so well-used that feathers came off often and was replaced 3 or 4 times a year. My brother was not good with maths back then. He was made to stand in the sun for hours. If we were Malay, Muslims, or from well-off families, we would not have been treated that way. Hence, guess what type of family background those students who queued up to be punished had.

Outside school, hitting children was the norm. Not hitting your child(ren) was unheard of. The Malay likes to use the term "Kurang Ajar," which meant that not being properly disciplined at home = bad parents.

It was common in Asia to get your child(ren) tutored. I remember being knocked on the head by my tutor and getting my knuckles hit by a ruler because I could not tell my right and left in the mirror. Obviously, all these teachers and tutors did not take into consideration whether their mode of delivery and how they teach would be effective to help the students learn in a happy environment.

I discovered through my teaching experience and through being a mum, that children and students can only learn and retain information if they are happy and enjoy the class.

So, can you imagine how surprised I was when we moved to Auckland, New Zealand and my schooling did not involve being punished for not doing homework or getting homework incorrect.

I loved my high school years. We were taught with compassion, love, and care. I was fortunate enough to attend a school that knew my potential and wanted to push my abilities. I was able to do a level above my year in certain subjects.

A lot of schools I know now do not provide this option. I am deeply grateful for the opportunities and the faith my teachers had in me. By the time I graduated, I had completed many subjects compared to my peers.

I knew that only being academic was not the way to go, so I made sure to fully immerse myself in what my school offered. I was involved in sports (soccer and hockey), music (orchestra and string ensemble), and culture (Chinese dance group, Asian committee, and the Duke of Edinburgh Award).

I was honoured to be the first in the school's history to hold two executive positions in my final year of high school, when I was the head librarian, and the only Asian ever to become the Multicultural Executive. I helped to plan and run the annual school Multifest.

That is how I knew how to greet people in several Pacific Islands' languages and Maori, of course. The look on their faces was priceless when I greeted them in their home languages. This is how I connect with my Islanders and Maori students.

During the two years in intermediate school (Form 1-2) and prior to going to high school (Form 3-7), I had the opportunity to become a deaf buddy to assist the hearing-impaired students in my class. This is where I learnt Australasian Sign Language, finger type, and lip-reading.

Decades later, I completed a short course of Level I and II Auslan. My exposure and empathy in this has enabled me to work in schools as learning support, in the Special Education Units and in a Special School.

Upon interviewing to further my teaching career, I was given a choice to either be in the mainstream classes or to teach special needs students, and I choose special needs students in a heartbeat. I love their honesty, rawness, and authenticity.

I had learnt to distinguish if the particular student was masking his/her abilities intentionally so he/she could do easier work or to get out of doing work completely. I do not allow their disabilities to be an excuse in regards to what they are able to achieve.

I can also say that with the mainstream students. However, they had no similar excuse for their bad behaviour.

Teaching Aussie students is tough. Australia is a country where children's rights are greatly observed; there is no way we could teach like I was taught back in my primary school days. I would have been arrested and jailed!

Students were not taught the subject of Morals from a young age like I was taught in Malaysia. We were tested on manners, applying respect, what to do in social situations, etc. Teachers were highly regarded; here…nope.

Some parents do not work with teachers; they challenged, even sue teachers. My friend, a former teacher, was stalked and tormented by the parents of her student, which resulted in her developing a mental illness and eventually she decided to leave the industry after hospitalisation.

She wrote her story and her book gave insight into what it was like for her back then. My other friend also left the industry because of the parents' high expectations (very common, teaching in private schools) and not getting enough support from the school management. Another friend quit — she'd had enough of the students' behaviour.

From the second day of my final practicum, I was so appalled at how my mentor teacher was treated. This is someone who had been teaching for decades and I could see that he was trying very hard to engage with the students, without avail.

It was heartbreaking. He said I have my work cut out for me because not only am I of short stature and of Chinese origin, but also a female. That did not stop me. I am determined and I am a fast learner. And now I am thriving as a teacher.

I would like to touch on Special Schools for the Gifted. I encountered one when my eldest was little, before he started primary school. He is 15 now. The private school was not structured: no uniforms, no timetable; it is all student-guided.

I chose not to enrol my son as I wanted him to be in a mainstream-learning environment. I wanted him to learn the social skills needed to interact with others when he is out in public, especially when he grows up.

I have tutored many, both privately and in some education centres. I could not believe how some parents put so much pressure on their child(ren) to get into "better" schools, like Queensland Academies, Brisbane State High School, and other schools that teach International Baccalaureate.

Each course is a few hundred dollars and some exams to get into these schools can be over AU$500 each time. I saw students in my class after school and weekends. One particular student re-sat the exams every quarter because his marks were not high enough. I will never do that to my boys. I would rather they have happy, healthy childhoods.

People were so surprised when I told them I do not tutor my own boys. I sometimes help them with homework when I have time, but they need to learn themselves and discover their grit and motivation to want to learn. Without that, no matter how you push, they will never stick.

Because they need to do it of their own free will. They need to want to do something for themselves. Doing it for others, especially to please your parents, is not a road I recommend.

A friend recently shared with me that only when her mum passed away did she realise for the first time in her life (she is in her early 40s) that she can do things of her own accord. Her whole life was about pleasing her mum. If you are a parent, do not ever do that to your child.

Last but not least, how can we miss out on Alternative Learning or Education. Due to the current situation of the COVID-19 pandemic, all learning has to be made available online.

There are a few drawbacks to this:

- Firstly, not every student has access to a computer or tablet and internet.
- Secondly, not all subjects can be taught virtually, especially those hands-on subjects such as VET (Vocational Education and Training) hospitality, childcare and aged care, car maintenance, etc.
- Thirdly, despite the teachers' support, ultimately parents are not teachers. They are not trained as teachers and do not have the necessary knowledge to help the students. The Queensland Education Minister said that it's

Home-based Learning or Remote Learning, not Home-Schooling, but a lot of people have married the concepts.

As a teacher in the SEU (Special Education Unit), we had to produce booklets (learning packs) with differentiated content to accommodate most of our special needs students. Most of our students with varied learning abilities are not able to be engaged solely with the internet for their learning.

We are all trying to do our best to get through this. Hopefully when this pandemic crisis is over, teachers will be appreciated more for what they do.

One thing that will benefit students, especially during this time, is introducing *Mindfulness*.

Some schools worldwide have already included it in their curriculum, as studies show a great reduction of behaviour management in classrooms. Students are calmer and staff are calmer when they are all self-aware, able to self-regulate and be in the present.

As a practising Buddhist for many years, I am an advocate to the benefits of mindfulness and strongly believe that it is very helpful, not only in schools, workplaces, and at home, but just about everywhere. It can be applied and incorporated into our daily practices, like walking meditation and mindful speech, thoughts, and actions.

I am also a Yoga Nidra facilitator, trained by the Daring to Rest Academy in the U.S., and have been offering yoga nidra in my schools since 2019.

Yoga Nidra is a yogic sleep, sleep of the yogis, which enable participants to do meditation lying down, where they can totally surrender and let go.

If you would like to try yoga nidra, feel free to contact me. My details are in my Bio.

ABOUT THE AUTHOR

Cenly Wong is a wellness advocate and soul guide who inspires others to want to be a better version of themselves at their soul level; whether that pertains to their environment, relationships, finance, health and/or wellbeing. She is a Certified Tao Hands Practitioner which enables her to give Tao Hands (Tao as in the Source/Creator. Tao Hands is very high frequency and vibrations of unique Light transmission) blessings and a Trained Yoga Nidra facilitator.

She is an international bestselling author having contributed to a book called *LEADERS – Women who change the world through their business*. She is also one of Diane McKendrick's Pixie affirmation card deck as the Pixie of Identity. She has recently launched a unique therapy called Ribbon Therapy.

Cenly has a background in Medical Science and complementary Eastern medicine such as Traditional Chinese Medicine (TCM) and the Chinese Metaphysics such as Ba Zi, Feng Shui. Currently a well-sought school teacher and a tutor, she has served children of all ages with varied abilities, especially those with special needs.

Website: www.cenlyswellnesscorner.com
Facebook: www.facebook.com/cenlyswellnesscorner
Instagram: www.instagram.com/cenlyswellnesscorner
Email: cenly@cenlyswellnesscorner.com

CHANEL MORALES

STARTING YOUR OWN ONLINE BUSINESS

The world is changing. We all know that. Changing for better or for worse, depending on who you ask. But we all agree it's changing.

In my opinion the biggest catalyst for change came on the August 6th, 1991, when the internet first became publicly available. It would be another five years before the invention of Hotmail, seven years before the invention of Google, and 13 years before the invention of Facebook. But the wheels had been set in motion for a series of events that would make the world a very different place.

The internet has given us so much. The ability to connect with people from all over the world. The ability to learn new things, see new things, and explore new places without ever leaving our homes. It has given us the ability to share music, video, photos, words, and ideas. But most importantly of all, is had given us freedom. Freedom that comes from the ability to make money from anywhere in the world, doing almost anything.

Jobs in the age of technology promised so much. We could work less because our jobs would be automated and we could spend more time on recreation. But that's not what actually happened, is it? We continued to work the exact same hours we did 50 years ago. So where is all the extra productivity going? Into the corporation's pockets of course. And we either toe the line or we don't work. Not much of a choice, is it?

I always thought it was strange that almost every job was expected to take the exact same amount of time: 8 hours a day. I also always thought it was strange that every person was expected to work these same hours regardless of their productivity or personal circumstances.

So out of interest, I decided to look into it. 200 years ago people often worked 10-16 hours, 6 days per week. This was classed as 'normal.' The working classes accepted it. People built their lives around it.

Eventually unions and people started to protest against these working hours. It was impacting the worker's health, and left no time for anything else. After a time, the 8-hour work day was born. This worked well during our industrial period when so much of the 'work' was manual labour and people were needed to physically carry out these jobs.

The idea was, 8 hours work, 8 hours recreation, and 8 hours rest. And it stuck. So almost 200 years later, we still have the same system, even though we now live in a totally different world where so many jobs are automated or done by machines and technology. All the extra time spent working must be going somewhere. And it goes to the profits of the big companies and corporations.

Think about it. You still work 8 hours per day, even though 70% of your job is now automated or done by technology or machinery. This is one of the main reasons I am such an advocate for running your own business. When you build a business based on technology or using technology, YOU get all the benefits. When the technologies evolve, YOU are the one who earns more money in your business. The idea that you NEED to work 8 hours a day to make a living is social conditioning. It's completely false. You can work for yourself. You can work less and earn more. You can spend more time doing the things you love.

Everything is possible if you can open yourself up to the amazing number of opportunities in the world. I honestly believe that one day we will all look back at the 8 hour work day the same way we look at the industrial revolution. It's not healthy. People are suffering from stress, anxiety, depression. Humans were not built to sit and do these repetitive jobs inside an office for such extensive periods of time. We were born to create, have ideas, make art and music, spend time in nature, and build relationships with one another.

There is actually much research that shows these kinds of working conditions and hours make us less productive. For those that do work we should be pushing for shorter working days, more flexibility for individuals, and better options to help relieve stress. For those who can, stepping away from the 9-5 and going it alone will give you so many more options to live life on your own terms.

Because of the internet I have more freedom than I ever could have dreamed of. Being able to earn money from anywhere in the world sometimes feels too good to be true. But it's my real life.

So if you have ever wondered how people make money online, this is the chapter for you.

I first started looking into online businesses and "make money from home" opportunities in 2016. And at the time, I was totally overwhelmed by the number of 'experts' and 'gurus' trying to sell me their thing. I knew there had to be a viable third choice to the two life choices I was being presented: Work full time and never seeing my daughter or stay home with my daughter and being broke. But no matter how long I spent looking for this mystery third option, I felt like every time I got somewhere, I would discover there was a piece of the puzzle missing or something they hadn't told me I would need to invest in.

Then of course there were the network marketing companies, selling the dream of having your own business while still selling someone else's products. And of course the outright scammer looking to make a quick buck from desperate and naive wannabe entrepreneurs.

Nothing seemed simple or straight forward. Nowhere could I find a list of options for online business that told me the skills, experience, and work required for each option. No one tried to help me figure out what I may actually be good at. Every guru just wanted to sell me their thing.

It literally took me months to filter out the genuine opportunities from the scams. Not only full blown scams, but also lots of people who were just really misleading and over-promising. Saying things like: Make 6 figures in 60 days, Copy my formula for 10k, The secret to making 5 figures online. I bounced back and forth from one idea and guru and system to the next without ever getting anywhere.

There are so many people out there who have had success and then promise to tell you their secret. They also guarantee that you can do the same, which is really strange because you aren't them and they don't know you. How could they possibly know what you would be good at or what you could become successful at, having never met or spoke to you?

After many years of research and learning, I did eventually become successful in the online business world, and that's when my life really changed. Digital products and services give you the freedom to work anywhere in the world, set your own schedule, give your family an amazing lifestyle, and make a huge impact.

Working online took me from being a broke single mum to making six figures in less than two years. I paid off debts, saved for a house, travelled the world, gave to charity, home schooled my daughter, and got her private tutors. I live a life that many people say is the life of their dreams.

At one point it was nothing but a dream to me too. I had always wanted to travel. I had always desired freedom over anything else. When I realised that I could have all of these things, when I found the right strategies to make it happen, everything fell into place.

My first online business was as a freelance social media manager. I then grew it into an agency with a team of seven based all over the world. But becoming a coach was never actually part of the plan.

After I started travelling the world and writing my blog, many women started to ask me: HOW? How was I travelling the world with no savings as a single mum? Was I receiving child support? Did I have a sugar daddy? The answer to both of those questions was and still is: No. I was working online and running my digital marketing agency as I travelled the world.

But I wanted to do more to help other women, because I knew first-hand what a minefield it was to try and work this stuff out. I knew that just one Google search could open up a whole can of worms that could take you months to work through and never get you anywhere. And that's when I decided to create my 12 step programme, The Dream Club, and launch my online coaching business.

When I became an online business coach, I decided to do things totally differently. When women ask me what kind of business they should start, the answer is always: That depends on you! I can't tell you what kind of business you should run. Not everyone will be able to implement the exact formula I used to make money online. There are far too many variables, personality and passion being just two of them. I work with women to first go deep into themselves, and then we can work on the strategy.

There are six online business models I most highly recommend, but the business itself has to come from you. I have coached women in all kinds of different businesses because, for me, it's always about discovering your passion, and creating a business that can give you the life of your dreams.

Many people don't do it this way. They do it backwards. First they create a business, then they work out how they can make it fit with their lifestyle. The best way to do it is to work out what you really want from life first. Then build a business to suit that.

But before we look at business or lifestyle, I want to talk about something else. Something that will shape your thoughts, ambitions, and ideas about business and lifestyle. Money mind-set.

From a young age we are all conditioned to believe certain things about money. We learn things from what we see, what we hear, and what we feel. And by the age of seven our subconscious beliefs are set. We have a certain expectation about how much we will earn, how we will earn it, how hard it will be to earn it, and whether or not we will be able to keep it.

When we grow up in a family where money is hard to come by and our parents spend a lot of time worrying about money, we have the subconscious belief that money is hard to get and causes stress. We have a negative money mind-set.

So when we go into the business world, what do we do? We set our expectations low, we assume it will be hard to sell and hard to find clients, and we also assume that most people, like us, cannot afford to spend much money.

It also impacts our lifestyle goals. When we grow up without much money around or in a simple, frugal home, we often set our lifestyle expectations to match what we are used to. My mother and grandmother both live in very similar houses, as did I up until recently. And that may be in part due to our mind-set of what defines home and security and success.

This is why kids that grow up on a council estate often go on to live on a council estate as adults, and kids who grow up in a luxury detached, 5-bedroom homes, often go on to live in luxury detached, 5-bedroom homes. It's simply what we expect from life. And that is what we then create.

If your parents work every day in manual jobs and go on holiday to Spain once a year, the chances are you will grow up expecting the same. But if your parents were entrepreneurial investors who worked from home and travelled the world for months at a time, you would find yourself expecting the same. So little of who we are is down to choice. As much as we like to think we are in control of our own destiny, the truth is much of it is subconscious, social conditioning.

But why is this important to an online business? Well, when we set our lifestyle goals, our business goals, our financial goals, all the things that will determine the kind of business we create and the amount of money we make, we need to check ourselves and know deep down that we are creating what we really want. Not what we expect.

Let's not set our sights too low. Let's not aim low for fear of failure, or so that we will still be loved by our family. Let's not aim low because we think everyone is as broke as us - because they aren't.

Money mind-set is an important part of online business because it helps us to understand why we find some things more challenging. We may feel terrified of charging premium prices or having sales calls.

So before you go any further, spend some time working on these questions:

- What was the money situation like for you growing up?
- Did your family struggle with money?
- Did your mum have financial responsibility or was that all left to your dad?
- What was the overall feeling about money in your house as a child?
- Did your family often say, "we can't afford that," "money is the root of all evil," "money doesn't grow on trees," and other negative things?
- Did your family say negative things about people who had money, things like "rich people are greedy."
- Can you now see how some of these experiences, thoughts, and memories could be impacting your current money situation?
- Are you repeating the same money patterns as your parents?
- Have you sabotaged your own finances to stay in line with those beliefs from your childhood?
- What did your family think about success and wealth?
- Did they make you feel it was only for certain people?
- Was there a connection made between working really hard and making money?

Once you have done the money mind-set work, we can move onto the next step. If you want to create an online business, we first need to decide what kind of life you want. We can't create the perfect business unless we understand the perfect lifestyle for you.

Let's start thinking about your dream lifestyle. What does your dream-life look like? Where are you living? What are you doing? Who are you with?

When you have a clear picture in your mind, now ask yourself, how much money do I need to earn each month to live this life, and how many hours per week do I want to work?

When was the last time you asked yourself these questions? It always surprises me how little time people spend on considering what they really want from life. Maybe some people find the question too overwhelming, or maybe they simply don't have time, as they try to keep their head above water. But it could quite possibly be the most important question there is. What do you want from life? And the second most important question should be: how can I get there?

One of the things I love most about digital products and services is that they can really help you to create whatever lifestyle you want. Say your dream is to travel the world or buy your dream home, or have multiple homes, or stay home with your kids, or create an off-grid community. Whatever it is, online business is a tool that can help you make it happen.

As much as we all hate to admit it, money makes the world go round. Money is power. Money is opportunities. As much as you might want to focus your energy on just helping people and doing good, ask yourself the question, how much more good could I do, if I had the money to back up my ideas or beliefs?

Making money means we can do anything we want. More money, more influence. And that is why showing good women how to make money is so important to me. More money in the hands of women wanting to do good things, and less money in the hands of bad men doing horrible things. And that's why I believe that if you are a good person, it is your duty to make as much money as you can and to invest and spend it on things you care about.

Now you know the life you want, it's time to look at what you love and what you are passionate about. Every business needs to be backed by passion.

What are your hobbies and interests? This does not have to be business-related, just think about all the things in life that you love.

Ask yourself these questions:

- What am I really passionate about?
- Where am I happiest?
- Who do I enjoy being around?
- Who do I aspire to be like?

- What have I been through in life that I am proud of? Could I help someone else through this?
- What am I an expert in?
- What do my friends ask me for help with?
- What do I want to be remembered for?

Think about all the things you have done in past jobs, things you have achieved, things you have been through in your life where you managed to come out the other side. Because remember, there is probably someone out there wishing they had the answers. The answers you have.

These are also questions to help you start to think about what you really want to spend your time on. What could you really dedicate yourself to? I teach women how to build online businesses the fast and easy way, but that doesn't mean it won't take some hard work. Because it will. And there is nothing worse than working hard on something you aren't even passionate about.

Every day when I wake up, I know I have calls with clients, I have specific activities that I have to do for my business, and there are very few things I really dread. Accounts is one of them, which is why it's outsourced. And sales calls used to be one of them, but now I really enjoy them!

That's why it's so important to go deep into this question about your passions. When I worked in a 9-5, I dreaded going in every single day. The last thing you want to do is create another job for yourself. Your business should always be based on something you are genuinely interested in.

Once you have some ideas in your mind, we can go back to the top six highest paying online businesses. If you want to make good money online, if you want freedom to travel, if you want to give your family the best of you rather than what is left of you at the end of the day. Then I highly recommend you choose one of these business models.

COACHING

Coaching is all about helping someone get from point A to point B. You can coach people in business, health, life and more. What have you achieved that you would like to help others achieve? This is super high paying and with low tech, which is one of the things I love so much about it. All you really need is you, wifi, your process, and zoom.

It's also very people-focused, so you need to like interacting with people. You don't need to be officially qualified, you just need to know how to help someone achieve something you have achieved or that they want to achieve. Boiling your offer down to health, wealth, or relationships means you are more likely to make sales. You should also look for the big transformations: how can you go really deep with people and impact their lives on the deepest level? Ask yourself the question: How can I solve the biggest problem in someone's life? The bigger the problem, the bigger the impact, the higher the price.

ONLINE COURSES

You can teach people anything with an online course. What have you uncovered that you are passionate about or that you know a lot about that could be turned into a course? This is a huge market; people are learning in new ways and want to learn new skills from the comfort of their own homes. Online courses are more scalable than coaching. Although, as a coach, you can charge more. With a course, you can really create one great thing and then sit back and watch it make money.

DIGITAL MARKETING AGENCY

Helping other businesses promote themselves through marketing. No marketing experience required; you can build a fully outsourced agency where your team does all the work. Do you have great team-building skills? Want something that may be hard work at the beginning but in the long term offers maximum opportunities for automation and outsourcing? If you are good with project management and people, then this is a great option for you. Everyone wants to get online, everyone needs to get their businesses into the online space, and you can be the one to help them.

CONSULTING

Helping businesses to improve or taking over aspects of a business for a limited time. Do you already work in a professional job that could be transferred over to consultancy? What problems do businesses have that you could solve? Many businesses hire consultants on a contract basis. If you can save a business time or money, improve their processes, and train their team members, then you can be a consultant. This business can be extremely profitable if you work with big companies who have expensive problems.

MEMBERSHIP SITE

Monthly subscription businesses that share regular content, training, or coaching to their audience. Do you have something great to share with the world? Do you have consistent value to share? A membership site, much like an online course, could be about anything. It's a place people come to learn and have a community so that they can learn more about something or develop new skills and get accountability. Membership sites are usually lower cost, but they offer secure, recurring monthly income and greater reach.

VIRTUAL ASSISTANT

Helping business owners with any aspect of their business that is taking up too much time. Are you organised? Do you have admin and customer service skills? Are you interested in getting some business experience and learning more? VA's are becoming such an important part of the online space. As more businesses go online, they need more support to keep things ticking over. They are usually paid hourly, which is one of the reasons it's not top of the list, but there is the potential to create a VA agency further down the line so you can start to scale the business further.

Which of these business models really stands out to you? Which one do you think you could apply to your current skills, passions, and expertise?

At this stage, you will have to do your own research. Both desk research and market research. So search on Google and Youtube, find competitors, join Facebook groups. And talk to people, talk to competitors and experts doing what you want to do. Talk to potential ideal clients and find out what they actually want and need.

Do not miss this step. You can't build a business in a vacuum. And stop talking to broke people. Talk to people who have money and find out what their problems are. There is no point selling cheap shit to broke people. Find out what people with money need help with. Then you will be creating something with a viable market from day one.

Once you have chosen a business model that's right for you, it's important to commit and stay the course. It's easy to get shiny penny syndrome and move from one thing to another when times get hard. But if you lack focus in your business - by trying to offer lots of different services to lots of different people - then you are going to struggle to sell anything.

The best way to start making money online is by focusing on offering ONE SERVICE to ONE IDEAL CLIENT.

Talk about nothing but that one thing and connect with lots of your ideal client. Make sure it's something people actually want AND are willing to pay for. Make sure it actually solves a problem for someone who has money to spend. Make sure it's something you are passionate about because you are going to talk about it a lot.

I see so many entrepreneurs making this mistake, starting out from day one with three or four offers, totally confusing everyone and diluting their message. It's great to be multi-passionate, but save the other ideas for when you are actually making money.

Once you have your one thing, and you are committed, you need a marketing strategy. How are you going to generate leads, how are you going to close sales? There are a million different ways to do this, so find someone you trust and get the full strategy from them. If you try and follow lots of different freebies, you will only ever get half of the story and these are going to be all totally different stories. So hire a coach or buy a course or join a membership site that will teach you the full strategy.

Build your personal brand. Get known. Speak. Write. Be visible. You can't sell a secret. Put yourself out there so that people begin to know, like, and trust you. Only then will they buy from you. Visibility and consistency are the two most important things when it comes to getting business online.

And of course there is a whole lot that goes into creating a successful digital product or service. But the fact is, once it's perfected, you can start to automate it. Automate your marketing and then automate your sales and, of course, automate your delivery. This gives you the freedom to scale, which means uncapped income. This means you can live your life whilst your business makes you money. This means location independence, and physical and financial freedom.

You don't have to work hard all your life to have good things. There is no correlation between hard work and money. This is an archaic lie we have all been sold. Look at those with the most money; the aristocratic classes don't WORK, they invest and create. Look at the lower classes, they work hard in physical, manual, laborious jobs and earn the least.

And yet we convince ourselves that 'hard work pays off.' 'You have to work hard to get the good things in life.' Well, the truth is, working hard doesn't make you rich. Working SMART does.

Working hard can help, but on its own it can only get you so far. If you want to make real money, you need to step back, relax, and take a look at the bigger picture. This is the future of work. This is the future of business.

ABOUT THE AUTHOR

Chanel Morales is a Serial Entrepreneur and Online Business Coach. She has spent the last 10 years honing her craft as a digital marketer and successfully launched and scaled multiple online businesses. A single mum and full-time digital nomad, Chanel helps women to craft and sell premium online services so that they can replace their 9-5 corporate income and live an amazing lifestyle anywhere in the world.

> *Website:* www.digitalnomadmums.com
> *Facebook:* www.facebook.com/mumbiztravel
> and www.facebook.com/groups/digitalnomadmums
> *Email:* chanel@digitalnomadmums.com

CHARLOTTE BJÖRNDOTTER

SACRED CONNECTIONS WITH NATURE & ANIMALS

A very young boy was throwing stones at a duck in the lake. I asked him why he was doing that. He stared at me angrily and said, "Because my mom and I hate ducks."

I asked him why. He couldn't answer; he really didn't know why.

So I told him that I love ducks. He looked at me as if I was crazy.

I continued to tell him why I love ducks and asked him to take a closer look at the duck, its beautiful feathers and colors, its beautiful and kind brown eyes, and its cute feet, paddling in the water.

I asked the boy, "Wouldn't you like to have feet like that to paddle with?" He suddenly dropped the rest of the stones that he held in his hand on the beach and said, "Yes, yes I would. Do you know what, I don't hate ducks anymore. I also love ducks, like you. Bye." He smiled at me, turned around, and started to play with something else.

This is a true story from my life and it clearly shows that parents are very important role models for their children, which parents need to be consciously aware of.

My name is Charlotte Delphi Björndotter. Björndotter meaning daughter of bear, and Delphi meaning womb. I live in the north of Sweden with my two wonderful sons and our amazing cat family members.

My parenting is imbued with my love for nature and animals, and I think it is crucial for children to learn to connect with animals, nature, and animal and nature spirits. I have worked as a parenting course leader for 15 years and have attended several courses myself in parenting, nonviolent communication, and mindful parenting.

With all this knowledge, my knowledge from my own parenting, and my love for nature and animals, I created my own lectures and courses.

It is a pure joy to watch families and especially children on my dolphin and whale retreats in the Azores, opening up their hearts and seeing them connect so easily with the energy of the dolphins and whales.

The children are really amazed by the dolphins. It's like they wake up from a slumber, seeing the earth and animals in a whole new and different way. They even question the time they spend with computer games.

"When I look into the eyes of Navi and Yoda, I see human beings, mom."

This is a quote from my beloved son Leo, who spontaneously expressed this with great conviction, passion, and love. He was talking about our two beloved family members, our cats. It was his way of saying that animals are like us, even though we are not the same species. My heart jumped with joy and hope for future generations, because it's about time that we recognize animals as sentient and divine beings.

SUPER HEROES

When I became a parent, I continued spending hours and hours every day outdoors by the lake and in the forest with my children. I taught them to respect, care for, and love nature and animals. In the summer we saved lots of baby fish from being killed by children, who caught them in small plastic buckets.

We talked to the children and explained that the fish were only babies and that they were really scared and stressed and that they would die soon if they didn't release them. The other parents didn't care about the fish and said and did nothing. We managed very easily to convince almost every child to release the fish. My sons were very happy and proud about our animal rescues and said we were super heroes.

My son Elliott was about four years old when he, one day at kindergarten, experienced something horrible. He witnessed two of his friends hitting a dragonfly with a heavy spade, and laughing. Elliott was devastated and so sad, he screamed and asked them to stop and cried for a long time.

The children who hit the dragonfly didn't understand why he was so angry and sad. It was only a dragonfly. The kindergarten teachers comforted him and they understood that this was important to Elliott.

So they gathered the children and asked Elliott to explain why he was so sad. He explained to the children that the dragonfly is like you and me and wants to live and deserves to live just like you and me. It's not only a dragonfly, it is a life. He really touched many children, who changed their views about animals that day because of him and his strong compassion, love, and connection with animals.

ANIMAL COMMUNICATOR AND A HEALER

I have always loved and felt a very strong connection to animals and nature. I was born with spiritual gifts, such as clairvoyance, clairsentience, interspecies communication, and healing.

I am an autodidact and educated animal communicator and healer. Some of my passions and missions in life are animal communication, healing, singing, and parenting. I love connecting with nature and nature spirits and I channel songs from nature and animals. It's magical when nature sings through me and with me.

I also convey the wisdom and messages from dolphins and whales to humanity so that we can integrate it into our lives and live a life of joy, harmony, flow, balance, unconditional love, freedom, and unity consciousness.

The dolphins and whales want to help us to release limitations and obstacles in our lives and discover who we really are, divine beings with infinite creativity and manifestation powers!

I have created a healing modality called Delphi Healing, focusing, among other things, on guiding the client to connect with the heart, heal the heart, and stay heart-centered, in order to embody unconditional love, compassion, and oneness. Oneness with humans, nature, animals, mother earth, and the universe.

Animals are wise souls; they are sentient beings, meaning that they can feel feelings of love, joy, sorrow, and pleasure, just like humans. I know because I communicate with animals and heal them.

What's important to understand is that animals adapt very easily to situations and people. They can feel our feelings and sense our thoughts. So they adapt to the people they are with. If the people treat an animal like a "lower" being that doesn't have any feelings, then the animal adapts its behavior according to that concept.

But if you start treating animals as sentient beings with feelings and needs just like humans, then the animals adapt to that and will show you more affection and will be more content. You can be really surprised at how wise they are if you only give them a chance.

Many animals that I communicate with are really baffled that I can communicate with them and some are even hesitant and afraid. Many animals do try to talk to us, but they eventually give up.

Once I was called to a home with a cat that was really afraid of every visitor. The cat hid every time, and it tried to do the same with me. I started to communicate with the cat and it told me that she was afraid that the people would pick her up and hold her, because she had trauma from that kind of situation from when she was a kitten.

I started to heal the trauma, and promised her that no human would be allowed to touch her unless she wanted them to. She was really relieved when the healing session was finished. She came to me and brushed against my legs.

The owners were really astonished and shocked. No way she would have done that to a stranger. They later reported that the cat was no longer afraid of visitors, because she knows that her owners have instructed visitors not to touch her unless she wants them to.

This is a very good lesson for us humans to learn. How is it that we can be so insensitive to another living being? How can we assume and take it for granted that we can walk up to an animal and start touching it and try to cuddle with it without permission? It's the same as a total stranger walking up to you and hugging and holding you.

So please think about this when meeting an animal for the first time. The least we can do is be polite and sensitive and let the animal come to us and lead the way. Many animals will let you come close and pet them and for many of them there is no problem. But many animals have traumas because of this.

ANIMALS ARE GUIDES AND HEALERS

We have so much to relearn from animals, because we also once lived with nature. They are focused on living in the moment, although they also remember the past. Animals are deeply in sync with and connected to nature. They have highly evolved senses, they can sense the subtle changes in the weather, and they get information from scents, sounds, energy fields, and their intuition.

They are also aware of and very sensitive to the spiritual realms. Animals heal us and harmonize and balance the energies constantly. Dogs are loyal and faithful to their family members. They will do anything to heal and harmonize the energy of their family members. They absorb imbalances, like sorrow and grief, and mirror it. This can actually lead to that the dog getting sick.

When I was at a home with a dog, the dog was very nervous, imbalanced, and stressed. It also had joint pains, and the veterinarians suspected a rheumatism disease. The dog showed me that the family was about to split up; there was a divorce, and the family was of course sad and stressed. The dog wanted to help everyone, so it absorbed the sadness, the stress, and the nervousness and mirrored it.

When I healed the dog, starting with its aura, I felt so many emotions from the family members. I cleared these emotions and the dog suddenly looked at me, gave a big sigh of relief, and fell asleep. The dog could finally detach from and let go of all the emotions it had been absorbing. I started working with its body and, unsurprisingly, the emotions it had absorbed were causing the joint pains.

After the treatment, the dog was so relieved, so happy, and balanced. The family members could see it clearly. The joint pain disappeared as well after a while. How was it that I, a total stranger, could be allowed to communicate with and heal the dog? It's because I connected with respect, heart-to-heart and soul-to-soul.

If you connect with animals respectfully and with their hearts and souls, you will develop a beautiful and loving bond. Animals feel your energy and intention so strongly. They know right away if they can trust you or not and if you have honest and loving intentions or not. Respect the animal's boundaries.

Always ask yourself, if I was this animal, would I like being treated like this?

For example, when you are picking up a pup or a kitten, do this very slowly. We need to put ourselves in their position. How would it feel for me if a huge something grabbed me really fast and put me on a rollercoaster ride high in the air, separating me from my source of safety, from my food, from everything I need in order to survive?

"Look into the eyes of an animal and you will feel a direct connection with your heart and soul"

The animals connect directly with your heart and soul because that is most important to them, and so it should be for us humans also. The more you live from the heart, the better you can connect with animals. The more you connect with animals and nature, the more you will perceive. It is like entering a whole new magical world. Your dulled senses will start to awaken.

In the Azores, on one of my retreats, I was swimming with the dolphins and they asked me if I wanted to heighten my senses and experience what they perceived. I said yes and when the tour was finished and we stepped on dry land again, I was really stunned by the harsh sounds from cars and machines.

It was really painful for my ears, like knives. I don't think we realize that the sounds that surround us in modern society are not harmonious and healthy sounds. They are in fact detrimental for us.

The toxic fumes from cars and toxic fluids were also painful to breathe and smell. So too, I experienced touch in a whole new way. I felt the sensations of water and the sand on the beach, touching and vibrating on my skin.

I used all of my senses in a whole new way, sensing with both my body and my soul. It was truly amazing and educating. So please be careful around animals with strong sounds and smells.

It's like many humans have separated themselves from the real world, and they have created a world within this world, a world of technology and devices with radiation and electricity, which stresses out our bodies.

Our bodies need contact with nature and water. It revitalizes, heals, and balances us. Many humans live indoors most of the time, without nature and animals. They have lost the connection to nature and animals and don't consider nature and animals as living, conscious, and sacred beings, which they are.

Many humans have numbed their senses and their souls. We need to wake up, detach from the superficial world, and reunite ourselves with the real world. Many humans around the world don't like animals; they fear animals and even hate animals.

Last summer I saw a beautiful jackdaw lying on the grass upside down. I contacted its soul and asked permission to pick it up. It accepted, and I slowly and lovingly picked him up.

I understood that he was severely sick. I arranged a safe space for him in a cat carrier and gave him water to drink and worms to eat. He was a little bit afraid at first, but then he relaxed. I healed him and sang songs for him. He looked at me with his beautiful, light blue eyes and we connected deeply, heart-to-heart, soul-to-soul.

He even leaned on me and wanted physical contact, love, and support. He told me that he was so surprised that a human could be kind to him. All of his life humans had chased him away, been angry at him, and even tried to harm and kill him. He didn't understand why.

It was a beautiful moment of unconditional love. Love is love no matter if it's love for a human, love for nature, or love for animals. He sadly passed away the next morning, but he was so thankful that he got to experience unconditional love and compassion from a human.

It gave him hope, he said. Hope for living together in oneness and love once again on Mother Earth.

"The animals and nature are waiting for us.
It is truly time for birthing the new earth and it starts from within. It starts with you and me."

EXERCISES YOU CAN DO ALONE OR WITH YOUR CHILDREN

In order to create a loving and caring relationship with animals, you will have to change your usual perception and preconceived ideas about animals.

1. When you see an animal, think about the animal as an individual and as a soul.
2. Be curious about the animal and its personal qualities. Send love to the animal and bless it. You will notice the animals starting to react and connect with you more and more if you do this exercise regularly.

TO CONNECT HEART-TO-HEART AND SOUL-TO-SOUL

Another exercise you can do if you have an animal family member is to do a meditation and invite your animal's soul to join.

Connect heart-to-heart and soul-to-soul. Talk aloud to your animal's soul; it will understand. Tell the animal that you now know that the animal is not just an animal, that it is an individual with feelings, needs and, wishes and that you know it has a soul. Tell the animal that you would like to connect more deeply and that you will treat it differently from now on.

Ask the animal to do something, to give you a sign that it has received this information. After the meditation, be mindful of signs from your animal.

If you have any issues or problems with your animal, you can talk to its soul about it. It's important that you give the animal an option of what do to other than the inappropriate behavior. You will be amazed by the result.

TO BE GUIDED BY A TREE

An exercise that will help you a lot is to connect with nature, clear yourself, balance yourself, center yourself, ground yourself, lower your blood pressure, energize yourself, and connect with Mother Earth and her healing energy.

Go out into a forest, for example, and connect with a tree that you feel drawn to. Talk to the spirit of the tree and ask for permission to connect with it.

Trees are very powerful beings that are connected to the core of the Earth, as well as the universe. Carefully hug the tree and close your eyes.

Feel its powerful energy, feel its love and healing energies embracing you. Feel time slowing down; be in the moment. Thank the tree and give love to the tree.

If you can't access nature every day, you can connect with your plants or do a guided meditation to the sounds of nature.

ABOUT THE AUTHOR

Charlotte "Delphi" Björndotter is a passionate and inspiring advocate for oneness. From Sweden, her mission is to guide humans to discover a divine heart connection with animals, nature and the Universe. She is an experienced interspecies communicator and healer who cooperates with advanced dolphin and whale spirit guides in the powerful healing modality, Delphi healing. She channels the energy, wisdom and messages from nature and animals in singing and drumming ceremonies, retreats, healing sessions, and guided meditations.

She offers retreats worldwide, in places like the Azores, where you learn to connect with your heart, intuition, nature, wild dolphins, whales, and the Universe.

Charlotte is a dedicated mother and an experienced parenting course leader. She also offers parenting retreats worldwide, in places like the Azores. Her passion is to empower and inspire parents to create an authentic, loving, compassionate, and intuitive relationship with their children, nature, animals and the Universe, for the benefit of all.

Website: www.charlottedelphi.com
Facebook: www.facebook.com/livingthedolphinway
and www.facebook.com/Sacred-Heart-Journeys-103441391126052
Email: withlove@charlottedelphi.com

DIANA BEAULIEU

AWAKEN YOUR WOMB WISDOM

I am a Womb Awakening teacher and a modern Medicine Woman. Since creating Sacred Womb Awakening, my Womb mystery school in 2015, I have helped hundreds of women around the world connect to their Womb Wisdom.

I have also trained women on three continents to become Womb Awakening Practitioners. They have gone on to share Womb Awakening and Womb Wisdom teachings in over 15 countries.

Womb Wisdom is the name I have for the deep, embodied feminine centre of intuition that I draw from every day to guide me. I will be teaching you to connect to this centre later in this chapter.

But first I want you to know that I travelled a long and sometimes difficult path to find my Womb Wisdom. It was difficult because it required me to get "out of my head" and into my body.

"In my head" was where I started my healing journey some 20 years ago. I was a postgraduate anthropologist and researcher. At that point, my life was all about the mind. I lived in the world of ideas, books, and theories.

I was pretty comfortable there — until one day, my healing crisis happened. I lost someone I loved. This opened me up to my emotions and connected me to the feelings in my physical body. I realised that I had a whole lot of pain inside me. My healing journey had begun.

I spent 8 years learning, practising, and teaching Shiatsu, which has its roots in Chinese energy medicine. Through this I learned how the body stores and processes emotional states. It was a ten year detox for my body, mind, and soul.

Along the way, I treated many individuals through their heavy trauma: IN drug addiction, homelessness, and women's services.

I then spent seven years as an apprentice of core shamanic healing. This is the art of connecting to the spirit world through the drum.

As I worked to help clients reclaim their energy and power through shamanic healing, I learned to listen to the wise voices of my spirit guides, who appeared in human and animal forms.

Their wisdom was miraculous for me. They provided deep answers and perspectives that could never be reached through logic alone.

However, I knew I needed to go deeper. I had become highly intuitive, but there were places I had not yet travelled. I still harboured old wounds. I still wasn't attracting fully healthy relationships. I still struggled with money. In short, I had not mastered life. Far from it.

That was when my Womb woke up. She'd waited 40 years for me to be ready to hear her. When she awoke, it turned my life upside down.

I became aware of old sexual traumas and fears that I'd hidden away deep in my body. I did the difficult work of healing them.

Then I began to remember deeper memories still - the lifetimes where I had been a Womb priestess, when the Womb had been at the centre of human spiritual life.

I have been listening to my Womb Wisdom ever since.

This has caused me to grow in many ways. I have become more grounded in my body and more capable of generating abundance. I have attracted far healthier relationships.

Although my life still presents many challenges, and of course I have plenty of learning and growing to do, I feel that I have found the strong, still core within me that anchors and guides me each day. It is my Womb Wisdom.

Now I want to help you to do the same, if it resonates with you to learn this.

BIRTHING A NEW EARTH - WHY WE NEED WOMB WISDOM TO GUIDE US

We have come to the point in humanity's story where all the old rules and structures are breaking down.

Women, just like me and you, are being called to birth the New Earth. The question I wish to invite us to consider is - how will do we this?

From what space of awareness or consciousness will we create the new?

Are we ready to fully let go of the old patterning that our world was built on: fear, greed, scarcity, and competition? Can we release the conditioned desires that our society has seduced us into: the desire for more, bigger, and better?

Are we ready to be stripped down to our essential selves so that we can create with trust, sacred vision, surrender, stewardship of the earth, and service to humanity?

One of the ways that we can do this is by connecting to our Womb Wisdom. For me, it is one of the keys to a new paradigm, where we are fully aware of our divinity and our sacred relationship to the Earth and each other.

In this paradigm we don't give away of our power to external authority figures, whether they be political, religious, or spiritual.

In this paradigm we are the wisdom keepers and way-showers for our own paths. We find our deepest truth within our bodies, the houses of our souls.

WELCOME TO YOUR WOMB WISDOM

Your Womb Wisdom is the sacred voice of your deepest, embodied wisdom. Imagine that your highest self, and your most ancient soul memories, are all embedded in this part of your body. Your Womb is an Aladdin's cave, a treasure trove of information. Your Womb knows exactly who you are as a soul, and why you came to be here on Earth right now.

Your Womb Wisdom is the voice and wisdom of your Womb. Your Womb is an energy centre within you that overlaps with your physical uterus, but is so much more than that. Your Womb is a magical space within you, a physical Akashic record, the place where your soul remembers itself through the matrix of your physical body.

It does not matter even whether your Womb is physically healthy or not, or even if you have a physical uterus or not. It does not matter whether you are still menstruating or if you have stopped menstruating. You can still access your Womb energy and your Womb Wisdom.

Your Womb Wisdom is the voice of your personal, sovereign power, the deep knowing you hold as a woman. Your Womb Wisdom has the power to guide you through the many, complex choices that you must make each day as you navigate your unique and sacred soul path.

Your Womb Wisdom knows when a relationship is right for you, and when a partner's energy is healing and loving.

Your Womb Wisdom holds fierce boundaries, and prevents you from giving your energy and life force away.

Your Womb Wisdom knows when it's time to act, and time to be still.

Your Womb Wisdom bypasses your logical mind, creating possibilities that you could never imagine.

Your Womb Wisdom knows who you really are, not the limited version others might see.

Your Womb Wisdom always has been, and always will be there.

Your Womb Wisdom, if you choose to connect with her, can become a compass within you.

Your Womb Wisdom is here to assist you, whatever your soul's purpose is.

She will help you tend a new life and new creations through your mother energy.

She will help you forge new ways of transforming through your warrior energy.

She will bring truth and vision through your wisdom-holder energy.

She will help you restore balance through your healing energy.

She will help you create beauty through your artistic energy.

Find her. Listen to her. Be true to her.

ARE YOU ANCHORED IN YOUR WOMB WISDOM? FINDING YOUR SPIRITUAL CENTRE OF GRAVITY

Many of us are not connected to our Womb Wisdom. As you know from my story, it was quite the journey for me to arrive there. We are often not even in our bodies; we are "somewhere else" - in our thoughts, in the clouds, in our imaginations.

I have created some questions that will help you to see where you tend to "be" habitually. I will call this your "spiritual centre of gravity."

The three principal "centres of gravity" for us are our feminine energy centres, the Pineal Gland (or Third Eye), the Heart, and the Womb.

The ideal is to be consciously connected to all of these centres. Then, we can enjoy a perfect balance of love, wisdom, and creative power while being grounded in our bodies and connected to the Earth.

Let's see.

WHEN YOUR PINEAL GLAND / THIRD EYE IS YOUR CENTRE OF GRAVITY...

The beauty: You have an expanded awareness of the astral and spiritual realms. Perhaps you have a strong sense of your Spirit guides and ancestors. You are able to hear spiritual messages and even transmit these to others.

The challenge: You receive lots of beautiful, wise information on how to live your life from higher sources. But it's a challenge to manifest money and solid relationships. You feel like you haven't quite "landed" on Earth. You may even feel that the Earth is an "unsafe" place for you. Perhaps you have had traumas you haven't fully dealt with and you don't know how to face them.

WHEN YOUR HEART IS YOUR CENTRE OF GRAVITY...

The beauty: You feel love and an empathetic connection to all beings. You experience a great deal of love and joy in your life. You truly feel that "we are all one." You have healed many of your hurts, and experienced great forgiveness in your life.

The challenge: You have difficulty with personal boundaries. You want to be a source of love, but what about your personal space, rights, needs, and wants? You often find yourself giving away energy to heal and help others. You end up being drained or even burned out. You lack the energy to define and create your personal direction in life.

WHEN YOUR WOMB IS YOUR CENTRE OF GRAVITY....

The beauty: You source your wisdom from within your body. You "know" what is right and true for you in a direct and simple way. You feel strongly present in your body and rooted to the Earth. Your boundaries are strong. You honour your personal energy and preserve it for yourself. You are open to abundance. You attract sacred relationships. These things come to you more effortlessly.

The challenge: You no longer tolerate relationships where your boundaries are violated. You become very clear about your needs and your truth. You stop worrying about other peoples' expectations and perceptions of you. *In short, you become badass and not everyone will like it.*

* * *

Having read these descriptions, where would you say your "spiritual centre of gravity" is? Have you arrived in your Womb? If not, would you like to? If so, read on...

* * *

THE BENEFITS OF BEING IN YOUR WOMB WISDOM

In the next section I am going to describe a daily practice that you can do in order to access your Womb Wisdom and help shift your "spiritual centre of gravity" towards the Womb.

If you choose to practice this, you will find yourself synchronising more and more with the physical rhythms of your body and the greater unfolding of your soul's purpose.

You will find yourself moving deep into deep knowing, deep receptivity, and deep trust.

Womb Wisdom will call you to walk along the sacred thread of your deep knowing every day.

HOW TO CONNECT TO YOUR WOMB WISDOM

I am going to share a daily practice that you can use to unlock your Womb wisdom. Before I do this, I want to make it clear that the key to unlocking your Womb Wisdom is to have clear intentionality. The clearer your questions or query as you practice, the clearer the answer you will receive from your Womb Wisdom.

AWAKENING

Here are some examples of the questions that you can bring to your Womb Wisdom, from the most mundane to the most spiritual:

- Where should I live?
- Is this relationships aligned to my soul?
- Is now the right time to take a particular step?
- Is it time to push forward? Is it time to rest?
- What are the gifts that I need to bring forward in service to the world?

THREE STEPS TO HEAR YOUR WOMB WISDOM - A DAILY PRACTICE

Step One

Sit quietly with your pelvis relaxed and your belly open. You may wish to have some shamanic drumming or meditation music playing.

Place a hand over your Womb by cupping your hands over your lower belly, just two fingers width up from your pubic bone. Breathe slowly and deeply into your lower belly and Womb.

Imagine your breath to be a healing, liquid light that washes all the way through your body and down into your Womb. Ask this light to clear any trauma memories or fears that are in the way of you connecting to your Womb's wisdom.

Ask a question that you wish to answer through your Womb Wisdom. For example: "What is my most aligned step today with regards to my business?" or "Is this relationship for my highest good?"

Step Two

Holding this intention clearly, now imagine that you in front of a great tree that has a hole in its trunk that you can climb into. As you sit in its hollow trunk, ask for a pathway to open down into the Earth. Let the Earth open up a tunnel through the roots of the tree.

Allow yourself to descend through this tunnel into the Earth until you emerge into a warm, safe, cave-like space under the Earth. You are entering into the cave of your Womb Wisdom. Breathe again into your lower belly. Notice any objects or symbols here, as they may be significant. Remind yourself of the question that you have brought here.

Step Three

Call upon your Womb Wisdom to make itself felt. Perhaps your Womb Wisdom will take the form of a woman. You may see her appear in the cave, or feel her presence. Perhaps you will feel your Womb Wisdom as a voice, or a sense of deep knowing. You will have your unique way of recognising it.

Breathe. Soften. Bring your question to your Womb Wisdom. Repeat your question up to three times.

Allow the answer to arise in whatever way is right for you. Perhaps you will hear a voice speak. Perhaps you will be shown visual images or symbols. Perhaps you will get a deep feeling of "knowing" as her answers come through.

Once you have received your answer, thank your Womb Wisdom. Allow yourself to rise up out of the cave, through the tunnel, back into the hollow tree trunk. Step of the trunk, back into the forest.

Open your eyes when you are ready and journal your experience along with the answers you received.

ABOUT THE AUTHOR

Diana Beaulieu is a writer, storyteller, spiritual teacher, coach, and the founder of Sacred Woman Awakening.

She specialises in supporting women to restore their sexual, intuitive, healing and creative energy by clearing past traumas and calling back their authentic power.

Diana gained a BSc in Human Sciences at the University of Oxford in 1996. She trained in energy therapy and shamanic practice for 15 years before establishing her own internationally recognised modality, Sacred Womb Awakening, in 2018.

She co-authored the Amazon best-selling book "Gratitude and Grace" in 2015 and is currently working on her own book, "Original Woman" due for release later in 2020.

Diana loves to spend time in the forest and walk barefoot on the Earth. She currently lives with her beloved daughter on the magical island of Ibiza, Spain.

To join Diana's online community for monthly global meditations, free articles and more, visit her website at the link below.

Website: www.sacredwomanawakening.com
Facebook: www.facebook.com/groups/sacredwomanawakening
Email: info@sacredwomancoaching.com

DOMINIQUE OYSTON

CONNECTING TO YOUR GODDESS VOICE

Your voice is like gold; it does not lose its value, no matter how deep it is buried.

I was fortunate to be born the daughter of an internationally acclaimed theatre director and Shakespeare expert, and of a mother who loved history, metaphysics, and the Arts.

The journey of my life has seen me on stage since the age of 4, as a dancer, through to an international operatic career performing for CEO's and Presidents in 35 countries, culminating in being chosen as the soloist for the wedding of much loved Australian Prime Minister Bob Hawke and writer Blanche D'Alpuget.

I have experienced the power of the voice to lift the hearts and minds of people throughout the world.

My passion to learn more about healing and spirituality saw me training as a Steiner teacher, Yoga teacher, in Aura Soma, Intuitive Sound Healing, and Ayurveda.

I thirsted to know everything about sound, goddesses, mythology, the magic of nature, history, sacred cultures, and poetry. This was not surprising, as when I was small I sang to the trees and flowers whenever I could. Unconsciously I was channelling the light of Spirit each time I let my voice express itself untethered.

My spiritual curiosity was private. I never made public my interest in the divine, as the idea of revealing this side of myself felt shameful and made me afraid. My wonderful career masked this other self.

Consequently, I felt split as a person and was accompanied relentlessly by confusion, inexplicable fears, and even self-hatred for who I was. I could not feel my core. I hid behind professional confidence and people pleasing. I continually stepped up and then shrank back. I offered my creative enthusiasm and abilities to others because I was terrified of my own purpose.

Perhaps you have experienced the feeling of profound longing, held back by hesitation and fear of the unknown, and the resulting self-criticism.

Unbeknown to me, I was preparing for a very peculiar purpose –to guide others to be the goddess they are by finding their authentic voice. And to reintroduce lost voices of the divine feminine to the world.

But first I had to learn what a goddess actually is and dare to speak to her and let her shine forth fully in my own life.

VOICE

Unlocking the silent voice of your inner goddess matters. Your voice is the central, aligning component that embodies your energy and your identity. It anchors your energy, your essence, and your personality in your physical body.

Your voice is both sacred and profane...an alchemical tool. When you harness its power, you have the ability to manifest Spirit on the earthly plane. It enables you to align to spiritual ideals while being grounded in practical matters. If you nurture and empower the goddess in your voice, you can do anything.

Women's voices have been silenced for over 3,000 years. Now women are hungry to both embody their feminine nature and find their authority. Somehow we know that when we are courageous enough to speak our truth, we can become the women we long to be. Aligning with the goddess in your voice is the missing piece you need to find this inner strength and share your brilliance. Your voice will lead you into a new life.

Imagine what your life would be like if your voice resonated like a goddess!

THE GODDESS IN YOUR VOICE

Most of us have only a small idea of who we really are and what our full potential is.

So what DO we have?

We have a feeling inside that is like a voice that keeps calling, "Get living. Wake up, because you've forgotten that you are a Goddess!"

You know the feeling when you open your eyes on a glorious sunny day feeling fabulous, but you don't know why. As if while you slept, you'd been filled up with sparkles that dissolved every thought of what you can and can't do. You leap out of you're your heart lifting, feeling your wings stretch, knowing that you are going to fly today.

And in that moment something moves from deep within you and you have the impulse to…is it to sing? Or at the very least you feel your sternum lift because something is there: a sigh, a hum, a noise, a conversation, a story, an audible breath, a yodel, a pure note of joy, a song, a laugh, a roar.

That is the goddess voice. It is an irrepressible part of your nature.

We all have this. In my father's workshops at the Royal Academy of Dramatic Art in London, he would gather his students into a circle and explain the principle of the talking stick. "When I hand you this talking stick, you are empowered to speak with authority. It is like the sceptre bestowed upon kings and queens." Their voices would change instantly. The goddess is not so far away as you might think.

The moment you connect with your sovereign, unquestioning energy to meet life, that voice is there. It is simply waiting for the right conditions to unveil itself, bubble up, and flow out. It is waiting for YOU, to open the door to your cage and remember.

SO, WHAT IS A GODDESS?

The goddesses are the representatives of the vast spectrum of the feminine. They encompass all of earth's creations and exist in the realm of nature. Think of all the earth, water, star, planetary, landscape, and sky goddesses there are.

You too have a goddess nature and goddess-like qualities. When you connect with these qualities, you can express yourself in a completely new and epic way.

Women have been labelled. Perhaps you saw the episode of *The Simpsons* where Lisa takes the 'career aptitude normalising test' and is told that she is destined to be a homemaker, but she speaks up and says 'no', because she wants to be the President of the United States of America.

You too can relabel yourself as a woman who communicates with authority. No matter what your niche, field of work, or interest, you can find your way home to your own goddess nature and create a life of sovereignty.

THE GODDESS AND YOUR SOUL PURPOSE

Speaking your truth means speaking from your soul. Your awakening will be accompanied by a longing to hear the voice of your soul more clearly as you seek your purpose here on earth.

Goddesses are both divine and earthly and bring your spiritual and human selves closer together so it is easier to hear your soul speak. You hear the voice of your soul's 'purpose,' so you can listen, recognise, know, speak the words, and take the actions your soul offers.

UNBLOCKING YOUR TRUE NATURE

Goddesses can help heal blocks in your human nature so your soul can shine through, speak up, and achieve its purpose.

- If you don't love yourself, there will be a goddess to help you heal your self-love.
- If you are sexually shy, there will be a goddess to unblock your pleasure.
- If you need to understand your grief more fully, you can work with a water goddess who will connect you to the depth of your feelings, and shift them fluidly and powerfully so you're not stuck.
- If you are blocked in your power, your truth, or your voice, there are goddesses who teach you to sing, command, and roar.

Goddesses help unblock your true nature and amplify your ability to express yourself with an epic frequency boost. They show you how to hold this divine frequency and light in your day-to-day life and work.

You might ask, "Who am I to call myself a goddess? Is it overtly sexual? Is it self-glorification? Do I need to participate in pagan rituals? Am I worthy of this title?"

The word goddess comes from the Norse 'gott'. You can imagine it's a little like showing everyone what you've really got!

EVERYONE HAS A GIFT WITHIN THEIR VOICE

Goddesses have gifts and abilities. They have voice gifts, such as prophecy, healing, and commanding. Your voice has gifts too. These may be obvious, or they may be lying dormant within you, untouched through lifetimes, or they may carry trauma and have shrunk into invisibility for refuge. Perhaps you've learned not to value your gifts, as they are not obviously 'useful' or important.

Your gifts are there and they are made for giving.

Are you ready to discover and share your truth with those who need it most?

Finding your gifts means exploring the landscape of your communication and sound. Your voice, like every other instrument, requires time and practice in order to be mastered and to build self-confidence.

If you listen to your inbuilt radar, follow your subtle intuitive messages, and stop hesitating, your path will emerge. Even if you can't see your talents, take action regardless, because when you catch a glimpse of the goddess power in your voice, a flame of excitement flickers in you and calls you to expand that power.

WHAT STOPS YOU?

Most people are afraid to let the goddess in their voice be seen. Perhaps the brutal thought, "I'm not enough," runs like a cold river through your mind. Feelings of fear and shame will stop you from even starting to develop your abilities, especially from your deeper self. But those deep down gifts have power and presence and your soul will push you to bring them into the light.

Perhaps you terrorise yourself with horror stories of what will go wrong if you don't do what you think you are meant to do in a day, or don't meet your own, or others', expectations. The inner critic, which likes to terrorise you, will dull the goddess voice that urges you to expand the space inside your body and make more room for your own light.

In your natural state you radiate divine, magnetic power and presence. You use it to heal, unfold, and guide your gifts for the world. It opens doors to infinite possibility. It is important to attend to overcoming critical, inner voices that would hold you back, and prepare yourself to radiate and confidently speak your truth.

It might be scary at first, but we all get nervous. When I get nervous, my whole body shakes. Even thousands of hours on stage doesn't make this go away completely, but I use my toolkit of skills, my training, my sense of purpose, and my connection to goddess energies so a power to perform surges through me.

WHAT HAPPENS WHEN YOU WORK WITH YOUR GODDESS VOICE?

Every woman has a different role to play when stepping into her goddess voice. Goddess wisdom isn't a prescription for how you 'must' be. It's a spark to ignite your own unique way of being.

For instance, you might:

- Create your own vision based on your inner motivations.
- Find the courage to go against your childhood programming.
- Act upon your inner authority, instead of seeking permission, approval, or validation.
- Trust what you have to say, without explanation, excuse, or the need to impress.
- Offer wisdom and healing.
- Express the joy of life on earth.
- Confidently communicate from your intuition.
- Speak up for the earth and all its creations. Call out injustice. Use your voice for the wellbeing of future generations.
- Teach the feminine cycles of life, death, and rebirth from a place of power.
- Generously acknowledge others so everyone can benefit.
- Share your emotions intelligently and fully: rage, despair, exhilaration, might, passion, ecstasy, and laughter instead of becoming numb to who you are.
- Stop putting yourself down emotionally, financially, energetically, physically, or spiritually to please others.
- Stand your ground with conviction.

- Set boundaries and ask discerning questions.
- Call forth peace, unity, and a love of all life.
- Balance the voice of your masculine and feminine to find true love.
- Choose the career you have always longed for.

The goddess in your voice might wish to appear to bring hope or healing or transformation, to connect people with their own light, their strength and the truth of their nature.

Begin the journey and you will know.

WHAT I DECIDED TO DO DURING COVID-19

Something happened when Covid-19 came. I noticed it in my clients. Things that we had been afraid of for a long time simply dropped away. I wanted to share my knowledge so I announced something I had been dreaming of for a long time: an online Divine Sound Healing Festival, "Voice Medicine Global," to be held in 2021.

30 extraordinary sound and voice specialists from around the world speaking about singing the land, indigenous traditions, chakra healing with the voice, reclaiming the powers of the priestess voice, sound healing for animals and with the elements, healing and shape-shifting businesses and finances, sound healing in the ancient cultures, the song of the heart, conflict resolution, the erotic feminine, astrology, and so much more.

What do you long to do? I'll help you begin.

BEGINNING TO CONNECT

The starting point for experiencing the goddess in your voice and the goddesses themselves is to connect through feeling. You find your place of potential, wisdom, and knowledge by connecting to a sensation. Feeling, walking the talk, and embodying and living what you think and know is where the goddess will take you.

The true beauty of goddess work is that you get to feel and bring to life the goddess qualities in your own nature. Can you afford not to move on to a better place? Can you afford to stay where you are?

THREE TOOLS TO CONNECT TO YOUR GODDESS VOICE

The feminine has 'soft skills.' When connected to these skills, pathways develop that enable confident personal expression. Here are three exercises for you to begin this journey to the new you.

Exercise 1: Imaging the goddess story within

Imagine a goddess story within. Mentally create an image of yourself as a person you would be at maximum goddess power. Imagine you are pushing the EQ slider up to 10 on your capabilities one by one: insightfulness, fearlessness, creativity, whatever your unique attributes are, the things that make you YOU, to increase their potency.

Use your voice to tell a short story of your power. For example, say out loud, "If I were Joan of Arc, walking into the court of the King of France, I would be fearless, because I know that my mission would not fail. I would feel the river of energy pouring through me and I would know that my words would be heard by the King. I would look out over my audience, knowing some of them would be cynical or laugh at me, but I wouldn't care because my words would be for the King alone. His is the only ear I needed to fulfil my task."

Speaking the feeling of that image out loud helps you rise to the occasion. You see a picture of what is possible to achieve and you bring it into your voice. It's a first step to creating a new reality. The image gives you the vision or concept of what it would be like and inspires you with voice and feeling. It works.

A study by the University of Colorado[1] shows that mental imagining can activate and strengthen regions in the brain involved in real life execution and improve performance.

Sports people use visualisations regularly to program themselves to behave in certain ways under pressure.

Exercise 2: Toning your heart with Green Tara

You can connect to a goddess through a simple sound. Goddesses sing. They don't have to BE 'singers.' They aren't concerned with having 'good' voice; that's not important. They use their voice as medicine, invocation, prayer, and connection to their power and joy. The gentle vibrational massage of sound penetrates every area of your body, mind, and emotions and helps you relax, focus, and release negative states.

Try this. Tone 'Aah' as a single vowel sound on any pitch. Imagine (and feel if you can) the vibration of the tone in your heart region. In yogic philosophy, the sound of the heart is an 'Aah' tone.

As you tone 'Aah', tune into a goddess, such as Green Tara, who can pull you into your heart and help you hear your heart's voice.

Imagine the green light of Tara starting at the back of your heart. Follow as she moves her light around the heart in order to encase it.

Once that has come to a conclusion at the front of the heart, feel yourself pulling down into your heart. Let her light pull you out of your head and your mind. Come into your heart to be fortified and held in your heart. Feel the 'Aah' tone supporting her green goddess light.

If you've never done something like this, experiment and know you are awakening your goddess voice.

Exercise 3: Invocation to reclaim your goddess voice

Let's get physical. Place your hands on your thighs if you are sitting down or your belly if you are standing.

* Breathe gently and feel the rhythm of your breath.
* Expand your lower ribs.
* Relax your throat, your belly and pelvic floor.
* Speak the following statements out loud.
* Feel the energy of the statements circulating through your body.

- *I awaken my inner light*
- *I awaken my goddess voice*
- *I reclaim my power*
- *I reclaim my strength*
- *I prepare to be seen and heard*
- *I release the inner barriers to fulfilling my purpose here on earth*
- *I heal what was broken and set myself free*
- *I spread my glorious wings and fly*

Let your voice step out from its usual pathways and speak differently. Play with the feeling of the vibrations that come through. Imagine your inner goddess declaring these things at the start of her adventure to find her voice. You are magical, powerful, and encoded for brilliance.

Let your voice shine.

Welcome home, beautiful goddess.

---

1. University of Colorado at Boulder. "Your brain on imagination: It's a lot like reality, study shows." ScienceDaily. ScienceDaily10th December 2018

ABOUT THE AUTHOR

International opera singer, speaker, visionary, ancient wisdom expert and bestselling author Dominique Oyston is founder of the Goddess Voice Academy, a platform designed to re-introduce the spiritual, energetic, creative and awakening feminine forces of the voice to modern speakers, leaders and conscious entrepreneurs.

Dominique's dynamic 25 year stage career, magical voice, technical brilliance and powerful intuitive channel plus 30 years' study of mythology and healing make her a unique teacher of how to authentically serve and inspire.

Dominique guides clients to fully embody their goddess nature and gifts and turn their mission into a luminous message that resonates powerfully to create ripples of change.

In her "Finding your Goddess Voice" chapter you will learn prime secrets to becoming a beacon, shining confidently and clearly from within, so the world sees you, hears you and acknowledges your light.

Dominique lives in Melbourne, Australia with her two boys where she chats to goddesses, writes, teaches and plans her next revolutionary adventure.

Website: www.goddessvoiceacademy.com/blog
Facebook: www.facebook.com/goddessvoice
and www.facebook.com/groups/327329514332337
Instagram: www.instagram.com/dominiqueoyston
Get My Book: www.goddessvoiceacademy.com

ELEONOR AMORA MARKLUND

THE NEW GENERATION OF CHILDREN: THEIR FREQUENCIES, TRAITS, & HOW TO AVOID TOXINS

"Hi, my name is Eleonor and I'm an Indigo!" is what I usually start my courses and seminars on The New Generation with.

THE BIRTH OF THE NEW ERA

Indigos are often viewed upon as the truth seers and the rebels, and they know instantly if being lied to. They have a sharp intellect and a quick mind, such that they get bored if things happen too slowly or if life is too repetitious and monotone.

They often take on leadership roles, because they don't like authority figures, and this way they can steer the ship themselves, both when it comes to direction and speed, with "freedom" as their leading energy.

Being a clairvoyant since birth means that I have always been able to see spiritual beings, energy structures, and energy fields, like auras and the planetary grid, with my physical eyes. For several decades I travelled the globe to learn advanced spiritual subjects from different Masters, until I remembered who I was through many reincarnations, and found the place within myself to start my own Stellar Academy, where, for the last decade, I have since taught many thousands of international students.

I started searching for answers about The New Generation shortly after the turn of the Millennium, when I was pregnant with my son and realized that he was of a different energy than mine, and perhaps one that I had never encountered before. It has since been my mission to teach about this New Generation of individuals, in order to bringing forth a better understanding of not only their traits, but also their strengths and weaknesses.

We have been chosen to be their parents and guardians, and therefore it is our responsibility to give them the best possible way of upbringing and to do our best in trying to understand them and why they are here.

THERE'S A NEW KID IN TOWN!

More and more Highly Sensitive Persons (HSP) are being born in the world. Research shows that these people have an energy and nervous system that are more sensitive than the average person's. Today, about 20% of the world's population is estimated to be highly sensitive, but many of the children who are now born are in this group, which means that the number is constantly increasing.

I look upon HSP as an umbrella term for the New Generation, which consists of different spiritual energies and traits associated with each group. We often divide these into three different categories: Indigos, Crystals, and Rainbow children. For as long as humanity has existed, about 10% of the population have been Indigos, and although some say the number has increased, my belief is that the number is correct when we include the other categories in the 20% of HSPs.

My family consists of all three of the categories, which has sometimes been a struggle, since the energies are quite different from each other. Where the Indigo is perceived as masculine or active in its energy, the Crystal is often viewed as feminine or receptive. The Rainbow children on the other hand often come in as an energy that is balanced in both their feminine and masculine aspects, if they get the chance to.

My expert advice is to always give an Indigo two possible choices; the Indigo wants to be able to choose for themselves what to do. If there is only one choice, the risk of just getting a plain *"No"* is more than likely. The Indigo is of Warrior energy and can be perceived as quite fierce and strong willed. The Indigo that is out of balance will only have its mind set to *"My Way or the Highway."* They are often very intuitive and pick up different energies, where they can either find a meaning to life or loose meaning if they feel that the world is too damaged; as a result, many of them self-medicate with sugar, food, or drugs if they become too unbalanced.

The Crystal on the other hand is the diplomat in the group. While the Indigo is perceived as hard and strong willed, the Crystal is flexible and very loving. Instead of being a warrior, they want world peace and everything that resonates with it. They are natural telepaths and healers who also pick up the emotions of everyone around them if they are not taught how to control their boundaries.

The difference between an unbalanced Indigo and a Crystal is that the Indigo tends to get extroverted and explosive where the Crystal tends to get introverted and depressed. The Crystals are not that comfortable with their physical bodies, as many of them have not been in a physical form before.

Many parents of Rainbow children have received messages far before the birth, and there are many who see the Rainbows as re-born Avatars, i.e. *Ancient Ones*, who now choose to come back to improve their work on the Earth plane. Many of the Rainbows have clear memories of who they are, from birth.

A Rainbow is very clear in its energy; it takes care of itself, believes in itself and walks the talk, just like the Indigo, while being very responsive and sensitive, without the Indigos' highs and lows, which is something the Indigo needs to balance much of its life. An unbalanced Rainbow cannot separate the different lifetimes from each other.

The Rainbow is more physical than the Crystal, but not quite as physical as the Indigo, so they use music and dance to balance their energies and ground themselves in the body with natural movement and flow in the energies. They also use the energy frequencies of light and water to bring balance in their physical vessel.

The HSP's heightened sensitivity is really a strength, as Highly Sensitive Persons notice much more details and contrasts than others. They experience the world differently and treat their fellow human beings on the basis of empathy and compassion. However, many of these have not had the tools to manage their sensitive bodies and energy systems, which has created long-term illness as a result. But why is this happening among this particular group of individuals?

HSPs are extra susceptible to their emotional and physical environment, which also means that they are very sensitive to toxins. Of course, everyone is negatively affected by poisons, but for an HSP it can basically mean life or death. Many of my clients and students have typical illnesses caused by toxins, such as autoimmune diseases, and all of them are also highly sensitive.

The HSPs all have a task when it comes to creating the new world, and everyone is needed to balance and complete the energies of the other groups. Many Indigos become parents to Crystal children to balance their fierce energy, and the Crystals often needs the energy of an Indigo to get into action. The Rainbows choose families that can support both the active and receptive energy that they consist of, and they are the product of both of these energies.

THE DIABOLIC PLAN

I have studied for many years at different universities, up to preparatory research level. The different subjects that I chose have given me a broad knowledge, and, as an Indigo, I question everything, which fits me perfectly when I worked as an editor, reading many different articles and scientific studies. This attitude is also something I bring forth in my own teachings, so that everyone realizes we should question everything we have been told in the past, and to start researching for ourselves.

What I have come to see is that there is a plan in motion to poison the New Generation, and it focuses mainly on destroying their pineal gland.

The pineal gland is also what we spirituals see as the seat of the soul, thus it is both the key and the path we have to our higher selves, as well as being in direct contact with our third eye. It is also portrayed in all religions symbolically as the pinecone, as well as Horu's all-seeing eye, which is a cross-section of the glands we see as being related to clear-sightedness.

For those of us who are spiritual, we know that the pineal gland is what our third eye is connected to, and is our 'ET-Phone-Home' button.

By attacking our third eye and disconnecting it, you are basically creating a population of zombies who are unable to distinguish right from wrong and who, without question, follow mainstream media and authority figures.

The perfect plan for creating the perfect workers, who cannot use their distinctive powers to break free from the system and create a New Earth.

The pineal gland is a tiny endocrine gland found in the brain. It produces the hormone melatonin, which is a hormone that helps regulate biological rhythms, such as sleep and wake cycles. The secretion of melatonin is inhibited by light and triggered by darkness.

If we are to look solely at the physical, then the pineal gland is thought by many to be a gland that does pretty much nothing other than regulate sleep and what is called the circadian rhythm, but there is also research that shows it affects different hormones in the body.

What is melatonin good for then, and does it really matter?

Well, except for the sleep cycle, it also protects the heart, lungs, and kidneys from oxidative stress.

But is that really everything it does?

DMT, or dimethyltryptamine as the substance is called, is a great mystery to researchers and nobody really knows where it is created, although it can be found both in the brain and the spinal cord. What is most likely is that DMT is created with the help of the pineal gland and through a similar biological process as melatonin.

What they have also seen is that DMT is used in nature for communication between plants, and that there is an opening in our system to communicate with DMT. But scientists don't understand if we do, or how. Because, unlike the plants that have contact through root systems, we are all "separated," as scientists see it.

What we must not forget is that our physical bodies are not only flesh and blood; we also have etheric bodies and electrical energies; our brain, our nervous system and, our hearts are controlled by electrical impulses. There is much that we do not see, but that is energy within (and outside) us!

What can be seen as the connection in this are the astral journeys, which in and of themselves are the explanation for why DMT has been found in an increased amount in the brain after near-death experiences, because this is exactly what happens when the energy bodies partially release from the physical body to travel in the astral dimensions.

What you can also imagine is that DMT is released when we meditate, and that it is the chemical that helps us get in touch with our soul, which makes us understand that DMT is a substance that works multidimensional, and thus does not only need to be released in the physical body, but in the energy bodies.

MK Ultra was a secret, illegal behavior modification research program run by the CIA in the 1950s where they used American and Canadian citizens as test subjects. Indeed, MK Ultra involved the use of many methods for manipulating people's individual mental states and altering brain functions, including by secret administration of drugs (especially LSD, but also DMT). What emerged about the program is that they also trained agents to do both remote viewing and astral traveling by using what they learned from the subjects.

What many spirituals agree on is that the pineal gland is the key, therefore we need to protect it by every means necessary, so that we are not completely cut off and distanced from our souls and our higher selves.

5G is the introduction of the extremely high-frequency millimeter wave bandwidth in the microwave spectrum, and the introduction of new delivery systems and scattering techniques, such as beamforming techniques now flood our energy fields.

The difference between this and previous technology, which is also not good for us, is that this is much more high-frequency and what we notice is that it almost works like microwaves on our cells, which means that the water in them vibrates as a result. The pineal gland has water inside it, as well as crystalline cells, which means it is directly affected, and in addition much worse affected than the rest of our body.

In addition to the pineal gland noticing light and darkness, science has seen that it notices energy fields. The problem in this is that it interprets these fields as light, so it then holds back the melatonin and DMT, which in turn affects the rest of the body and limits our ability to astral travel. DMT is produced naturally in our system, and we do not need to use any substances to achieve it.

Astral travel is not only something we do for fun. We have separate lives in the astral worlds where we not only live, but travel and educate ourselves, and travel "home." Many of you who are reading this will understand exactly what I mean, and understand why we often sleep so much when we are depressed, when we are unable to be in this reality.

I have been able to astral travel consciously since I was a young child, and therefore I know the need for this practice for our health and life here on Earth.

WHAT CAN WE DO TO TAKE ACTIVE PRECAUTIONS AND HELP THE NEW GENERATION?

- **NO FLUORIDE:** The pineal gland is calcified over the years if we do not take action, and we know that this happens, as do other things, when we use fluoride in toothpaste. This cannot be compared to the fluoride found in our soils and our nature, but it is about the synthetic substance, which is in fact also a nerve poison. Instead, we can use oil pulling with different vegetable oils, which have numerous benefits not only for dental health, but for the whole body. Fluoride should also be removed from beverages and other sources of ingestion. (Read studies in PubMed). *Holy Basil helps the body to clean itself of fluoride.*

- **NO VACCINES**: Avoid vaccines that contain substances like polysorbate that open up and penetrate the blood-brain barrier, thereby allowing aluminum, and other adjuvants of the vaccine, to reach the brain. Everything that goes into the brain affects the pineal gland. (Watch the documentary *VAXXED* by Del Bigtree and read the book *Make an Informed Vaccine Decision* by Mayer Eisenstein & Neil Z Miller). *There are ways to help the body heal from adverse reactions to vaccines, but the best way is to never take one, since the reactions can be too severe to heal in time.*

- **NO ALUMINUM:** Avoid adding aluminum to our bodies, which means that we need to avoid vaccines that include aluminum. But we also need to choose deodorants without aluminum salts. The fluoride binds the aluminum in our bodies and in our brains, and thereby affects the pineal gland negatively. (Read studies in PubMed). *Silica helps the body to remove aluminum.*

- **ONLY ORGANIC FOOD:** Avoid environmental toxins like glyphosate, which also opens up the blood-brain barrier and creates a pathway for pesticides to reach the brain and the pineal gland. (Read studies in PubMed). *Choose organic and GMO-free food.*

- **ELECTROMAGNETIC FIELDS (EMF):** Avoiding EMF can be difficult in a time like this since they are created in everything from smartphones to televisions, but we can avoid areas with 5G and even high voltage lines that affect us very negatively. Be aware of the fields in our homes and shut them off as often as possible. (Read studies from experts questioning the new techniques.) *Earthing helps the body to balance the energetic fields. Algae, such as kelp, has natural iodine that helps the body withstand EMF better.*

There are many ways to help the body heal and get rid of toxins. One way is to find a naturopathic or homeopathic doctor; a good healer is also an asset on the calling list of every household. The best way to gain good health is to bring focus to the natural immune system and intestinal flora.

I am very committed to a sustainable and ecological lifestyle, and I am happy to explain, in my role as a teacher, how it affects our energy system and energy bodies. In all my trainings I share basic knowledge about how everyone should take responsibility for their own energies, so that they are able to control their energy fields and stand in their own power!

As a Swedish visionary and spiritual rebel who has been on the forefront of the Conscious Movement for more than a decade, I am also the founder *of The Church of the Conscious Movement,* where I have changed the rules of living based on the laws of religious freedom in the Nordic countries. Since we have laws that give us the freedom of religion, why not use them to our benefit? My mission has been to create this religion for the children of the New Generation, to be able to protect them from harm, and I have succeeded! This movement has since spread to the rest of the world.

I will let some words from Dove Cameron's song *Born Ready* end my chapter:

"Ready, set
Time to be a fighter
Don't look down
Keep on climbing higher
Be yourself, 'cause heroes shine in different ways

And when your voice can't make a sound
Just know we hear you all around
Don't need to fit into the crowd
To be a force of nature

'Cause we're gonna be, we're gonna be, we're gonna be the best
They're gonna see, they're gonna see that we were born for this"

ABOUT THE AUTHOR

Eleonor Amora Marklund is a passionate Swedish visionary, world changer and thought leader who has been in the forefront of the Conscious Movement for more than a decade.

She is a gifted entrepreneur and a spiritual teacher in her own Stellar Academy, where she is the creator of different popular spiritual programs online and offline.

After a near-death-experience, her psychic gifts magnified and she is now considered as one of the world's leading experts in psychic self-defense and astral work, where she is often described as "The Oracle" from the movie "Matrix."

As a gifted Clairvoyant Medical Medium, she has created the popular healing modality Multidimensional Healing™, which has practitioners all over the world.

Eleonor Amora is often described with humor as "The Unfuckwithable" because of her fierce and powerful yet loving Indigo energy.

> *Website:* www.EleonorAmora.com
> *Email:* Elle@EleonorAmora.com
> *Facebook:* www.facebook.com/EleonorAmoraInternational
> and www.facebook.com/stellaracademyandstellartravels
> and www.facebook.com/medvetnatrossamfundet
> and www.facebook.com/ChurchConsciousMovement
> *Instagram:* www.instagram.com/eleonor_amora

ELLEN SIRENA

MONEY, A DIVINE SPIRITUAL BLESSING

I was a broke, burnt out healer (a.k.a Witch) who had a long, toxic and abusive relationship with money.

Like a lot of spiritually gifted people, I'd fallen into the negative belief system that money was evil, unspiritual, and that I should just give my work away for free or charge the bare minimum, lest I be punished and sent to the bowels of hell for making a dime with my gifts.

It used to be so bad, I would charge $5 for 2 hour potent Angelic healing sessions, which would get rave reviews. But even then I wouldn't keep the money; I would donate it all to charities and maybe keep some to cover the bills.

And I started to feel resentful; the people I helped were healing and flourishing, and yet there I was: tired, exhausted, starting to detest my "spiritual work," hating money and feeling so DONE living pay-check to pay-check.

I was also super sick and tired of feeling riddled with deep shame, guilt, and anxiety whenever anyone approached me about money or wanted to pay me for my time, energy, and gifts.

I remember a good friend of mine at the time sat me down and said to me, *"Ellen, it's great you donate all your money to Landcare to support the environment, but what about Ellen-care? What about looking after you, nourishing you so you can have the time and energy to serve and support those who you care about? Utilise some of that money to nurture and restore yourself."*

Until then, I hadn't looked at money as a tool to help support and nourish myself; I was too focused on the toxic belief that money was some separate entity out to punish me and make my life a living hell. Everyone else deserved it, but not me.

However, after that conversation and also after receiving a message from the Angelic realms telling me, *"it's time to heal your relationship with money, beloved one, and create wealth with your gifts,"* things started to shift and change.

I decided to start charging higher prices for my work. At first it scared the hell out of me to do so, but when a client was more than happy to pay me $150 for an hour of my time (at the time this was A LOT of money to me, though it seems so small now!) I was over the moon. As I allowed myself to receive more money for my healing gifts, I felt more energised, more lit up, and I wanted to serve and help more people.

The burn out, exhaustion, and resentment started to dissolve as I came to realise money was simply an exchange of energy. That just as I gave, I needed to receive. The reason why I'd become so burnt out was because I was over-giving and not receiving, so I created an out-of-balance energy exchange.

I learned money was one and part of my energy field, not separate from me and that, in fact, it was the energy of love manifested as paper and coins, which constantly flowed in and out of my life to support me. But at the end of the day it was up to me if I opened my arms to receive it or block its flow by shutting it out and down with fear.

* * *

Money is the loving neutral energy of the Divine, which flows to all. It doesn't differentiate between good or bad. It just is.

* * *

So I FIGURED if toxic corporations were making millions of dollars polluting the planet, then why couldn't I make millions of dollars to help support and heal the planet?

I'd like to say my relationship with money radically changed overnight and that I was off making hundreds of thousands of dollars, unapologetically, from that day onwards, but it wasn't until a couple of years later when I left a toxic relationship with a narcissist, 6 weeks pregnant, broke, and having to go on welfare, that shit hit the fan and I had to take a good hard look at my life and money situation.

I remember one particular night, I cried in the bathtub, feeling like the world's biggest rejected loser, wondering how my life had come to this. I felt incredibly ashamed and embarrassed, fully believing I was destined to live life as a poverty princess.

But something in me said NO! This voice rose up within me and said, "No matter what, you are NOT going to be a victim or a broke ass single mum, living in a cardboard box on struggle street! It's time to heal and rise to the next level of your life. This breakdown is your breakthrough and a divine blessing; you need to get out of this bathtub, dry your tears, and get out there and SHINE."

So I did. I had no other choice but to pull up my big girl panties, cause no way in hell was I going to bring a baby into this world on struggle street or buy into the limiting, toxic stories that single mums must struggle. I was determined to ensure my bubba and I would have a safe, secure, and loving home with luscious loads of money to support us both.

And being a healer, I knew the only way to change was by turning within to clear out all the deep fear, pain, shame, and limits that had brought me to this point in my life. I had to raise my vibration to a whole new frequency, so I could then be a match to the money and life I truly desired. I knew if I wanted things to change, I had to change, No more excuses.

As WITHIN SO WITHOUT.

BUT MY INNER healing journey took an unexpected twist. I ended up accessing the power of the energetic womb space, the seat of the subconscious mind where all things start and finish, the feminine frequency of God consciousness, the Creatrix of all life. A powerful energetic portal that both men and women have located in the base of the body and also houses the root and sacral chakras responsible for money and creativity. I like to call this space the inner garden of creation.

I believe becoming pregnant and having my baby gave me this incredible gift to access this divine space within me.

I discovered that the universal intelligence was creating my physical reality with whatever was growing in my inner garden of creation, including my money situation. And for LIFETIMES, without realising it, I'd carried a deep subconscious belief that money = punishment, because in previous lives I'd been killed, tortured, or condemned for being a powerful and prosperous healer/witch by a patriarchal society.

So by going directly into my womb space, I was able to heal and clear out major money blocks and beliefs, not only from past lives, but from my family lineage and the collective consciousness in a short amount of time. I rewired and overhauled my subconscious mind to the new belief that it was safe for me to be powerful and prosperous, to live my soul's purpose, and to make great money doing what I love, guilt free!

And with this new belief firmly in place, incredible things started to shift and change. Within a few short weeks clients showed up out of the blue wanting to work with me and pay me awesome money.

Opportunities and incredible support started to appear; I was able to invest in an amazing, high-end business coach and the worries of how was I going to provide for my child and I dissolved as I started to feel lit up, rich, and divinely secure and supported from within. I knew everything was going to be ok.

And since then, I haven't looked back. I now run a successful and prosperous business as a single mamapreneur with a safe, secure, loving, and peaceful home for my son and I. We have loving, supportive, and healthy relationships and, yes, luscious loads of money rolling in and out to support us and others we care about.

Making, giving, receiving, and having money to me is a divine spiritual blessing. It enables me to serve, care, create, and have the time, energy, and resources to do good in this world.

And if there is one thing I'm so DONE seeing, it's people staying in soul-sucking work, under-earning, undercharging, and living in fear-based money consciousness, which at the end of the day serves no one.

So it's now my passion and my mission to teach and inspire others the truth about money and how living one's soul's purpose is a money-makin' magnet and that wealth is available to all, not just the "lucky" few.

* * *

Money, wealth, prosperity, riches, and abundance start from within you, not outside of you.

* * *

So to help you create a love-fuelled relationship with money, over the following pages I've put some exercises to help you heal and release old toxic money stories that are keeping you stuck in struggle street. It will help you connect to the power of your inner garden of creation so you can start to get your energy aligned with the money you desire, so it can flow into your life to support you and the work you are here to do in this world.

May these exercises bring you blessings and infinite love, health, and juicy wealth.

EXERCISE 1: CUT THE MONEY-FEAR STORIES

On a blank piece of paper, write out all your fears around making, giving, receiving, and having money. Don't hold back. Write them all out.

Then once you've written out all your money-fear stories, in a safe space away from flammable objects, light up and burn the money-fear pages you've written.

As the pages are burning away, please say the following prayer 3x:

I now cut, clear, and remove all money fears and money karma drama from my mind, body, and spirit in all times, spaces, frequencies, and dimensions.

I now replace all money fears with divine love, abundance, prosperity, wealth, health, and wellbeing. I now give myself full permission to make, give, receive, and have divine loads of money and prosperity -- guilt, shame, and fear free!

I am wealthy. I am rich. I am holy. I am lit up with love, abundance, peace, and prosperity today and every day for the rest of my life. I am free to create wealth and make riches rain.

I am FREE to live my soul's purpose, to share my gifts with the world, and to make money doing what I LOVE!

Thank you and so it is.

PLEASE NOTE: You can do this ritual any time and as many times as you like, but feel free to do it especially around new moons or full moons, as the healing energy is extra potent and magical at these times.

EXERCISE 2: THE MONEY WOMB HEALING

1. Before you begin the below exercise, please state clearly in your mind how much money you want to make in your life right now. You may even wish to write the amount down. Once you've got the amount clear, begin the below exercise.
2. Remove any eyewear, place your left hand over your lower abdomen, right hand on top of your left, press your thumbs together, and close your eyes and your mouth in a soft smile.
3. Bring your awareness into the base of your body, into the base of your spine. Inhale and exhale deeply into the base of the body for 3x cycles. 1 inhale and 1 exhale = 1 cycle. Relax your entire lower area. Soften. Open up. Let go.
4. With your awareness in the base of your body, say the following out loud or quietly in your own mind 3x: *"My divine inner garden of creation, please show me where and what pain, shame, and blocks are preventing me from creating and receiving (STATE MONEY AMOUNT)."*
5. Become aware of any areas that light up and may feel tight, tense, painful, uncomfortable, or where you feel your awareness drawn to. Feel free to repeat the above statement a couple of times if needed.
6. I now want you to go into the space where your awareness has been drawn to and inhale/exhale deeply for 5x cycles of breath.
7. Then repeat out loud or quietly in your own mind: *"I now release this block(s) that is preventing me from creating and receiving (STATE MONEY AMOUNT) to the divine and my angels in exchange for love, peace, health, wealth, and wellbeing. I now allow myself to create*

and receive (STATE MONEY AMOUNT) with divine ease, grace, and playfulness. Thank you and so it is." (Repeat statement 3x.)
8. I now want you to spend a few moments resting in your inner garden of creation and ask: *"What do I need to create, share, and take action on in order to receive this amount of money I desire?"*

Allow any ideas, insights, visions, whatever is given to you to be. You may wish to journal what you received. Don't forget to take action on ideas given to you! It's guidance on steps you need to start taking to create and manifest the amount of money you desire.

You can do this simple, healing exercise as many times as you wish and practice as much as you like until it becomes second nature.

Don't worry if you find it difficult or hard to connect to your inner garden of creation at first or don't feel anything. Keep practicing and she'll soften and open up for you. It will get easier, I promise.

EXERCISE 3: THE NEW MONEY LOVE STORY

Write out a love letter to money and what your new luscious, loving relationship with it looks like. What do you want to do with money? What holidays, vacations, and experiences do you want to have with money? Who do you want to spend it on? What do you want to spend money on?

Don't hold back. Be as wild, free, and imaginative as you like, because moving forward, I want you to maintain a loving relationship with money. So if/when you find yourself getting into a toxic fear-based story with it, read this new, money love story out loud a few times or until you can feel your energy shifting back into alignment with love, prosperity, peace, wealth, or wellbeing.

Also as a quick exercise, having a daily attitude of gratitude is a money magnet. Spending a few moments each day saying or writing down what you are grateful for and appreciate in your life will activate the law of attraction and bring you more things to be grateful for, including money.

Sending you love and high rich vibes,
Ellen Sirena xoxo

ABOUT THE AUTHOR

Ellen Sirena is the founder and creator of *Lit Up & Rich Academy*, a leading abundance activator, money womb maven, and purpose and prosperity priestess. She is on a mission to activate men and women to create love, health and juicy wealth with their divine purpose and natural gifts, talents and abilities.

Ellen believes money is part of our soul's purpose and is a spiritual blessing which can be utilised to heal and create wonderful changes for Mother Earth and all beings which call Her home. She is determined to break down the old toxic patriarchal money stories and create a new global money love story movement where light workers feel safe and confident to make riches rain with their natural gifts.

To find out more on how you can unleash your soul's prosperous purpose and natural money-makin' gifts, check out: *www.litupandrichacademy.com*

Website: www.ellensirena.com
Facebook: www.facebook.com/groups/litupandrich
Email: ellen@ellensirena.com

EMMA TURTON

HEAL FROM WITHIN: HOW TO HEAR THE WHISPERS OF YOUR SOUL & BECOME YOUR OWN MEDICAL INTUITIVE

As a leading international Medical Intuitive, and Founder and Director of Medical Intuition School, I talk about health all the time. I reveal how the body really works and I teach people how to heal from within using an integrative form of Medical Intuition.

People often assume, however, that because I appear to be healthy, vibrant, and connected with my body that I've always been this way, but that is not the case.

As a Medical Intuitive I work with people all over the world. I use my powerful non-local intuition to uncover the root cause and meaning behind a person's physical illness, injury, or symptoms, and guide them to heal from within. I teach them to decode the vital information hidden within their physiology using an approach that integrates science with spirituality.

But first, I had to learn to do this for myself.

In the process of learning, I uncovered powerful lessons about who we are and how we, and our health, fit into the Universe. These lessons have become some of the pillars of my work to this day. I am going to share some of these lessons with you now so that you can begin to apply them in your own life.

Let me start with the heart-cracked-open turning point that changed everything for me and set me on my path to learn how to heal from within.

When I woke on the morning of my 29th birthday in early 2006, I curled into a ball on my side and cried.

I did not want to face the day. I knew that when I hauled my body out of bed to see my two beautiful little boys I'd be struggling to walk. My joints ached and were stiff with arthritis. My stomach felt like I'd been punched, even though I hadn't. At this point in my life, I was 50 pounds overweight, miserable, and had a chronic cough that wouldn't budge .

I felt 89 instead of 29, and it showed.

Even though I am an experienced health professional in my own right, I couldn't figure out where I'd gone wrong. As a physiotherapist, I knew how the system worked, so, I put my faith in the medical system. I took nearly every test under the sun and saw a seemingly endless team of doctors.

The medical team presented me with a grocery list of diagnoses and a fistful of medication to take daily. My specialists said that there was nothing I could do, that I would have these diagnoses for life. They told me that medication was something I would have to get used to if I wanted to function daily. Except I was not getting better, I was getting steadily worse.

So, when I woke on my 29th birthday, knowing I would be hobbling through another day of pain, I decided it wasn't worth getting up. Instead, I rolled over, gave in, and cried.

Before that day, I had never really allowed myself to completely give up or to really experience what I was feeling deep down inside. In that moment, I felt raw despair and hopelessness. I felt like I was on a fast-track to old age and disability.

I was desperately unhappy in my life. I felt all the years of worry, pain, embarrassment, fear, confusion, loneliness, and shame rise in me and bubble over. I allowed myself to feel it all; to let it move through my body like water in a river. To wash over me in wave after wave of sensations and emotions until I felt small and empty. And for the first time I could remember, I sat in presence with my body. I breathed and sat with what I was feeling.

As my tears eventually subsided, something shifted inside me. I felt cracked open like an egg. Different. Suddenly more aware. Awake.

In that space that opened within me, even as emotion was pouring out, I knew there was more. There had to be. This couldn't be how I was supposed to feel for the rest of my life. I wasn't even half-way through! I began to wonder if the doctors didn't know the most about me and my health. I realized there had to be another way. I knew I had to take a stand for my body, for my life, and for myself.

In that moment I decided that I couldn't depend on the health system to help me any more. I had handed over my responsibility to others. I had placed the responsibility for my physical wellbeing in the hands of my doctors, my mental wellbeing in the hands of my psychiatrist and psychologist.

Even more, I had put my marriage and happiness in the hands of my husband. They had all tried to support me, but it was in this moment I realized it wasn't their responsibility at all. It was mine.

It was time for me to take back responsibility for my life.

LESSON 1: YOU ARE YOUR OWN BEST HEALTHCARE PRACTITIONER.

You know you best. You may choose to outsource to the experts occasionally for tests and treatment, but never hand over your power or your responsibility for your own health to someone outside of you. They cannot heal you. Only YOU can heal you.

You are the protagonist in your own story, the lead actor in your own film. If you aren't happy with your life, you get to choose what that new story will be.

As I rose painfully from my bed that day and stood to face my family, I squared my shoulders in a new way. I felt calmer than I had felt in a long time. I was awake and clear, and I had a new determination to find the answers on my own. I had made a decision that day. It seemed small at the time, but that decision would change every aspect of my life from that point forward: I had decided to take back my power.

I was seeing with new eyes.

When I looked at my then-husband, I could see the effect our toxic relationship was having on my body. When I looked in the mirror, I could see how the sharp pins of constant negative narrative inside my head were harming me, like I was a voodoo doll.

I began to see that my food choices were not serving me well, and that the reason I drank wine every evening wasn't to relax, or even as a reward for surviving the day. Instead I realized that the wine was to escape from the life I had created; a life I was desperately unhappy with. I started to unpack every single aspect of my life to see how it might be contributing to my physical suffering, starting with food.

Food seemed like the logical place to start. I wanted to lose weight so I could keep up with my children, but it was all so confusing. I'd read all the diet books. Each one told me something different and all the information was conflicting with each other. I soon realised I was doing what I had done with the doctors: handing over my responsibility for my food-choices to one diet or another.

So, I experimented on myself instead. I studied nutrition and how to use food as medicine, letting my inner science nerd come out to play. I worked out a way to find out which foods nourished my unique body and which foods acted like poison in my system. I found a way to create my own ideal way of eating, specific to my unique body, and in the process I began to listen to the language of my body.

I changed the way I ate and it made an immediate difference to my symptoms, despite my doctor insisting that "it won't change a thing." My journey with food and the subsequent effect on my physical health was so profound that I later went on to become a certified nutrition coach, so I would have the expertise to support others with their nutrition too.

The most fascinating thing was, as I cleaned up my diet and started eating the foods that aligned with my body, I started to receive clear intuitive guidance. At the time I didn't call it that, but that's what it was. I now know that with every positive shift you make in the physical world, you raise your vibration on a metaphysical level. My vibration was rising, and as it did, anything that was not a vibrational match began to fall away.

LESSON 2: YOU ARE AN INTUITIVE BEING — YOU WERE BORN THAT WAY

Intuition is not reserved exclusively for a few lucky, gifted souls.
It is your birthright.

As your physical body becomes cleaner, your metaphysical body becomes clearer. Your consciousness upgrades and your connection to your highest self (the divine aspect of you) becomes stronger.

Put simply: As you align with your soul your intuitive ability will sky-rocket as a result.

As my dormant intuitive ability became activated, I found myself drawn to things without being able to explain why. These things served me very deeply. Like the time I was in a funky clothing store in Fremantle and stumbled across a flyer for a "Food As Medicine" workshop series that would start the next day. I felt the intuitive nudge and immediately signed up. That course kickstarted my journey to use food to help heal my body.

After that, in a leap of blind faith, I booked a ticket to a full-day spiritual event on the other side of the country without knowing why. I just knew I needed to be there.

I couldn't explain it. Even though I'd had my third son only months before, I knew that I had to attend. It all felt right. The flights, accommodation and childcare presented themselves to me effortlessly a couple of weeks out. By the time I arrived at the beautiful historic convent where the event was to unfold, I knew exactly why I was there. It was to ask a famous Medical Intuitive a question, a question to which her answer would radically change my work - and my remaining physical symptoms - from that day on.

It all felt like the Universe was conspiring to support me, and I delighted in this new-found feeling of support.

LESSON 3: THE UNIVERSAL LAW OF SUPPORT HOLDS TRUE — THE UNIVERSE IS ALWAYS SUPPORTING YOU

Even when it feels like it isn't. Especially when it feels like it isn't. Your life's events happen FOR you, not TO you.

By "the Universe" I mean God, Source, divine consciousness, Oneness, the unified field, the divine matrix, the quantum jelly that connects us all, <insert your preferred term here>.

You are a mirror for the divine, so know that your body is always supporting you, too. Especially when it feels like it isn't. Your body is always supporting you to awaken further. Calling you home to your soul.

As my life began to align with my soul-calling, I found myself stepping further and further out of my spiritual closet. I studied intuition in depth and began teaching others how to access their intuition, too.

My guidance invited me to choose a completely different path in every aspect of my life, but it does not always have to be that drastic! I had found myself in a pretty bad situation - correction: I had chosen it. So my body, at the tender age of 29, was pleading with me in the only way it knew how, to make a new choice.

I discovered that the physical issues I was suffering from, the life-long diagnoses and crippling symptoms that went with them, were directly linked to the choices I had been making every day. When you are unhappy with your life but stay in it, you continue to choose what makes you unhappy, every single day.

LESSON 4: YOUR CHOICES HOLD WEIGHT IN YOUR PHYSICAL BODY

Not just your choices around food, lifestyle, or exercise. ALL your choices. Including relationships, environment, work, beliefs, fears, perceptions, self-talk, and trauma perception. These can create very tangible disruptions within your physiology, which lead to illness and injury.

You are metaphysical first, physical second. In terms of health this means that your feelings, emotions, beliefs, fears - the intangible aspects of you - exist before the physical results.

This doesn't mean that your suffering is your fault. Your body is never punishing you for the choices you have made. Rather, your body is trying to communicate with you through the language of symptoms. This is to guide you to make a different choice. It is inviting you to support your body to heal and it's doing the best it can under the circumstances.

In the year after that fateful birthday I changed everything. I packed up my kids and left my first husband. I started eating in a way that served my body instead of harming it. I did what felt good for me and what nourished me, instead of punishing myself or trying to escape my life. I reconnected with the long-lost love of my life - my high school sweetheart - who has been my rock ever since. The puzzle pieces of my life began to fall into place to become a new, more soul-aligned picture of me.

LESSON 5: YOUR BODY IS A CHANNEL FOR DIVINE GUIDANCE

Every symptom, every medical sign - even an injury - is an invitation to open a line of communication with your body. Really it is communication THROUGH your body as information channels through you from your highest self.

So often, spiritual teachers talk about the body being inconsequential, but this is so far from the truth! Your body is the temple that houses your soul. It is the physical manifestation of your soul in a three-dimensional world, and it is a channel for guidance from your highest self if you allow it to be. Not just about what to do to physically support your body to heal, but also about what job to work in, what house to live in, which partner to choose, whether to turn left or right. Everything.

Your body is a powerful compass for your life if you allow it to be.

So, what can you do to activate this natural Medical Intuitive power within you?
Here are 3 steps to become your own Medical Intuitive to start using your body as a compass to connect with your soul:

STEP 1: ELIMINATE THE BACKGROUND NOISE

The best way to begin to hear the whispers of your soul through your body is to eliminate the background noise. Inflammation in your physical body creates background noise for your intuition. It's much harder to receive and interpret the messages coming through your body if there is more inflammatory noise within the system.

Some foods may create inflammation within your system without you knowing. Find out what nourishes and heals you and what acts like a poison in your system by removing processed, inflammatory, stimulatory, and addictive foods from your diet. Eat as close to nature as possible. Saturate your body with fresh vegetables, fruits, water, fish, and high-quality meats. Use fresh herbs and spices to flavor your food, instead of processed condiments. Experiment and find out how your body prefers to be nourished.

If this sounds too overwhelming, then start small. Remember one small step towards eating and living cleaner will begin to raise your vibration and decrease the background noise on your intuition. Simply take the next step in the direction that feels good to you. I created The RESET Protocol to make it easy for people to take this step with me. Check out my website for some delicious recipes to get you started!

STEP 2: TURN UP THE VOLUME

Turn up the volume on your own Medical Intuition by meditating every day. Meditation is how we focus our attention on the gentle whisper of our intuition. It doesn't have to be lengthy or at the same time each day (although many people will tell you otherwise). Just find a little time for meditation every day. Even a few minutes a day will make a huge difference.

In addition to meditating, it is important to also learn about the chakras - the energy centres within your metaphysical body - and begin a dialogue with them in your meditations. Get familiar with your own energy field, even if it's new to you.

Sit in silence, presence, and stillness each day and learn to focus your awareness and receive.

STEP 3: ASK AND RECEIVE THE ANSWERS

Ask your body questions and allow the answers to land within you. Sit with what you are feeling in your body and where you are feeling it. What is that part of the body used for? What metaphysical meaning is associated with it?

Then ask yourself:

- What else is happening in my life right now?
- Why am I experiencing this now?
- Where am I pushing too hard?
- Where am I holding back?

- Where am I out of alignment?

Tune in to what is specific for you and allow the information to arrive however it chooses to. Sometimes you may have a deep knowing of the answer, other times you may see an image or hear a word with your inner senses. And sometimes the answers may arrive later, in the words of a song on the radio, or in a sudden craving for a food you don't normally eat which has the exact nutrients your body is asking for.

If you'd like a more comprehensive list of self-enquiry questions you can download one at *www.emmaturton.com.au*.

That day, back in 2006, was the beginning of my journey to regain my health. A path that took me on a deep dive into Medical Intuition. One that changed every single aspect of my life, including completely recovering my health and healing ALL of my "life-long" diagnoses.

What I learned changed everything, and it is my earnest wish that it will help you, too.

So, if you want to make some changes to your physical health and you have been looking outside yourself for the answers, I invite you to go within, instead, using the steps that I have provided here. This journey will change your life, and I am here to support, encourage and challenge you to take back your power, every step of the way.

ABOUT THE AUTHOR

Emma Turton is a leading international Medical Intuitive and founder and director of Medical Intuition School. A rare combination of both health-science nerd and intuitive bad-ass, she sinks her teeth into the place where medicine and metaphysics meet. Emma uses her powerful intuitive eye to see inside people -- and guides them to heal from within using Medical Intuition as a compass for life and health.

An international #1 bestselling author and award-winning university lecturer with 20+ years of clinical experience as a physiotherapist and nutrition coach under her belt, Emma also teaches a world-class Medical Intuition Practitioner Training course that is set to change the global paradigm for health and spirituality.

Website: www.medicalintuitionschool.com
and www.emmaturton.com.au
Facebook: www.facebook.com/emmaturtonhealth
Email: hello@emmaturton.com.au

GABRIELA BRUNNER

SHIFTING OUT OF "HUSTLE" INTO ALLOWING & FLOW THROUGH CONSCIOUS CONNECTION

Lately it seems as though we've moved away from glorifying "busy-ness" to glorifying "hustle."

All I seem to hear these days is "The hustle is REAL," "Bosses Hustle," and "Hustle to build your empire."

But, do we even know what *hustle* means?

Hustle - verb:

1. force (someone) to move hurriedly or unceremoniously in a specified direction.
2. obtain by forceful action or persuasion.

Essentially, to hustle means to create by force. (Insert a cringey face.)

HERE'S MY THEORY: The hustle is *not* real.

Let me give you an example:

You show up every day at the same time. You work hard, really hard. You get all As, not Bs or Cs, As. You start taking college level classes before you even graduate high school. You are done with two years of college before you ever step foot on a college campus. You graduate with all A's, valedictorian of your class.

Next thing you know you are swapping the college hallways for the corporate hallways. You haven't stepped foot outside in months. You haven't touched the Earth in years. You haven't seen the sun shine except through the blinds that are pulled down over your office window to reduce the glare on your computer screen. You've typed hundreds, if not thousands, of memos. You don't even remember the last time you went outside for a walk.

And you are doing this because your mother/father/spouse/mentor or even society expects you to.

That's the hustle.

The hustle is not real.

"Excuse me," you say, "but that's all I have been taught. I don't know any other way." Yes, I know my child, you don't know any other way. But that is changing right now because ... the hustle is not real.

WHAT DOES THE HUSTLE FEEL LIKE?

Here's what I think. Before I found my true calling (passions\gifts\strengths), I felt like I had to hustle every workday just to get by. I felt as though I was forcing everything: tasks, that smile on my face, my sense of happiness and well-being, everything.

Everything felt like an uphill battle. *Everything* felt like a fight. And when everyone around you is trying to make light of their situations ("I'm always busy! No, I am waaaaaayyyy busier! Actually, I'm busier AND I hustle too!") they tend to find comfort in voicing their unhappiness in this way. I wanted to learn more. I needed to learn more.

As I researched and studied this concept of "hustle," I learned that when you perform tasks (job related or otherwise) that are out of alignment with what you are truly *meant* to do, aka your Soul's Purpose, then, *the hustle will be real.*

And since that is one side of the coin, the other side must be that once you bring your life into alignment with your Soul's Purpose, you will be full of a peaceful momentum that will gracefully guide you through your day. In other words, little to no *hustle* at all.

So, what do you do? How do you be? How do you allow yourself to stop forcing and creating something that was only happening because of that exerted energy and effort? How do you allow yourself to just be and allow things to come to you?

Those are the questions. And the answers come when you awaken your inner peace through conscious connection.

AWAKENING INNER PEACE THROUGH CONSCIOUS CONNECTION

In order to begin the process of releasing the hustle, you must first connect to your heart. It's that simple and that complicated all at once. There's nothing more to do than connect to your heart. It is one of those things that you have to learn through experience. No one else can tell you what that will feel like to you. You have to be willing to open yourself up to different experiences so you can begin to understand what it feels like to be connected to your heart space.

There are a lot of different things out there that will help you let go of the hustle and step into your heart space. The very first step is to identify what it feels like to be in YOUR heart space. To be in that space where your heart guides your decisions, where your heart tells you without a shadow of a doubt to turn left instead of right, even though the entire world is telling you to turn right.

So where do you begin?

The honest truth is that there is no right answer to this question. There is no "one-size-fits-all step one." There is only a step, your step, whatever that may be. To assist you in this process, I am going to review a few of the modalities that have worked for me and for my clients. What works for me may not be the exact thing that works for you, however, by allowing yourself to experience and touch and feel and move and breathe, you will awaken your conscious connection and be guided towards your first and next best step.

Let's create the menu, a buffet of sorts, to help you see the choices, to help you understand how to connect to the best choice for you right now. It's important to note this last piece, "the best choice for you right now." Tomorrow, that choice might be different. Next week it certainly will be different. And guess what? You want it to be different, because this is the mark that you are moving forwards in your journey. So, open yourself up, receive guidance from your heart, and act upon that guidance.

Let's begin, in no particular order, with Conscious Breath.

CONSCIOUS BREATH

How do you know you are alive? Because You Breathe.

Our breath is our prana, our life force. Through breath, we bring in this vital energy, which is essential to an aligned life. Yogic breathing techniques, or *pranayam*, are designed to expand our life force and bring vitality to our lives.

"Once we increase our awareness, we can consciously bring *prana* into areas of our body that need healing. We weave together the scattered parts of ourselves and reclaim them, renew them with the pulse of life."- KRI International Teacher Training Manual Level 2 | Vitality & Stress, pg. 235

Through Conscious Breath, we activate our *prana* and align our chakras. Chakras are energy centers that run along our spine. There are many chakras, but the most common are: Root, Sacral, Solar Plexus, Heart, Throat, Third Eye, Crown, and Aura. Breath is the connection between them all.

Breathing is automatic and very few of us actually realize that we are doing it. It is something we have learned to take for granted. Today, take a few moments to really focus on your breath. Notice how it feels as you inhale. Notice how it feels as you exhale. Just notice.

Next time you feel anxious, rushed, stressed, or run-ragged, simply breathe.

Practice Tip: Sit in a comfortable position on the floor, in a chair or lying down. Begin by bringing awareness to your breath. Once you know you are breathing, practice inhaling for 3-5 counts, holding for 3-5 counts, exhaling for 3-5 counts, and holding for 3-5 counts. Repeat.

As you engage in this breath awareness practice, your lung capacity will increase, and you may find yourself inhaling for ten or more counts. Be patient with yourself. Honor where you are. Breathe.

As you become aware of your breath, then become aware of the inner voice inside of you that is sharing your Soul Purpose with you.

CONSCIOUS MOVEMENT

Movement is essential to well-being. Through movement we harness our physical bodies to feel and process our emotions, get physically strong, and calibrate our nervous systems. A strong body is the vessel that supports our sacred work in this world. Through movement, we honor our physicality and use it to serve.

One of the most complete ways to engage in Conscious Movement that I know of is through the ancient technology of Kundalini Yoga. As a KRI Certified Kundalini Yoga Instructor, I guide students to use movement, dynamic breathing techniques, meditation, and chanting to build physical vitality and increase consciousness. I also incorporate sound healing through the vibrations of a 30" Paiste Symphonic Gong.

Kundalini Yoga is called the Yoga of Awareness. It is a dynamic, powerful tool that is designed to give you an experience of your soul. In Kundalini Yoga we harness the mental, physical, and nervous energies of the body and put them under the domain of the will, which is the instrument of the soul. Through this process, we become re-connected to our minds, our bodies, and our hearts. The best way to see if this works for you is to experience a class.

Regardless of whether you choose to practice Kundalini yoga, the key takeaway here is to find a form of Conscious Movement that allows you to connect to your body, your soul, and your mind so you can awaken your inner peace and release the need to hustle.

Practice Tip: Get out in your local community and experience a movement class! You can also check out my Events tab on my website to experience a Kundalini Yoga class with me.

CONSCIOUS EXPRESSION

Expression of your most authentic self is powerful and a key to living a life that feels wonderful to you. It is also a big piece of the 'less hustle, more heart' journey.

So how do you awaken your unique Conscious Expression? That will be unique to you. Each one of us enjoys the act of expressing ourselves differently. When we combine Conscious Movement with Conscious Breath, our unique Conscious Expression naturally flows. When we are in alignment, we tend to share our true selves with the world. And when we are in alignment, we are more inclined to trust in the natural flow of life, and, you guessed it, hustle less.

. . .

PRACTICE TIP: Experiment with different ways of expressing yourself. Perhaps you like writing or painting. Perhaps you love cooking or nurturing your family. The more you listen to your heart and express it, the less hustle you will feel.

CONSCIOUS SOUL

Your Soul is the gateway to your Essence. Wake up to its magnificence. Wake up to *you*.

The Soul is magical. I believe that it is the very encapsulation of our essence. Yet, how can we access our Soul's wisdom? How can we hear its voice?

To be honest, I struggled with this for a while. I learned to listen to and trust my intuition most definitively with my work in the *Akashic Records.*

"The Akashic Records are the record of your soul's journey, from the time you first arise from Source until you eventually return home. This can take millennia. But no matter how new or ancient of a Soul you are, the Akashic energy holds all your thoughts, feelings, actions and deeds from each lifetime. Many people imagine the Akashic Record as a library with each book representing a lifetime. Some people look at the Records as a computer with all your info stored in the hard drive.

You have your own Masters, Teachers and Beings of Light that keep track of this information, just for you. We can access these Masters & Teacher and they will answer your personal questions about this life and the past lives which are affecting you today. When you realize that you came into life with a plan, it becomes very useful to access information about that plan. We come to complete some Karma, fulfill our past life Vows or to be with someone special and to support people who are part of our soul family. The human challenge is that as soon as we're born we forget this plan. At times in our life we feel blocked or constricted or disappointed in our life because we don't remember why we chose our families or situations. We may feel life is unfair or very difficult. I access the Akashic Records to help you learn information about these situations and to heal and clear the emotional pain. You can ask questions in relation to: health, career, relationships, life purpose, self-esteem and abundance." Copyright – Lisa Barnett and the Akashic Knowing School of Wisdom.

You may find that you awaken your Conscious Soul through Astrology, Reiki,

Yoga, Meditation, or any other type of conscious connection. I'm sure you are starting to see a pattern here; the key is to experience all that you are a guided to experience and do more of what resonates with you!

Practice Tip: I invite you to use any or all *of these powerful prayers*, for 33 days, to watch big shifts happen in your life. How will you know which one to use? Listen to your heart, she knows the way.

You are on your way towards awakening your inner peace and letting go of the hustle!

* * *

This practice, moving from hustle to alignment, is a shift in perception. It is a shift in having to seek external validation for all that you are. You are. Period. There is really nothing else beyond that. Because you are, *you are.*

I know that sounds circular and esoteric, but at the end of the day, you do not need to prove yourself or validate yourself to anyone else. Not through degrees, not through salary, not through approval of your boss or approval of your parents. The challenging piece is that we have been conditioned to believe that we must constantly be proving our worth to others. And it feels impossible to break through this pattern, to collapse this idea that we need the validation of another to have value or meaning in our life.

That is why it is crucial to learn how to tap into your own heart energy. The moment we begin to open up this channel of communication between our heart and our actions, then we begin to feel the fact that we are who we are and that is enough.

One of my favorite examples is the experience of having a child. Perhaps you are the parent who birthed the child, or maybe you did not birth the child, but when that child comes into your life, you see nothing but love, possibility, and hope. There is not a single flaw or imperfection. All you feel is pure love. Even if that child engages in an activity that is not "correct" according to society, they are still perfect. They do not need to do anything to earn or deserve your love. They simply have it because they are.

Now, take that notion and flip it onto yourself. Look at yourself in the mirror and shower yourself with the same love that you would a child (or other person in your life that you love unconditionally).

Turn the light on and have it shine on exactly who you are because that is the same truth for you. You do not need to do anything other than be who you are, live from your heart, and walk the path that is guided to you by your heart. Awaken your inner peace through conscious connections and dismantle the theory that the hustle is the only way to get anything done because, the hustle is not real.

And remember, "Grace will take you places hustling can't." -Elizabeth Gilbert.

#MoreGraceLessHustle

ABOUT THE AUTHOR

Gabriela Brunner, J.D., is the founder of Gabriela Brunner Coaching and co-author of "Awakening During the time of Corona." Her approach to personal development is one of cultivating compassion and curiosity towards oneself. As a result, her clients (re)define success by identifying and honoring their own inner voice and taking action on it.

Gabriela is a KRI Certified Kundalini Yoga Instructor, Reiki Master & Teacher, Akashic Records Practitioner and Intuitive Coach. She is the author of the illustrated book "Mama, Where Is the Truth?" She currently works at Richland Community College as a Career Coach.

Gabriela is also the co-founder of Conscious You – a not for profit designed to make spirituality accessible.

At her core, Gabriela believes in gently and lovingly supporting those around her to awaken their inner peace through conscious connection.

Gabriela was raised in Honduras and currently lives in Illinois with her husband and their two children.

> *Website:* www.gabrielabrunner.com
> and www.mamawhereisthetruth.com
> and www.consciousyou.life
> *Email:* gabrielabrunnercoaching@gmail.com
> *Facebook:* www.facebook.com/gabrielabrunnercoaching
> *Instagram:* www.instagram.com/gabrielabrunnercoaching

HELEN MARTINEAU

MARY MAGDALENE: THE FEMALE CHRIST INITIATE

There are rare individuals, high initiates who, when they incarnate come to earth, have a particular purpose that assists soul evolution. And at a certain point their greater destiny opens up. Mary Magdalene is a soul like this.

ON HER GLOBAL SIGNIFICANCE

Mary incarnated in first-century Palestine, imbued with ancient feminine wisdom gained in former lives. She awakened to a new dawn when she received the world-changing impulse from Jesus the Christ, in whom the archetypes of myth became mystical fact on the plane of human existence. In the mystery of love and death she fulfilled the destiny that began for her when the world was young, and her beautiful soul continues to have a significant influence in the world today. Mary Magdalene helps us to rediscover the spiritual path that became known as *the Christ Mystery.*

As a child I loved the church with its rituals and Bible stories, but my questions only ever enlisted a simplistic response, especially about God 'out there.' Believing without knowing was not enough and so began a lifelong quest for spiritual knowledge.

By my early twenties I was living in England and a mum to my daughter and son. Involvement in dance and drama connected me with the spirit in nature and with myths and symbols that speak of the mighty Gods and Goddesses not as external powers, but as archetypes within the soul. And the feminist movement inevitably led me into the realm of the goddesses. It seemed to me that there was no room for Christianity, at least as the church's patriarchal teaching defined it. Yet I still yearned for something lost.

There is an old saying that when the soul is ready, the teacher appears. Back in Australia, I found that teacher, Mario Schoenmaker (1929 –1997), a most unorthodox priest and seer in touch with the eternal. I entered a modern mystery school with a yearning heart and Mario helped unlock the metaphysical and mystical depths within the gospels, and, most importantly, the eternal feminine aspect of the divine was in there.

I know now that genuine Christianity is not about churches or any man-made religion. It is the journey towards the true humanity of the future that promises wholeness in body, soul, and spirit – but as a potential.

In the present we are seeing the outcomes of materialistic, destructive, egocentric, yang-dominated ways. In Australia, my home, terrifying bushfires ripped through temperate forests that had never been burnt. Many people and a billion creatures and plants unique to this land perished. These devastations were followed without pause by the world-wide corona virus pandemic that shut down the lives we assumed were normal. It is breaking apart the fabric of our societies. Fear is widespread.

Yet the larger view reveals that renewal is possible through a revolution in consciousness, so that love and care for one another and for the earth herself becomes the norm. But we must change our minds. And high among the solutions is the need to restore the balance of the feminine.

Mary Magdalene was the first woman to be initiated into the Christ Mystery, where she discovered the active involvement of the goddess of many names, encapsulated as divine Wisdom. Her experience is especially relevant today for all, regardless of gender, as we undergo a seismic shift towards a new age. 'Magdalene Christianity' begins, then, with claiming the rejected half of the human soul. This is important for women and men with spiritual, psychological, and physical dimensions.

FINDING MARY MAGDALENE BENEATH THE VEILS OF TIME

As a Christian priestess, my teaching has covered a range of metaphysical themes. My writing has included articles for spiritually based magazines, a website, and three published books. The third in 2016, a novel, *Marriages of the Magdalene*, was motivated by a wish to restore the balance alive among the earliest Christians but lost as the church evolved. I called on an Eastern Orthodox church tradition that placed Mary Magdalene in Ephesus in Turkey, where she worked with John the Beloved, the gospel author, and in some versions married him. In the novel, Mary and the beloved disciple are portrayed as counterparts who are initiated through Christ into the 'marriage' within their souls.

Typical for an author, I had folders full of material I did not use in the novel. And Mary Magdalene was not finished with me. I was urged to share more of what she had revealed via my research, plus an injunction to 'Write my gospel.' That second request truly challenged me.

At least I had a starting point. I knew her story involved a Christ path that would shine a light on Wisdom, long hidden but not lost after all.

In Mary Magdalene's time, Wisdom was still a living being, and Mary would have experienced this intuitively as she listened to readings from, for example, the book of Proverbs, which is all about the getting of wisdom.

Still, in first-century Palestine, women had little status and no religious authority. The message Jesus brought was radically different. It was for all who 'hunger and thirst,' for the inner beauty of the soul, whoever they were. This was about inner freedom, including freedom for women, to discover their true beingness, a freedom inspired by empathy and love. It was natural for women to be among the disciples and to become apostles and early Christian leaders.

But doors would close again on a message deemed too radical. Women would be denied any authority as the church became an establishment.

The reputation of Mary Magdalene, the first apostle, suffered. The most damaging story originated in the sixth century – Mary the redeemed whore. Pope Gregory the 1st, 'the Great,' had a lot to do with turning an independent, loving, visionary woman into a licentious sexual sinner. He combined several women appearing in the gospels to build a composite character.

In 591 the pope declared in his homily number 33:

> *She whom Luke calls the sinful woman, whom John calls Mary, we believe to be Mary from whom seven devils were ejected, according to Mark. And what did these seven devils signify, if not all the vices?*

Those vices were known as the seven deadly sins – pride, greed, envy, gluttony, wrath, sloth, and lust. The Magdalene had them all. At best, she was a second Eve, atoning for the sins of the first Eve in the Garden of Eden, guilt all women should bear unless, like Mary, they repented. We are looking at a Roman Catholic establishment having real issues around sexuality and purity.

In a startling contrast, in 1945 a library of gnostic Christian texts was discovered stuffed in an urn in a cave near Nag Hammadi in Egypt. They had been hidden around the year 400, probably to keep them safe. Gnostics were not popular in a church that was becoming more dogmatic. These finds revolutionised understanding of early Christianity and Mary Magdalene in particular. Most of the texts were written at least a hundred years after Mary lived. But in them she is the one with greater wisdom and knowledge, unlike the prejudiced male disciples. Perhaps these writings contained memories of the real Mary.

There is so much that can be revealed about her by peeling back the veils of time. The kind of authority that lived in this woman in her full power can be reclaimed – an intelligence not limited to the linear, calculating, power-grabbing, 'masculine' mindset, but rather was a deep nature wisdom, with the ability to connect soul to soul and the knowledge of the heart so vital for the future of humankind and the whole earth.

Through Mary Magdalene's story we can see how the Christ spirit, uncontained by man-made forms, continued to operate, and in truth how Wisdom is always present, part of the all, part of us. We can awaken wisdom through our conscious efforts, and it is important that we remember this, always.

LEGENDS OF THE MAGDALENE

As the centuries progressed, the Roman church would dominate Western Europe. In medieval times life was hard, violent, and rough, and spirituality was part of everyday life in a way that's alien to most people in our secular culture. Human life was not valued, but the state of the soul was, and the church aimed to control souls through its hierarchical structure. Religion was a refuge, yet it failed to fulfil a deep spiritual need for the sacred feminine. Among the diverse impulses that emerged as counters to patriarchal orthodoxy were legends of Mary Magdalene as beloved saint.

In one legend Mary Magdalene is said to have come to Glastonbury in England, carrying her alabaster jar, the one she used to anoint Jesus, now containing his holy blood, which she caught as he hung on the cross. She was in the party of Joseph of Arimathea and brought this holy object to the ancient mystery site. The legend says that her alabaster jar was the true Holy Grail and so began her association with the Grail stories.

Some of her legends were accepted by the Catholic church, like that of her journey to France, included in a 'lives of the saints', called the *Legenda Aurea*, or Golden Legend, written in 1260. The author, Jacopo di Voraigne, drew this immensely popular compilation of miraculous escapes, healings, and fantastic beasts from a range of earlier sources.

The story goes that Mary Magdalene was cast out to sea by enemies in a rudderless boat with Lazarus, Martha, a new disciple called Maximin, and others. They ended up in the region of Marseilles. She made her way to a cave high in the Sainte-Beaume mountains, where she spent her last thirty years upheld by angels.

Our modern wish to 'prove' the facts about everything has no place in legends. They have an inner verity and their potency endures. Legends particularise universal myth. And in the case of the divine feminine, my sense is that the stories growing up around Mary Magdalene made up for what the church in western Europe had sent underground.

The sites themselves have power and resonate with the love of countless pilgrims. In France, Mary's cave, now a lovely grotto chapel, and the cool beech forest below watered by sacred springs, is a most ancient holy region, where Ligurian druids offered sacrifices and Greeks and Romans worshipped the great mother goddess as Cybele.

Today when you walk as a pilgrim through the ancient forest and climb the steps to the grotto, in some mysterious manner, Mary, who may well invoke the ancient goddess, is present in your meditations. Her love touches you in a profound way. This happens in places where countless imaginations have attuned to their sacredness and is often why we visit such sites. Such settings have an aura and it is the power within legends that gives them their longevity.

INITIATION AND THE CHRIST MYSTERY

Mary Magdalene's extraordinary impact has continued through the centuries. And through her soul's wisdom we can rediscover the rarely understood depth in the account of Christ Jesus. It exists as an almost forgotten stream beneath the patriarchal church, which in many ways has become an outdated institution. Here I will touch on certain aspects that relate to initiation.

Once humanity lived absorbed in the divine realms. But as consciousness evolved, that innate connection was lost. This is a vast evolutionary story, so I will jump forward to the time when humans had moved so far from knowledge of the divine, special initiations were needed to enable the reconnection.

Initiation took place within the cult or religion. There was a path laid out and it was followed rigorously. Entrance into the deeper levels required dependence on a more evolved hierophant – a priest or priestess. Today we have a debased remnant of this in religious leaders and their rules that demand obedience.

Yet counter to this came the human push towards individualism. It is still going on, even as comprehension of the spiritual realms has retreated for the bulk of society and the physical world seems the only reality. We can be thankful it is not like this for everyone. In our age there is a return to the spirit. This gradual re-acquaintance was made possible at a spiritual low point 2000 years ago (both physical and spiritual evolution move very slowly). An 'intrusion' from the spiritual realms took place when materialism was beginning to entrench itself, typified by the Romans, who were innovative engineers and administrators across the conquered lands. But they borrowed where the spiritual was concerned.

Divine Wisdom was powerfully involved at the pivotal point of time when the dove-like spirit descended upon Jesus the chosen one, and the high being that would be called Christ incarnated in a human. This leaves us in no doubt – the divine feminine is part of the Christ and part of Christ in us.

Jesus Christ was prototype of *anthropos*, the completed and harmonised human being. Mary, through her preparedness and profound inner experiences, reached the mystical marriage in her soul with the Christ spirit, which she encountered at the empty tomb.

THE WISDOM OF MARY MAGDALENE GUIDES US STILL

Through her free will she chose to become a disciple, and she had the courage to go alone to the tomb of her teacher. This was her own initiative and such action is significant for us.

Initiation as it was once practised ended with the Christ event. Along with the rise of individualism, now we must personally and individually undertake the initiatory journey. And it takes place in the world, through experiences and challenges. You don't need to belong to a church, a group, or any religion. Relationships that bless are found in people, especially those who can respond inwardly.

Through her transformed soul Mary Magdalene represents the wisdom that comes from within, through the soul's trials in the sense-based world. She bridges the earthly and spiritual realms. If we can know this Mary, she is revealed as a living example for us of the personal initiatory path.

It begins with the human soul, which consists of the contents of our consciousness, non-physical, yet vibrantly alive in us. At the very heart of our soul is the spiritual 'I' or the Christ self. The new kind of initiation leads us to true spiritual individuality. Mary loved consciously in her full humanity, body, soul, and spirit. My dedication is to the inner process clearly defined by her, and to teaching the balancing and harmonizing mystical way of 'Magdalene Christianity.'

We incarnate to discover and awaken the spiritual self, the essence of who we are, and through our own hard work and discipline, seek to penetrate beyond ordinary knowledge to knowledge of spiritual reality. The deepest purpose of human life is to manifest the spiritual self in the world.

Often setting out is triggered by a dramatic wake-up through a life-changing event. Sometimes a feeling of 'divine dissatisfaction' will grow until you know you must act on the longing in your soul. There may even be a moment when you seem to slip out of the ordinary world of time and space to glimpse the fullness of what you can be, and you are drawn to seek this wholeness.

In whatever way you experience the call to action, the path must be entered through a conscious decision to participate in a personal journey of transformation. It is a harder way than of old and a lonely one, involving fully delving into the forces of the soul, including the darkness that inevitably lives in us, which must be faced and transformed.

But Wisdom is there, as she was for Mary Magdalene. Initiated to her human fullness by Christ Jesus when he walked the earth, Mary speaks even now with truth and grace, singing her songs of love for all life, beautiful as only the fully empowered, fully Christ-filled female voice can be. Mary's enlightened soul is always available to work with the spiritual forces that assist the evolution of human consciousness.

But only if we ask her to. And this must be our own choice, uninfluenced by anything but our heart's wish. Unencumbered decision-making is a characteristic that leads us towards the spiritual self, and toward being a truly free individual, able to lovingly embrace all.

I did eventually write a Gospel of Mary Magdalene. And perhaps her soul let me know it was time. Her wonderful gospel unfolded during my meditation on the most unusual Easter Sunday 2020, in the midst of Covid-19 isolation. Mary's Wisdom gospel of the soul has a special place in my heart. It is the last portal on my website: www.magdalenechristianity.com.

A MAGDALENE MEDITATION

On the spiritual journey we have Mary Magdalene's symbolic attributes as entry points and as continuing inspiration. The meditation below can extend to a series of meditations on each of the symbols.

For this meditation you take note of the symbols but go inward without further research on their meaning. The intention is to discover what emerges spontaneously in your soul.

Here they are:

- *The alabaster jar* – Mary anointed the feet of Jesus with its precious oil in preparation for his death.
- *Her seven 'demons'* – Luke's gospel mentions that she is cured of them although there is no description of what they are.
- *The skull* – Mary is frequently depicted contemplating a skull.
- *A red egg* – Mary holds up the egg, a common symbol in Eastern Orthodox icons.
- *Her name* – Mary, Maria, Mariam, after Miriam the sister of Moses, whose first home was in Egypt, where the name was derived from *mryt* 'loved one.'

- *Magdalene* — from *migdal/magdal*, which means 'tower,' this was a title given to her.

Allow yourself to sink into a meditative state. Invoke Mary Magdalene's beautiful soul and ask for guidance.

Let the symbols emerge without conscious mind effort. Don't be concerned if not all come before you, or if only one presents itself. You are going to allow your inner being to choose one symbol.

What is this symbol? Let it become clearer to you; colours, atmosphere, surroundings. Where is it? Do you see an environment or setting?

Without judgement, become aware of any feelings and associations. Be with your symbol and let a word or phrase come to you. This is the message offered to you by Mary Magdalene.

Before you return, thank her. Her beloved soul is always ready to give of her wisdom.

ABOUT THE AUTHOR

Helen Martineau is a teacher, speaker, author, and lover of the mysteries. Her early career in the arts led her into humanity's great myths and spiritualities -- and to thirty years as a wisdom teacher and writer. Helen's published books include the powerful story of the spiritual essence of creativity and a novel about Mary Magdalene, the first woman initiated into the way of the inner Christ and a counterpart to the male beloved disciple in John's gospel.

Helen is dedicated to unravelling the deeper truths of Christianity as an initiatory path that embraces the goddess Wisdom. The beautiful soul of Mary Magdalene is her guide towards reclaiming the vital place of the divine feminine in a distinctive Magdalene Christianity.

Through ongoing mentoring and writing, Helen brings the Magdalene to light as a continuing inspiration for people today on the quest for the harmonious balance and wholeness that is the true Holy Grail.

Helen enjoys life with her beloved husband, as a parent and grandparent and attuning to the feminine spirit in nature.

> *Website:* www.helenmartineau.com.au
> and www.magdalenechristianity.com
> *Facebook:* www.facebook.com/helenmartineau.author
> *Email:* helenmartineauauthor@gmail.com

HOLLIS CITRON

CREATIVITY & EMPOWERING EXPERIENCES

Some people just know what they want, what college they are going to go to, what they want to be when they grow up, what their wedding is going to look like, and how many kids they want to have. I was not that person; were you?

As a younger person, up to my thirties or so, I would have described myself as a little serious, shy, empathic, and very aware, which made me very sensitive. I noticed some life experiences that could have disempowered me, but instead I became empowered.

EMPOWERING EXPERIENCE ONE

It was my senior year of high school. I applied to art school because I honestly did not know for sure what I wanted to do, but I always enjoyed art classes and found it to be a happy place for me. I had a guidance counselor that was not so supportive. When picking my schools, he said, "I don't think that you should apply to that school. You are not good enough to get in." Well, he was wrong. In hindsight, it was like one of those coming-of-age movies where I was the main character, growing and blossoming to find my true passion, so I can then say to Mr. P, *Look at me now*.

So I ended up going to art school and graduated with a BFA in Ceramics and later went on to get an MA in art education.

EMPOWERING EXPERIENCE TWO

It was my foundational year of college. We had to take drawing, a 3D art, and a 2D art class to have a well-rounded education and to determine our strengths and weaknesses, which would direct us towards a major. Drawing was never my thing really; I could get my ideas out on paper, but I didn't shine in that area.

In this class the teacher would do something that, when I became a teacher, I promised never to do. She would "fix" our work by drawing on our paper. It always bothered me; not that I did not need correcting, don't get me wrong. It just felt like a violation.

One day as she was making a change to my work, and I worked up the guts to say, "Please do not draw on my paper. Show me how to fix it on another piece of paper." Her response to me was, "I don't think that you are good enough to do it on your own."

Here I was, 19 years old, standing up to my teacher. I just could not keep it in anymore. As my voice trembled, I said, "I did not ask you if I was good enough. I just asked you not to draw on my paper." Well needless to say I got a D in the class. But to this day, I vowed to never draw on anyone's paper unless I ask permission first, and I will always demonstrate and allow them to try on their own.

Our experiences and things that people say often affect our beliefs about what we like, what we don't like, and what we think we can or can't do well. When I graduated from college, I fell into teaching art by accident. My mother was a teacher in the Philadelphia school system. I grew up around it, but did not know it would be my path. My first teaching experience was when I was 22.

EMPOWERING EXPERIENCE THREE

I got this amazing ceramic residency at the Clay Studio in Philadelphia, PA. The process of getting there felt like a nightmare. If you were to be considered for a spot, you would have to come in for an interview.

In my head I thought there would be 20 people sitting in a circle asking me questions, judging me, determining if I was WORTHY. Well the reality was, there were 15 people. I turned every shade of purple during the interview, but I got the spot.

Despite all the things I perceived as faults, the group saw me differently. I felt vulnerable, but was honest and they accepted me for who I was. It was really just a matter of me being open and rising to the challenge. I realized that it was in me this whole time and it took the process of failing, getting up, and waking up to figure it out.

EMPOWERING EXPERIENCE FOUR

With this opportunity, they told me I had to teach. Every insecurity that was not buried too deep came up. The screaming one was, "I am 22 years old and have to teach adults. Why the hell would they listen to me? What do I have to teach them?"

Well the pivotal moment for me was when I was in the classroom and witnessed two women standing across a table from each other. As they were getting ready to glaze their pieces, one asked the other to borrow a paint brush, and the other said, "Yes, as long as you give it back." I giggled to myself. Light bulb moment!

When you are just learning something for the first time, you have that childlike perspective and, in this case, I was the "expert" or the one with the most experience. Needless to say it was incredible and it really set me off in a career that would lead in many directions, with one mission: provide a space for expression.

My twenty five years plus in teaching experiences have not been traditional, which has its pluses and minuses. I do not have tenure in a school system with the big 401K or 504 and the comfort of retiring with my pension. But I have had the privilege of teaching ages of 2-100 in various states around the US in both general and special education.

The settings have been from traditional school systems to homeless shelters. The populations have been in both urban and suburban settings. At present I have been lucky enough to have the freedom to be an entrepreneur and start my own company, which is all about creativity.

Having been in many different settings, I have come to recognize basic categories of creative expression that people fall into. It varies, but it generally looks like this:

1. I am not an "Artist." I cannot draw a straight line or paint. People often think this is all you need to be creative. (By the way, this is not just an adult mindset. Young kids can say this as well, but it is usually because an adult said something to them.)

2. I want to do something, but I am not sure what and I don't want to make mistakes. We all know the answer to this. You have to make mistakes to get better. More on that later.
3. I am willing to try these different mediums and am ready to mess up so I can learn along the way. This last one is all about being open and comfortable with yourself. You can mess up and it is not a reflection of you as a person; it is so freeing to know that it is you just having fun and being vulnerable to know that you are not perfect.

My last stint as being an Art teacher in the traditional classroom was for five years in Philadelphia K-12. My main message always was that you do not have to know how to draw or paint to be creative, whether I said this to a child in the classroom or at the professional staff developments I led.

The formal definition of creativity is the formation of an idea or object. We do this all of the time, and are often unaware of the process. An important component of teaching, I have found, is that you have to meet people where they are.

If you are not showing them anything that interests them at all, or it seems unattainable, they will shut down and not even try. So much of navigating this creative process is about listening and observing. It is human nature to want to do something that you enjoy.

If you are pushing information without real inspiration on someone, you are fighting a losing battle. As a teacher, when you are truly listening and can provide a space for a person feel safe, so they can go out of their comfort zone, while providing them with the steps they need to feel it is attainable, then you are approaching the finish line.

People want to feel protected, to know that if they expose themselves they will not be harshly judged. Creative expression in whatever form it comes in is exposure to your thoughts and feelings, which can leave you feeling naked. The creative process is so often about trust. When we get comfortable with the process, we trust that we got this and we will get from point A to B somehow and someway.

There are so many stories to tell, but this one particular story sticks out in my mind. I was teaching in a catholic school in Camden, grades kindergarten to eighth. The interactions were limited because of the time frame and there were productive days and difficult days, often stemming from behavior issues.

This goes back to never knowing people's stories and their circumstances. Did they eat that day? Did the 11 year old wake up at 4 am to take care of the baby brother or sister? How many people live under one roof and are there enough beds? It could have also been coming from my end: Was I being clear enough in my directions, was the objective clear, am I talking too much, was there enough visuals to make it clearly understood? Basically, there are many factors that go on when communicating information.

EMPOWERING EXPERIENCE FIVE

How individuals handle their circumstances are each unique and many times you don't know others stories unless they are shared. This story is about an eighth grade class that was not the easiest to teach. There was lots of pushback and many personalities in one space.

This was so helpful. It taught me to be more effective and get to the point more succinctly and efficiently. This particular project was about designing their own businesses by coming up with the name, building a 3D model, and deciding specifically what they would sell.

One particular student was challenging. She was not always willing to participate and she was absent a lot. When in class, she would start a fight if so provoked. She was interested in this project, but was getting frustrated.

One day before class, she pulled me aside and told me that she could not come up with a name for her company. We talked about different possibilities based off her idea and then I tried to explain that a lot of the process is about connecting with the feeling. It is knowing something is right when you feel it in the pit of your stomach, like butterflies; then you know it's right.

I asked if she understood and she responded that she thought so. Later, I was in front of the class, doing a quick intro on what we were doing for the day. I will never forget what happened.

All of a sudden, I looked over at this girl and it was like a light bulb went on. Her spine straightened up and her face just lit up. I smiled and said, "You got it?" Her response was, "Yes." When we take the time to notice this visceral feeling, when we take the time to breathe and to notice, it has the power to be life-changing.

It is obviously easier to teach a subject to someone who wants to be there and who wants to do the work that is required to grow. When there is no resistance, it is all about ease and flow. But I have to say that being in that space, where there was push back and behavior issues, there was a massive opportunity for growth.

EMPOWERING EXPERIENCE 6

When teaching another class, I realized that I would never have a more difficult audience, and it was a gift. I had to learn how to make art approachable, how to make it something that someone at least had enough interest to stick their toe in the water and be willing to try.

I truly got to experience the saying, you never know who you are affecting and how. This scenario was a high school in Philadelphia. The class that I taught was for grades tenth to twelfth. We met the first period of the day at 8:30am.

The kids would trickle in and this one particular boy would do just enough to get by, like many others, but he stood out to me because of his polite, but lawyerly approach when describing why he did not want to participate. He was a senior and had to take art to fulfill the requirements to graduate.

I implemented a program that was choice-based, but structured. It was meant to satisfy many of the kids like him. It was about giving them the power to choose techniques based on their interests.

I would go around the class and with him he would often say, "I really don't care, no offense, I am not an artist." My response was always, "I get it, really, but since you are here you, have an opportunity to try some different things and explore your interests, so why not use the time well."

As far as "results" went, I would see him ebb and flow with effort, but as I said he was respectful enough. He did well enough to pass. At graduation that year, I made little gifts and wrote notes to the students, trying to individualize the messages as much as possible.

I remember when I gave him his little gift, he gave me a hug. He was so tall, and I am 5 feet tall. He said to me, "Mrs. Citron, I will never forget you."

It really took my breath away. When you realize that you are so blessed to have the opportunity to expose people to new possibilities, to allow them to shed their skin and be vulnerable, it is a true honor to be allowed to be part of the process.

So I have left the classroom and dove into my company, which is all about creativity and empowering people to access their own expression, explore interests, and expanding their thinking. I am loving working with adults now.

AWAKENING

We get caught up in life (work, family, meals, cleaning house) and we forget what really interests us. What really lights us up! What we are really here to do to achieve our life's purpose.

Now you might be thinking, "How can I be a more deliberate creator? How can I tap into what I really desire?" You might be saying, "Hollis, I don't know where to start."

What I would say to this is, it is really all in the baby steps. If you try to go from A to Z, you are going to get frustrated and just give up and tuck that attempt away and chalk it up as, well I suck at that! Never gonna do that again!

So here are some easy, manageable ways to make you feel excited about tapping into your interests and talents:

1. Carve out at least 15 minutes a day to do something that you like. Start there and it will grow in time.
2. If you are not sure what you like, journal it out and just get it on paper, as silly or trivial as it all might sound. I call it thought vomit: just think it and throw it up all on the paper, yum…
3. If you do not know how to do it and need a support system, join a class or get a partner to support you in the journey for accountability. It may sound simple, but it works.

Get the ideas out and take time for yourself. I see creativity as your voice, as your contribution to humanity. You can either step up and choose to show up or you can choose to hide and not be noticed.

I am not saying that you have to stand in a crowd and scream, "Look at me, it is all about me." But what you really do have to do is be able to stand in a crowd and scream, "I HAVE SOMETHING TO SAY, LOOK AT ME."

To sum up what have I learned so far in my fifty-two years in this life journey: Get out of your comfort zone. Try new things, revisit old things, do some things you don't like, and maybe you will discover something new; you might be surprised.

Learn to own your stuff. If you mess up, say you're sorry. If you love someone, tell them. If you are turning purple while talking and you feel like you need to acknowledge it because people might think you are going to pass out, make a joke out of it.

Life is too short to spend time wondering and thinking, well I might mess up and just not be good at it. If you are not good, then great, you just learned something about yourself and can move on.

If you happen to discover a talent, when you get those butterflies in your stomach that make you feel alive, then feel it and own it; you are worth it.

I wish you time to play and discover your voice to shout from the mountain tops or beach, if you so prefer. Just feel it is really living!

ABOUT THE AUTHOR

Hollis Citron is on a mission to make creativity accessible to everyone! She is a seasoned art teacher and founder of *I Am Creative*. Hollis is passionate and wants to shout from the rooftops that being creative is not just about drawing and painting! Creativity is within everyone!

 Hollis has been spreading this message from the west to the east coast in all of the various places that she has lived. There are so many ways to benefit from her services — ranging from an online membership program, to various workshops & creative boxes that offer opportunities for anyone to explore their potential, express themselves and expand their thinking.

> ***Website:*** *www.iamcreativephilly.net*
> ***Facebook:*** *www.facebook.com/iamcreativephilly*
> ***Podcast:*** *www.creativeconversations.podbean.com*

JACQSTAR DAVIES

THE ART OF SACRED SUCCESS

Is it possible to create a more meaningful experience of success? Our society has a very narrow definition of success that, for most, only includes money. I believe that a path exists that contains a depth of fulfilment far beyond the mainstream model of success.

Most people who have experienced financial success get to that place and then ask: now what? This version of success can feel unfulfilling because it only takes into account the individual, but doesn't necessarily take into account humanity as a whole.

I view success from an entirely different perspective. Success happens when we collectively weave our dreams together and realise that we are part of a larger ecosystem. To achieve success we have to view life as a grand symphony, in which we all play our part but come to fruition together.

To reach this way of living requires carefully sculpting one's way of being. I believe there are some fundamental understandings that are essential to reaching this goal.

In this chapter I discuss these fundamental, core credentials. They are:

- identifying one's core values through a deep reflection on one's personal story
- embracing change
- finding one's unique talent

- owning all the parts of one's self
- living big
- acknowledging the power of the spirit
- and recognising that we are intrinsically connected to a larger web of life

DEEP REFLECTIONS

> "When I looked into the 'true' mirror I wasn't looking AT myself...
> I was looking FOR myself"

A decade ago, I remember looking into the mirror one morning after yet another night of no sleep, suffering from a severe case of insomnia that had been going on for almost 9 months.

My body was completely out of balance and I hadn't had a menstrual cycle for years. There was an abundance of money from various businesses coming in, but I wasn't feeling fulfilled. Intuitively I felt something inside of me was wrong. I was having some very uncomfortable conversations with myself.

This was a moment that stood still in time. As I stared deeply into my eyes, they reflected back my heartfelt sadness. With tears streaming down my face, I remember feeling pain, discomfort, exhaustion, and fear of failure; I realized what I was looking for was reassurance, for reassurance that I was successful.

I was brought up with a strong value system based around monetary worth. This is what I had known success to be. However, even though I owned a successful business and managed many other big projects, I didn't feel a sense of success.

The value system that I had conformed to was not my value system at all. When I looked into the 'true' mirror, I wasn't looking at myself, I was looking for myself, not for reassurance, but for revelation.

This was a deeply moving moment for me as it was really the first time I'd stopped to ask myself the question: "Why don't I feel satisfied with my life?" What did I expect from life? And what did life expect from me? I hadn't allowed myself the time to be still, to truly feel.

I experienced all these feelings rise up. I realised they had been blocking me from living a life beyond my wildest dreams. In that very moment, with a glance at the real me, I experienced this strong desire to explore not just myself, but the world.

It was as if a gate opened inside of me and I could see the oceans, the mountains, the people waiting to be met and, more importantly, me waiting to meet my true self.

The next day, after that first 'date' with myself in the mirror, I received a phone call. Somebody had made an offer on my business. I was stunned. I could feel the direct connection between what I had resolved the day before and this new eventuality.

It was the first of many such experiences where I would observe the synchronicity of life and how miracles really do happen. I sold my business, handed over all the current projects, closed some other income streams, and set off around the world.

If you keep doing what you've always done, you may miss the magical opportunities that are waiting for you. This was the beginning of my road to real success.

DISCOVERING A NEW WAY

These many, many years of traveling around the globe gave me the opportunity to work with many types of people, including scientists, healers, performers, artists, singers, yogis, dancers, poets, archaeologists, marine biologists, historians, writers, producers, CEO's, directors, cinematographers, photographers, shamans, and chiefs.

From amongst all these people, the one thing that stood out was the indigenous traditions. I have been fortunate enough to have spent time with wisdom keepers, elders, and grandmothers all over the world, in ceremony, in circle, in prayer, sitting around the sacred fire.

When it was time for the grandmothers to share, I'd be spellbound by their stories like a little child with their favourite bedtime book. These moments would set my heart on fire and also trigger emotions and memories of my past.

In the ways of our dominant culture, life is mostly about wanting to get something. Whereas in the indigenous way, if you slow down and become still, it will come to you. In the wisdom of patience we see the richness of what's here now.

By opening ourselves to possibilities, we move into a way of thinking that is grounded in abundance, instead of scarcity. Exploring the knowledge of indigenous people and their connection to the earth teaches us resilience.

They've had to deal with drought, not being able to find food, and extreme heat; we can draw a lot of metaphors there for business. Drought — when there's not a lot of money. Extreme heat — when there's pressure, the need to make quick decisions, or the team is fired up.

- How did the indigenous people do it previously?
- What can we learn from them?
- How can we deeply connect to a place and feeling of being home in ourselves?
- How can we accept diversity and work collaboratively, remembering that the spirit does not have a colour or race?
- How do we learn more about patience, generosity, and the sense of being with what is?

A book I highly recommend is *Grandmothers Council the World* by Carol Schaefer. One of the grandmother's quotes has always stuck with me, "Because of spiritual blindness, people look at the bottom line rather than looking at life itself."

Our society has been driven by a desire for wealth, comfort, and material goods, built on a value system of monetary success. In this pursuit, we have upset the fragile balance of our planet. Self-indulgence and delusional materialism have brought us to the verge of self-destruction.

As the Earth increasingly suffers, we have become more disoriented and lost our way. The web of destruction has been as intricately woven as the web of life, and so we have to learn how to unweave ourselves from the aspects of ourselves that contribute to this destruction, and learn a new way that brings the whole of humanity forward. What is required is a new mind-set — and a new mind-set of success.

WE ARE ALL CONNECTED

First and foremost, it's important for us to recognise that we are all connected to a larger ecosystem, and realise that we are bigger than our individual dreams and aspirations. We all depend on each other and the planet.

The indigenous grandmothers are marvellous role models of how we gather our energies together to make the necessary changes that are needed to return to a life of balance and harmony. We must be willing to make conscious changes to the way we view life and be accountable for all our actions.

In the Indigenous understanding, the core of everything is our relations; not only to people, but to the elements, to "our animal brothers and sisters," and to our plant relations. Seeing the world in this way ensures that people acknowledge and respect the intricate web of life.

Spending time with the Lakota people was always a blessing, as they acknowledge all of their relatives in every ceremony. 'Aho Mitakuye Oyasin' is a simple, yet profound statement meaning, 'All my relations.'

Forming connections not only with our family and friends, but with our work colleagues, neighbours, and other various groups contributes to our well-being. Cultivating a sense of belonging with other people around a shared mission or identity is a major contributor to our sense of personal meaning in life.

Our personal resilience is interwoven with the resilience of the communities we belong to. It is from the web of our relationships and connections with other people that we draw our strength. Such communities can lift us when we are down and give us the capacity to deal with whatever challenges come our way.

Life is a grand symphony; we have to learn how to play the greatest part in this symphony that we can. The part we play must advance the Grand Harmony and not create dissonance.

We have the choice to work with "Life as A Whole," in which case we gain a great ally (the source of all synchronicity), or we work alone, in which case we risk creating dissonance in the Grand Harmony, that life itself must then correct.

The true music of success is about walking a path on more than one level, more than only the dimension of money. The "truly rich" journey in life is walking the deeper path that honours the unique gifts of your heart, and also is deeply connected to the heart of all things.

When you walk the path in this way you may be blazing a new trail of success, but you are never alone, because in this new earth, 'true SUCCESS' is when we walk this journey together. To enter into this harmonious relationship with all of life, one has to learn and adopt some essential understandings.

I call these 'the core credentials of sacred success.' They are outlined below:

EMBRACING CHANGE

There are certain times in your life that lend themselves to great change. In the modern world, people are usually terrified of these moments, because they represent a break with the past and an uncertain future. However, with an 'abundance mindset,' we learn to embrace these moments.

These experiences make change quicker and deeper; they are intervals of infinite possibilities and potential. If you are prepared to look deep enough inside yourself, you will know this as you sense the opportunity for change, and the call towards something greater.

Some of these intervals of possibility are indeed difficult, however, we have to see them as something that life has given us in order to wake us up. Perhaps your partner has left you or somebody you love has become sick, or you have become sick, or perhaps you have lost your job.

But you have to learn to see these moments as something that has happened to rock you back to your inner self and make you ask the question: Who am I really?

This chapter is being written during the corona lockdown, and as such it is clear that at the present moment in history, we are going through a mass identity crisis.

Who am I outside of this job? Who am I outside of this account? What am I? There is always a time when you come face-to-face with your expectations, because what you think is going to happen doesn't happen. So now more than ever in these pandemic times, one is brought up against the unknown.

Living this way, surrendering to the unknown, is how the indigenous live without trying to control the future. Many people are experiencing their proverbial houses burning down in terms of businesses, wealth, and attachments.

I am witnessing that this dissolution of attachment is actually creating higher levels of unity and connection possible on the planet. We are being invited to surrender and move into a place of reciprocity and sharing with an appreciation of what truly matters in every moment.

I feel more appreciative than ever because of the uncertainty. There is a liberation that happens when we embrace the unknown.

FINDING YOUR UNIQUE TALENT

We all have an innately human desire to contribute to the world in a meaningful way. However, we often grow up with values that stem from conditioning and this can distort what is really important, and can cloud our vision of what we are here to do.

Having worked with experts in various fields from around the globe, I have noticed that they have one thing in common. They have figured out their unique talent and gift, and put that at the service of their goals. They have found and then fined tuned their instrument to play in the orchestra of life.

We all play a different instrument; each of us are unique and precious. Your job is not to be anything like any other person.

In fact your job is to be as unlike another as you can possibly be. To find your unique talent, start by thinking about what you used to love as a child. See this passion hunt as a fun, joyful adventure.

OWNING ALL PARTS OF OURSELVES

In our modern world, people have become so well trained at putting on masks. That means they essentially hide themselves, and dim their light, scared to let their true self shine.

How do we create a level of depth and connection with ourselves so, if the uncomfortable parts come up, they don't take us hostage and they don't hold our power and our essence at bay?

We are called to dance with all of ourselves, saying yes to all of our conflicting parts. It is challenging to feel all of our emotions. However, if we can integrate these emotions, we'll be able to access more of our potency and more of our essence. We allow ourselves to be vulnerable, as that is our sensitivity that is our strength.

A potent memory of mine is one time when I was sitting in circle around the sacred fire, and then a grandmother said, "Our most sincere form of prayer is our tears. Sometimes words alone cannot express what is in our heart."

This triggered the memory of the moment I had experienced in the mirror many years before. It was at that moment that I understood that the tear was a representation of the prayer so necessary for the change my life had been waiting for.

There is a story behind every feeling that has been felt. We don't have to apologise for the sacred waters moving through us. No need to apologise for shedding our tears. This is energy in motion and we should celebrate; it's a gift to be witnessed, and there is nothing to fear. These are all the feelings that accompany a life of success.

And yet these are the very feelings we relentlessly avoid. At both spectrums of failure and success and all the parts in-between, there is the opportunity to really feel all those feelings that erupt. These feelings are not inconvenient; these feelings are information.

If you can't admit that you failed, then you'll never learn what didn't work. It is important to acknowledge when you are doing something well and when you are doing something that is failing.

> In wisdom shared by Daniel Schmachtenberger: *"One has to acknowledge success and failure, and feel the whole range of feelings as these emotions are part of the emotional intelligence system and if you reject any of them you can become a kind of a fragmented person."*

LIVING BIG

How big is the emotional roller-coaster of life you're willing to ride? Small dips and rises? Or huge rises, drops, spins, and twists? Life is meant to be lived, emotions are meant to be felt and experienced.

You get to design the ride and you get to experience living a life that only you can live. The choice is yours. Everything you want is available.

The more extreme the emotional shock you're willing to walk through, the faster you'll get the results you're seeking. If your dreams and desires are big enough, you may have to do different things than what you've been doing.

Your role is to be better and better every day, every month and every year at being your true self. How you do anything is how you do everything.

ACKNOWLEDGING THE POWER OF SPIRIT

Our true self, that which guides our intentions, is what changes the world and our lives. When we begin to understand that we are much more than our desires and needs, our egos and personalities, then we meet each other in a different place.

For some, the word "prayer" may feel uncomfortable; there is a connotation that the word relates to religious beliefs. In the indigenous tradition, however, prayer means the ability and willingness to be in constant communication with all that is and celebrate the life given to us.

When we begin to realise that there is a spirit and a prayer connected to all of life, we begin to fully grasp the divine nature of our human experience, and in that I have found the most beautiful expression of freedom and sovereignty.

I had a profound memory of this divine connection the night I slept outside under the stars in a 'dream kiva' in Ojai, California, which looks like a yoni, or amphitheatre into Mother Earth.

A 'dream kiva' is a sacred gathering place, originally made by Native Americans. I had a strong intuition that I had to sleep there as I could feel that something magical was going to happen.

It was right before returning to Standing Rock in North Dakota, where I had been assisting in protecting sacred lands from an oil pipeline and I prayed all evening for the resources to build the main gathering place for all the Chiefs and First Nations peoples at Oceti Sakowin Camp.

The following morning, a man walked into the dream kiva and wanted to start a conversation. That conversation lead me to the man that wrote a $35,000 cheque only 5 hours later that made our mission possible. As he handed me the cheque, I burst into tears of gratitude.

BRINGING TRUE WISDOM FORWARD

True wisdom is timeless. Humanity would be well served in bringing the best of our past forward if we truly want to co-create a better future.

I have been deeply impacted by the seven values of the Lakota Life: prayer, respect, compassion, truth, generosity, humility, wisdom.

As I have personally embodied these teachings, my confidence has grown, I have increased my compassion for others, and I feel more grounded in my work, more powerful, and more generous.

One of the profound gifts that I have received from embracing the seven Lakota values was a space for silence in me. This silence allowed me to listen to the true calling of my heart.

Your whole life experience changes when you not only live the music, but also feel the silence between the notes. This is my wish for you and for all of humanity, for people to find their true calling.

A call for deeper integrity, to listening to the inner knowing. A call for deeper listening to the note of our instrument. A call to feel our sacred obligation to do great work for humanity and the earth, recognising that we all have our individual truths and strengths. To be clear, grounded, and giving yourself fully in humble service, without coming from a place of fear.

Fear will still come up from time to time, but you no longer have to live there. The spiral of life will still continue to deliver you spins and twists on your journey of success, but now you have a more empowered way to handle it differently.

It is literally in your DNA to overcome and adapt to these challenges when you are honouring your true self.

Knowing the true notes of your soul allows you to find harmony in any situation. Shhhhhh…..listen…..I can hear a grandmother's voice right now, "When you choose to live from the heart, your life will blossom."

I invite you all to play in this magnificent symphony of life. Aho Mitakuye Oyasin, to all my relations.

ABOUT THE AUTHOR

Jacqstar Davies is a spiritual advisor and the founder of Sacred Signatures, a crisis management firm for men and women in business who want to discover the next version of themselves, experience true love, and contribute more meaningfully to humanity and the planet, so that they can live fully expressed lives.

For over 15 years as a successful business woman and entrepreneur, Jacqstar has worked with wisdom keepers, healers and global influencers to build effective partnerships, deepen her connection to self, mother earth, sacred ancient wisdom, and humanitarianism.

As a highly intuitive woman, she understands the importance of living in harmony with the rhythm of nature, and has mastered the art of bridging the gap between ancient wisdom and modern technology through effective negotiation for sustainable global change. Her clients work with her to learn how to access unlimited joy, feel more invigorated, and reach inspirational levels of success through purpose-driven investment.

Website: *www.SacredSignatures.com*
Email: *jacqstar@sacredsignatures.com*
Facebook: *www.facebook.com/jackie.davies.967*
Instagram: *www.instagram.com/jacqstar_*

JEM MINOR

DAOIST SACRED EMBODIMENT PRACTICES TO HEAL THE NERVOUS SYSTEM

How can we co-create a more peaceful, mutually respectful, compassionate, equitable, sustainable world?

It begins with:

- Being fully present within ourselves, empowered in our ability to navigate our own embodied experiences.
- Becoming aware of and clearing past trauma held in our cellular memory (our own, as well as what we've taken on from our ancestors and the Collective), so we can respond appropriately to what's happening Now.
- Understanding how what's happening internally, in our nervous system, is responding to and affecting all that's happening externally (and vice versa) — and letting that bring both compassion for ourselves and others, and empowered responsibility, as we learn new ways to cultivate healthier, more helpful responses.
- Rooting deeply into our Yin Beingness *before* and *while* utilizing Yang energy to take Inspired Action.
- Bringing Yin and Yang energies back into balance, so we can explore new ways of Being and Doing that feel harmonious, empowering, aligned, and sustainable in our lives and in the world.

TRANSFORMING TRAUMA TO BIRTH A NEW EARTH

All of those skills and resources become increasingly important during times of crisis, major change, uncertainty, and upheaval — whether personally, collectively, or both, as many have told me during this pandemic.

At every major transition or stressful stage of my life, Chinese medicine, alchemical meditation, and Daoist sacred embodiment practices have brought me back to my Center more quickly and powerfully than any other modalities.

Graduations, changes in relationship, having a baby, postpartum challenges, going back to work, grieving the loss of loved ones, moving, traveling, healing ancestral and personal trauma, divorce, navigating financial uncertainty, emotional and physical health crises, the current pandemic...

I've navigated ALL of these situations with greater Ease, Clarity, Vitality, and Courage, thanks to Daoist medicine and sacred embodiment practices.

Beginning in secondary school with an hour of tai chi every morning for six years, I learned the importance of cultivating my own internal flow of Qi ("chi," or Life Force Energy) to help balance my physical and emotional well-being. Those years of daily practice offered a powerful foundation for what would become my life work.

Of course, at various points along the way, I've forgotten that foundation, or let other "matters of consequence" be prioritized — and those are the times when I've been more prone to illness, injury, or emotional challenges. Each of those injuries, illnesses, transitions, and emotional breakdowns have brought me into a deeper relationship with myself, my life purpose, and the Daoist healing arts. Such is the nature of Alchemy.

In 2006, amidst months of miserable back pain from an injury on my college crew team (which five different doctors did nothing to alleviate), the physical pain also instigated an emotional breakdown. Being flat on my back, barely able to move for hours on end, brought up memories of rape and early sexual abuse, and I learned that "the body keeps the score" on trauma. It was time for deeper healing.

Fortunately, I took an introductory class on the Five Elements of Chinese Medicine, taught by Leta Herman (who is still a dear mentor). As I absorbed the information, I immediately thought: "This is it. This paradigm makes sense of my entire life, and of the whole universe!"

Within three sessions of working with her privately (including a 5-hour "Ghost

Treatment" to clear past trauma held in my body), my pain was GONE. Entirely gone. The light came back into my eyes. I felt more fully myself than ever before. And I knew this was the medicine I was here to work with and bring to others.

She sent me to Daoist Traditions College of Chinese Medical Arts, where I dove into the medical and spiritual aspects of classical Daoist medicine for four intense years (acupuncture, herbal medicine, nutrition, and their integration with modern functional medicine), deepened my qigong practice, and was introduced to Daoist internal alchemy meditations and sexual energy cultivation, including conscious breast massage and jade egg Womb-healing practices. In that time, I moved through many long-standing physical and emotional challenges, and felt so much healthier and more resilient!

However, after the home birth of my son in 2014, amidst postpartum physical and emotional health challenges, new layers of trauma came up for healing — both my own (as deeper layers of past sexual abuse), and intergenerational trauma passed down from my Cheyenne ancestors' betrayal by white men.

Few people talk about how giving birth can bring up past trauma held in the Womb, and I wasn't prepared for it, despite all I "knew" and all the internal work I'd already done. My nervous system was struggling to cope with the daily stressors of parenting (much of it solo), on top of healing the trauma that had resurfaced. I researched all sorts of new things, but it wasn't until I got back into embodied healing practices to work directly with the trauma in my body (and the Five Elements) that harmony returned to my internal ecosystem.

I learned (again!) just how essential it is to *continue to practice* embodied awareness, to learn more about the nervous system *and actually keep tending to it*, and to honor the pain held in the body, so that it could gently be allowed the space to transform, with compassion and conscious intention.

I "knew" all of those things before, but in the postpartum overwhelm of having fewer of my usual coping strategies or support people available, intellectual understanding wasn't enough. Actually *using the skills I had learned for tending to my nervous system* became more important than ever — just as at any other time of major transition or uncertainty.

(Many clients have shared similar realizations amidst the current pandemic, lockdown, and racial healing crisis too.) To make sustainable changes, we have to listen to our nervous systems and put our bodies first.

Herbal medicine, acupuncture, bodywork, somatic experiencing, and connection with mentors and loved ones helped me re-activate the power of my own Heart-Womb alchemy to heal.

As my body felt better nourished, it became easier to return to the qigong and sacred embodiment practices that re-birthed me into a fresh, more authentic, compassionate, and empowered version of myself, no longer held back by old patterns or ancestral trauma. (Of course, old triggers still come up, but now I remember to tend to my nervous system first!)

Since then, I've moved through massive life changes and have been thriving, in all levels of my health and relationships, even amidst the current uncertainties of parenting and being pregnant during a pandemic, and with all the other changes afoot in our country and the world. I feel more confident, accepting, trusting, and at home in my body now than I previously thought possible, even as my body transforms on a daily basis to create space for my growing daughter.

I feel deeply connected to Source Energy, to my own empowered sacred embodiment, and to my loved ones, in vulnerably courageous ways that nourish mutual safety, respect, freedom, and authentic Presence.

Now, I bring all of these experiences, practices, and modalities together to support others (primarily women, and especially mothers) in healing the trauma and stress held in our bodies, so that we can thrive in our True Essence, with the individual and collective vitality we need to co-create a more peaceful, mutually respectful, empowering, equitable, sustainable world.

WHY IS IT SO CRUCIAL TO HEAL TRAUMA AND STRESS, IF WE ARE TO BIRTH A NEW WORLD?

When our bodies are constantly triggered by past trauma or ongoing stress, *and we don't have the skills to move through it healthily*, it's very difficult to generate enough energy to create the changes we wish to make (or to support those changes long-term), either in our own lives or in the larger world. Our energy is co-opted by trying to survive, so it's unavailable for creating conditions in which we can thrive.

Stress responses mobilize energy for our survival (to fight, flee, or appease a person who feels threatening), or to conserve our energy (by freezing), to keep us safe. We're all subject to stress on a regular basis, which can build resilience and adaptability, as we navigate this uncertain world; it teaches us a lot very quickly!

However, if we wish to thrive, we need to become aware of when our stress responses are healthy, how to recalibrate afterward, when they're being set off due to past trauma held in the body (which might mean the current scenario isn't actually threatening), and how to listen to and work with these embodied warnings, before they cascade into unhelpful words, patterns, or actions.

Otherwise, our lives and world will continue to run on millennia of unconscious stress responses, such that it's very difficult to birth a more conscious world that can support ALL of our thriving.

This transformation has to start within ourselves, so that we can feel and *embody* the difference of responding more consciously, rather than letting generations of trauma responses dictate our future.

As we get better at regulating our own nervous systems, we can model that for our children, as well as help other adults co-regulate and come into more conscious relationships, which in turn allows us to co-create more functional, empowering, supportive social structures.

And, while many of us understand that intellectually, it's entirely different to embody it! The sustainability of change lies in its embodiment.

As modern culture has become increasingly driven by productivity, focusing on doing and having more, it often demands that we keep pushing through ongoing stress, at the expense of our bodies.

However, if we don't sufficiently nourish or tend to our bodies, or honor the signs that we need to rest or do something different than society dictates, eventually we burn out and collapse, often with some form of health crisis. (Just like I did in college, grad school, and postpartum.)

In Daoist energetic terms, the chronic stress dynamic most often shows up in our culture as depleted Yin (physical resource, beingness, rest, water/fluids, awareness of feelings, embodied presence, wisdom, capacity for listening to intuition), giving rise to excess Yang: hyper-productivity, mental hyperactivity, anxiety, heat/fire, constant doing, overstimulation, discomfort with quiet or stillness, emotional reactivity, etc.

> (Note: those are qualities of *excess* Yang, not healthy Yang! And, some people will be more prone to Yang deficiency and unhealthy Yin stagnation, or "dampness," which can be the opposite response to our cultural tendency toward Yin deficiency and excess Yang, related to our patriarchal society's devaluation of rest, connection, and embodied Presence and over-emphasis on productivity.)

If we have experienced significant personal *or ancestral* trauma prior to a period of increased stress, our bodies have an even bigger challenge to navigate, as they're wired more for survival (with fight/flight/freeze/fawn responses) than for thriving.

In that stressed state, it becomes harder to access our inner resources, or to utilize whatever skills we've learned to regulate our nervous system — or even to be fully aware that we're in a trauma-response at all. (It took me over a year to realize I was experiencing postpartum PTSD; my nervous system was so activated that I couldn't put it all together, even as a trained health practitioner! Humbling...)

If we've been accustomed to surviving traumatic situations, where a high level of stress may have been "normal" to us, we may also have a reduced ability to discern what is "healthy" or "sustainable." Especially in the current culture, "normal" does not equal "healthy."

Remaining in stressful situations becomes more depleting over time, and as we get further depleted, we also tend to get more stagnant, since our bodies start trying to hold onto whatever resources they can.

Sometimes that shows up as "dampness," "phlegm," weight gain, lingering chronic illness, depression, and/or pain. (Daoist medicine says: "Where there's pain, there's stagnation; where there is free flow, there is no pain.")

Such symptoms show us that we don't have the right balance of fluids, or appropriate energy available for change, to keep our qi, blood, ideas, and emotions moving through healthily, which then contributes to a myriad of other health challenges.

And all of this often comes back to trauma and stress!

These dynamics tend to beget quick fixes that don't address the root problems: stress, trauma, excess Yang activity, and/or Yin deficiency). We can fall into a vicious cycle where we keep burning up Yin resources; once they're depleted, they can't balance out the Yang energies as well, and the cycle continues to be exacerbated, unless we interrupt the process with rest, presence, and deep nourishment.

(Likewise, the Earth herself has shown us this dynamic in climate change. When we burn up all her resources without replenishing them, the environment becomes less conducive to our thriving. We see greater extremes of heat, fire, and wind in some areas, and flooding, dampness, stagnation, toxicity, and more intense storms in others (or, in the same places at different seasons).

Air and water quality have been so damaged by over-use that when humans took our recent Global Pause, and we saw how the air and water cleared in several polluted areas, it became all the more obvious how our excessive Yang activity is disrupting the sustainable health of the Earth's ecosystem. The Earth herself is inviting us to create a healthier balance of Yin and Yang!)

When Yin (substance, beingness) and Yang (spirit, doingness) come together, they create Life. As long as their interchange is healthily flowing, they nourish life with abundance, and there's infinite potential for transformation. If they're out of balance, we move toward various sorts of illness and pain, though there's still room for transformation and healing.

When Yin and Yang separate completely, the spirit leaves the body, and we die. Any symptom that shows up in our bodies is a message inviting us to bring Yin and Yang into better balance.

Of course, how an imbalance of Yin and Yang shows up in any individual will vary with their constitution, age, genetic/ancestral tendencies, environmental factors, diet, lifestyle, quality of emotional support, and, most importantly, with their *ability to notice and tend to any symptoms or feelings as they arise.*

Daoist medicine excels in noticing the nuances of our bodies, in seeing how all aspects of ourselves are connected, and making sense of how a curious symptom in one part of the body is related to another part, or to the change in seasons, or to an old trauma, or to an emotional energy that's asking to be processed.

Acupuncturists and Chinese herbalists tap into these nuances, and can often provide immense relief of symptoms (especially for anything related to female reproductive health, which is often thrown off by Yin/Yang imbalance).

Alchemical acupuncture can go even deeper into the spiritual trauma healing that many of us need, with Ghost Points, or by clearing various other blocks that have been preventing the body-mind-spirit from accepting a good suggestion when it's offered, as often happens with trauma or chronic illness.

When those blocks are cleared, and we come into a deeper understanding of our own bodies and spirits, we liberate the energy of our True Essence, such that we can self-actualize our full creative potential, and bring our best to our families and the world.

However, Daoist medicine is *most* powerful when it empowers individuals in their own practice and personal evolution, not just when someone is prescribing herbs or doing acupuncture for them. Because Daoist medicine is rooted in the ways of nature, it's easily felt and observed by all of us.

We know *in our bodies* what heat and cold, movement and rest, anger and compassion feel like. As we get more skilled at noticing Yin and Yang energies in ourselves, others, and the environment, we're empowered to balance them ourselves.

That's why I've shifted more into teaching qigong, meditation, and sacred feminine embodiment practices, including breast massage and jade egg Womb-healing work, to release intergenerational trauma often held in the Womb.

The Womb is a powerful portal for creating life -- not just for birthing a baby, but for re-birthing ourselves and the world we want to live in everyday. Building practical skills to Be With and transform our own embodied energy is vital for our ongoing healing, empowered radiance, and self-actualization, especially if we are to birth a new world.

While trauma takes us *out of our bodies*, Daoist qigong, meditation, and sexual cultivation practices *bring our awareness back into our bodies*, as the source of our power for healing and transformation in this lifetime.

We feel what's off-balance, and engage in a direct relationship with it, rather than giving away our power to someone else to fix us, or feeling doomed to feel like that forever. With these practices, we can both release what's ready to move through, and offer support to the aspects that need nourishment.

When we look courageously at the larger picture of our ever-changing bodies, spirits, relationships, culture, and ecosystem, rather than just at individual symptoms, we get a deeper understanding of what support is truly needed, and how we can bring the entire ecosystem back into balance.

Kind of like tending a garden — some plants need more sun, or water, or shade, or certain nutrients, while others need to be pruned, weeded, or harvested. Embodied awareness helps the gardens of our bodies, relationships, and communities to thrive.

How can we tend to *all* parts of ourselves, and to each other, for the overall flourishing of the ecosystem?

That's what we need to keep asking, on a daily basis, as we birth a new world, rooted in Healthy Yin.

When we cultivate practical, embodied, energetic skills to heal trauma and harmonize Yin and Yang within ourselves, we can navigate the Unknown with greater ease. We return to the center of our own deepest knowing, feel grounded in our internal resources, and magnetize the support of external resources into appropriate balance.

The more we live in our own bodies consciously, compassionately, and in healthy relationship with all aspects of ourselves, the easier it is to be in a healthy relationship with each other and with the We-Space (the collective relational field), such that we can create a world that sustainably supports ALL of our thriving.

HOW CAN YOU BEGIN SOME OF THESE PRACTICES TO HEAL YOUR NERVOUS SYSTEM AT HOME?

First, simply start bringing your awareness back into your body, as often as you can. Notice how your nervous system responds to various stimuli. Just observe, without judgment, with curiosity and compassion, as you get to know your own mammalian body more deeply.

Notice how your body feels in times of ease. Does it feel expansive? Light? Energizing? Relaxed? Open? Warm?

What helps your body come into a state of ease and safety?

What were you doing before you noticed the ease? Were you tending well to your basic resources of sleep, food, water, exercise, breath, connection, touch, creativity? (Notice and appreciate that, so you'll get better at tending those resources more regularly!)

Make a list of your "Essentials" -- activities that help you regulate your nervous system and come back to center -- and keep it handy as you become more conscious of replenishing your basic resources.

My own Essentials list includes: drink water, do spontaneous qigong and self-massage, practice healing sounds or breath work, meditate, take a shower, lie down to reset, get a hug or deep pressure from weighted pillows, eat something green, go outside, sing, dance, journal, tend to the felt sensations with compassion...

(Free meditations, and qigong, healing sound and breath work practices are included in my free mini-course, at: *www.nourishingalchemy.net/embodying-courage-in-challenging-times*)

Utilize your list of Essentials daily, any time you need to re-center yourself, and see what changes. Is there a sense of greater ease and safety? Does that open up more energy for the things you care about most?

Then, start noticing how your body feels in times of stress — when you get upset or worried, when you're in pain or overwhelmed, when someone is angry at you, when you're sleep-deprived, when you feel threatened and unsafe…

What parts of your body are you most aware of? How do they feel? Hot/cold? Tight? Shaky? Tense? Buzzy?

Maybe you hold grief in your throat, anger in your head or fists, anxiety in your chest or solar plexus, fear in tightening your lower back or belly…

Allow yourself to let go of the *story* of what happened, and focus on the *felt sensations in your body*. Shifting that focus helps soothe the nervous system in itself!

Notice what parts of your body get activated with each emotion, or in certain circumstances.

Allow those parts to feel what they do, then gently bring them compassionate acceptance.

Listen for any messages they might have. See if they soften at all when they feel heard with love.

For challenging emotions that feel deeply stuck, try some healing sounds for their associated Element (available for free on my website), to let them transform into that Element's empowered emotion.

Working with the healing sounds and colors of each Element helps bring them back into harmony, supporting the creative transformation cycle of Metal to Water to Wood to Fire to Earth.

(More practices for deeper levels of healing are included in my *Thriving Beyond Trauma* course, and in my membership, *Thriving Mama Circle*.)

Finally, if you're a menstruating woman, start noticing your energies at different times in your cycle, just tracking them with love, not judgment. Give yourself full permission to feel the way you do, knowing that your body has infinite wisdom to nourish your cyclic well-being, even if that's not often honored in our culture.

It's natural to rest when you bleed, to honor that Yin time and let your body begin building resources for the next cycle. How can you adjust your life, however simply, to make more room for your natural ebbs and flows?

What would it feel like to honor your body's cycle and wisdom, to work *with* your body and emotions, rather than feeling internal conflict or succumbing to external pressure? How much more energy would you have available for what you want to create?

It's immensely empowering to get to know our bodies and actually honor them;

we cultivate greater vitality, deeper trust in ourselves, and better boundaries around how we want to live that will truly nourish our thriving.

When we are thriving in our authentic Essence, freed from past trauma with the skills to navigate our responses to daily stressors, we can embody the changes we wish to see, and come together to co-create a more peaceful, mutually respectful, compassionate, equitable, sustainable world.

Every individual's healing and evolution supports our ability to birth a healthier world. Thank you for Being all that you are, and for supporting all that we are collectively Becoming.

ABOUT THE AUTHOR

Jem Minor, L.Ac, MAOM, is a licensed Acupuncturist, Herbalist, Alchemical Sacred Embodiment Coach, Feminine Power Facilitator, and Healing Tao Instructor of Internal Alchemy Meditation & Qi Gong — and the mother of one very loving, exuberant son, with a daughter expected in October 2020.

Jem has successfully used Chinese Medicine, Daoist Alchemy, sacred sexual cultivation, dance, qi gong, and somatic practices to renegotiate her relationship with the various traumas stored in her body (from early sexual abuse, rape, pregnancy loss, childbirth, and intergenerational trauma), to live a healthy, radiant, fulfilled life, comfortable in her Wholeness. She is passionate about sharing these practices with women who are ready to empower themselves in their own healing, liberate their True Essence, and co-create thriving relationships, in a culture ripe for change.

Born and raised in Alaska, Jem is now joyfully co-creating a thriving family life with her partner in Asheville NC, where they homeschool, dance, and have many outdoor adventures in the beautiful Blue Ridge Mountains.

Learn more about Jem and Nourishing Alchemy Healing Arts at:

> *Website:* www.nourishingalchemy.love
> *Facebook:* www.facebook.com/nourishingalchemyhealingarts
> and www.facebook.com/groups/thrivingfamiliesembodyinglove
> and www.facebook.com/groups/thrivingbeyondtrauma
> *Instagram:* www.instagram.com/nourishingalchemy
> *Email:* jem@nourishingalchemy.net
> *Free Mini-Course:* www.nourishingalchemy.net/embodying-courage-in-challenging-times

JULIA CHAI

HOW QIGONG & INTERDIMENSIONAL WORK CAN HELP US MOVE FORWARD

"Know this, we are interdimensional, and unlimited."
"Think of all the forces of the Universe ready to serve us.
Yet centuries elapsed before man penetrated their secret
and discovered the means of utilizing them.
It is the same in the domain of thought and mind:
we have at our service forces of transcendent value
of which we are either completely ignorant or else only vaguely conscious."
- Emily Coue

Child of the universe, I speak to you. Every step you take, Mother Earth supports you, her energy transmitted through the bones of your body. With every breath, molecules from Father Sky stream in to inspire your beingness.

Source energies[1] bounce from the ethers, magnetized by the earth, yearning to be embodied. Golden energy waves pulse from your heart centre. A celestial self and support team works tirelessly behind the scenes to protect and guide you.

Return to original unity and perfection by understanding your interdimensionality, child. You were not created, then dumped on earth to fend for yourself.

Pristine energies, infinite potential, and a loving spirit support team are available to you at all times. All it takes is to reach out with your mind and connect with them.

Your body was designed to resonate to frequencies across the spectrum like a harp. You spirit is interdimensional. Let the music of the spheres, the song of nature, and the joy of living spirit that surrounds you uplift you, child. Choose your frequencies wisely, for when you are sad and troubled, the whole world is troubled.

* * *

"Move beyond the known, into the unknown"

* * *

THE MESSAGE I wish to share in this time of Corona, for our Awakening, is that human consciousness is not limited to our current timeline. Our consciousness can move freely, forwards and backwards in time, but also beyond timelines – to access what I call "the Space beyond Time." As a past lives and between-lives regressionist, who has taken hundreds of people from different cultures, age and backgrounds, into this space, I know this to be true.

A popular German proclamation of independence is 'Gedanken sind frei' (Thoughts are Free). I say to you "Spirit is Free."

When we venture into the realms beyond the physically embodied one, this is what we find:

A home coming. A place of unity, One-ness, and belonging.

A place beyond right and wrong.

A place of light, expansiveness. A place of healing.

Spirit guides know what to do, and how to take you to the next stage of your path.

Angels bless, transform and uplift.

Ancestors have been keeping an eye on their lineage and know how to restore order and harmony.

Animal spirit guides are often the first to connect – with no judgement.

Unicorns, dragons. Colour rays, symbols, white spaces, womb spaces.

Other planets, magical, mystical, elemental realms,

as well as the space between the stars,

and the atoms.

* * *

"How do I get there? Go within."

* * *

THE ANCIENT CHINESE art of Qigong[2] (Qi = Life Force, Gong = to work with, or cultivate), of which I am a teacher, refers to Source Qi[3] that lives within the deepest part of us.[4]

Humans have access to three realms: the earthly, human, and the celestial.[5] The brain is designed so that in every moment we have access to quantum potential[6] and can simulate what the chosen path will be like. Then we make a choice, and the chosen path is manifested. This is how we are agents of change; this is how the light of the one-and-all-as-yet-unmanifest is made flesh. We are designed to be co-creators in a Free Will Universe.

Human consciousness is free to roam in dimensions invisible to the human eye. Interdimensional abilities are not limited to prophets of old. Every person is born with the abilities; it is just that we have not been taught that it is possible. It is time to become conscious of our abilities and use them.

* * *

"How do we do this? Where do I start?"

"Practice allowing the spirit of your consciousness to roam freely beyond the physical."

* * *

TO BEGIN AN INTERDIMENSIONAL JOURNEY, we go within. Qigong, and the Law of Attraction, teach that whatever we focus on is where our energy goes. We close our eyes; and concentrate our attention on the flow and rhythm of our breath. We let go of thoughts – and drop deeper within. As we listen and allow our awareness to meld with the energy within our bodies, our hands, feet, and face soften; it is as if boundaries dissolve. Then awareness enters the dimension of energy, not limited by form.[7]

As awareness rests within, be it at the level of an organ, muscle, tissue, or a bone, then the spirit in the form of consciousness can deepen to the next dimension: the level of cells; then deeper still to the informational blueprint (DNA) level. From there we journey into the dimension of electrons, to atoms, to the binary space of beingness and not beingness - pure Yin and Yang, until we reach the Source and all other realms that manifest from the Source.

Students of qigong experience the following:

- Power follows connection.
- Peace, as the mind sinks into the body, and comes home. The energetic body tucks into the physical body, like birds coming home to roost at night, rather than scattered in all directions through mental pursuit.
- Awareness flows deeper within. The diaphragm begins to relax. Breath becomes deeper and nourishing. The heart warms and activates. Wings unfold. Smiles form, delighted, like a child discovering something new.
- Rotating hips, shoulders, elbows, knees, ankles, and wrists initiate a spiral flow. Golden phi ratio energy spirals freely through the body.
- Joints and muscles relax, and their life force circulates freely to those spaces where it is needed. There is a hum as different components of the inner orchestra come into harmony.
- Head lifted and floating as if in clouds, the spine is free to move and distribute momentum and impulses: energies with no form.
- Light frequencies flow in, distributed through the three energy centres, illuminating and pulsing within. The inner temple is filled with pristine energies of the Here and Now, enabling a new beginning.
- The human is reconnected to Gaia's field, returning from a sojourn in the world of projections and speculation.

We may not be particularly good at controlling others, but we most certainly can restore harmony within ourselves.

* * *

"Is it safe to move between dimensions?" – *"Only seekers find out"*

AWAKENING

* * *

"Out beyond ideas of wrongdoing and right-doing, there is a field. I'll meet you there.
The breeze at dawn has secrets to tell you.
Don't go back to sleep.
You must ask for what you really want.
Don't go back to sleep.
People are going back and forth across the doorsill where the two worlds touch.
The door is round and open.
Don't go back to sleep." - Rumi

As CHILDREN, we discover that if we were to follow every instruction given by adults, instead of following our own inner wisdom, life would become complicated, and quite dull.[8]

As children, it also dawns on us that our perception of situations — and how to respond — is often at odds with that of our caregivers. Adults' perspectives can be trapped within society's parameters and the need to keep the family safe. "What if" and "Why not" questions are rarely welcomed by those upholding the status quo.

And so, we learn for our own sakes, to venture past the safe zones and discover what lies beyond. This is the classic hero's journey and, as the extraordinarily successful recent movie series *Frozen* illustrates, the heroine's journey too. Only by venturing into the unknown, within and without, is it possible to establish who we are truly, and what we are capable of.

Children carry the seeds of potential for the next stage of human evolution within them. Without our children to dream and conceive new ways of being, humanity would stagnate. A look at the films currently inspiring children: 'Guardians of the Galaxy', 'Spirited Away' or 'Inception'– and we can see which way humanity is headed. At the same time, we see the nightmares of the collective reflected in the Black Mirror and the Dystopian Society films.

THE DREAMS OF OUR COLLECTIVE SEED OUR FUTURE

As you read this, you may already inhabit the body of an adult. Yet the spirit child still lives within you. To forget or ignore this spells the death of dreams and new potential for you. By virtue of our imagination, each of us can dream, and should dream into being new scenarios for our lifetime.

* * *

Who am I that speaks to you?

* * *

I AM the One that is called the Great Connector in the Spirit World. I have remembered many existences on the human plane before this one. I lead many into the space beyond time, where they consult with spirit guides, are inspired, and transformed. Every day I gather fresh energies in nature and release stagnant or dissonant energies. They call me Spellweaver, Shapeshifter, Energy Harmonizer.

In past lives, I have protected my tribe as half man-half ape, swum in the waters of Atlantis, and hovelled with villagers in rags, placing stones to protect them from the pestilence. I have bathed in the unity light stream as a mountain dragon and walked with the forefathers of humanity in Lemuria.

I have wreaked fire and havoc as an aggrieved bandit and have been burnt for violating class rules. I have herded goats in the fields of Europe and watched helplessly as my daughter was raped by a king. Yet these are all stories that were of my dreaming, for in the dimensions beyond the stories, beyond our trials, tribulations, and redemptions, you and I - are unlimited.

In 2017 my friend Marilyn Caflish channelled this message from Archangel Melchizidek:

"*Many changes are happening in the world today.*
Our souls need to be reshaped to fit in with what is happening in the here and now.
If we continue as we are then we will not move forward.
To move forward we need to renew our souls and take them back
to the original blueprint of the Divine and change our future.
Only then can we proceed to be free." - Archangel Melchizidek

CORONA IS TEACHING US THAT THE WAY THINGS HAVE BEEN DONE BEFORE IS NOT SUSTAINABLE

The message from spirit guides is that we are here because we hold the potential for the next stage of humanity's evolution. There are many correlations between our present existence and the schism between technology and the seers of Atlantis. The spectre of the Galactic Wars, or entrapment in the Matrix, an enslaved society on a planet poisoned by human civilization, haunts us. Conflict looms as resources shrink.

* * *

Many dream of a return to a more sustainable future.

* * *

YOU AND I have come back to be the avatars: to transcend the past by cleaning up the dross in our psyche, DNA, societal structures, and environment from past lives and childhood traumas. Yes, we and our co-actors have been at war, in famines, locked up, betrayed, abandoned, or lost.

However, that was then; this is now. Step beyond the stories, the ego, and access new quantum potentials and the realm of the spirit world, where we can think of anyone and they are with us immediately. Each of us has our own support team of celestial guides.

Just like Wi-Fi, our minds can remotely tune in, and download information from the celestial realm (un-manifested realms). Telepath soul family members and ancestors, guides, and angels on the spirit plane; they enjoy a clearer overview, unhampered by the restrictions of being in a physical body.

They helped us come into this world, and we need not wait until we have left this world to talk to them again. Inspiration comes through intuition – assistance and support from spirit support teams is always available; we only need to reach out, ask the question, and await the answer. By walking behind the scenes and working with our support team, we become the directors and producers of our play, rather than mere actors.

We cannot let the leftovers of past stories and attractions smother the seeds of potential that we carry within us. We can choose to free ourselves from captivity, arise from the half sleep, explore our full potential. Like gardeners, we must take responsibility, dig out and expel that which would harm, restrict, or encumber us, and our children. We can choose to learn, and practice channelling pure pristine universal energies that exist in abundance to support all beings of creation. This is our birthright. This is what we were designed to be.

Download pure frequencies. Let them flow through us to birth new beginnings.

Once we have experienced interdimensionality, we know that Separation is an illusion, limited to the physical dimension. There are no borders that cannot be crossed if the heart so wills.[9] There are no dimensions in which hurt cannot be healed, and despair cannot be comforted by the power of spirit and compassion. There are no mistakes, challenges, or crises that wisdom cannot be learnt from.

And so, it is that wisdom and compassion become a part of our lives, which we then embody, and share with our fellow humans.

In this way the world becomes a better place.

---

1. The solar neutrino flux for us on Earth is about 65 billion neutrinos, passing through just one square centimeter of area on earth, every second. That means that every second, trillions of neutrinos are passing through our bodies, estimated at about 100 trillion. http://timeblimp.com/?page_id=1033
2. Qi Gong and Tai Chi are exercise regimes that are over a thousand years old and nurture the body and spirit. The practice involves slow and smooth movement patterns, clearing out the meridians and organs of stagnant energy. Awareness, breath, heart, and intent are combined in different stances to build up vitality, inner coherence, and freedom of spirit and mind.
3. Greg Williams, Awaken the Qi Within, page 103
4. As does Yoga and other Eastern, Western mystic and meditation practices.
5. The Scandinavians call it the Rainbow Bridge
6. In 2017, neuroscientists discovered that the brain can operate and build structures in up to 11 dimensions. See https://www.sciencealert.com/science-discovers-human-brain-works-up-to-11-dimensions
7. Just as a study of the electromagnetic spectrum and physics reveals the range of the seen vs unseen to the human eye (https://courses.lumenlearning.com/boundless-biology/chapter/vision/), ancient Taoists were adept at navigating the realms beyond form, differentiating between the realm of energy unbound by form (e.g. weather, emotions) and the realm of form (archetypes, astral, abstract ideas), that when mixed with energy become embodied on the physical plane. See Opening the Dragon Gate: The Making of a Modern Taoist Wizard By Chen Kaiguo, Zheng Shunchao
8. The Greek fable about the father and the son carrying the donkey alludes to this – you must find your own path.
9. Where there is a will there is a Way

ABOUT THE AUTHOR

Julia Chai knows "pristine energies and unquantifiable potential lie just around the corner." A teacher of Qigong and Tai Chi since 2009, Julia loves introducing people to the realm of pure energy and spirit. Since 2008 Julia has helped hundreds of people access quantum spaces, past lives, between lives, release vows, ties, and ancestral baggage with hypnotherapy and DNA recalibration techniques.

Having started working life with a degree in Chinese and Economics, Julia became an investment banker working in London, Singapore and Shanghai. She switched to fraud investigations, then gave it all up to focus on the Inner Realms.

"As within, so without." Julia is an inspirational speaker and facilitator at energy-healing and spiritual connection conferences, workshops, and meditation circles. Past engagements include Byron Bay, Gold Coast, Bali, Vietnam, and Colorado. Julia currently co-hosts a weekly radio show, "Dreaming the New Dream," and has published qigong and meditation videos and mp3s (see Youtube: Minds Ease).

Website: www.mindsease.com.au
Facebook: www.facebook.com/MindsEase
Youtube: www.youtube.com/
    channel/UCZRex797ClRRm4sOxNT59QQ
Email: julia@mindsease.com.au

KAVITA ARORA

QUANTUM PROSPERITY & PRODUCTIVITY DURING TOUGH TIMES

We are in a time of unprecedented uncertainty AND possibility. Institutions and structures are crumbling around us. We are rethinking how we relate to work, education, and other people.

Things that seemed like they were never going to change have changed. Just look at telemedicine, for example. Not that long ago, it felt so far away, and overnight it's become the norm.

Unparalleled times call for unorthodox, creative leadership. And, I am one of those leaders. I have been preparing for times like this my whole life (and for many lifetimes before this one.) When the Coronavirus hit, I pivoted easily because I have a rich inner life. But, it wasn't always that way!

In June 2010, life as I knew it fell apart. I crashed into life, and my only choice was to change, evolve, expand, and find new possibilities and ways of doing things. Everything looked great on the outside, but on the inside, I was miserable with my work and my marriage, I had a self-hating inner dialogue about my body, and I felt like I was dying inside. To hear the full story of my dark night of the soul, look up my talk on YouTube, "When Life Brings You to Your Knees, and Saves You."

In 2011, I made a Quantum Leap and left my secure corporate legal work and started a purpose-based business, supporting visionary entrepreneurs to use soul-driven business strategies and create prosperity without sacrificing pleasure and peace.

I was terrified of marketing and selling, my husband didn't support me in leaving corporate safety to take the risk to build this "weird" business, and I was going through the greatest inner conflict I'd ever experienced. My Inner Critic was telling me that I was Bad, Crazy, Too Much, and Wrong. Yet, I did it anyways.

It seemed like a crazy move. I took the leap and honored my intuition over my intellect. Much to my surprise, I discovered that Einstein agreed.

*"The **intuitive** mind is a sacred gift and the rational mind is a faithful servant. We have created a society that honors the servant and has forgotten the gift." - Albert Einstein.*

What previously seemed crazy was actually the sanest choice to make. There's likely some way in which this is true for you in your life right now. Where are you overvaluing the rational mind? (Which it turns out isn't really as rational as we think!)

* * *

No matter how bad things seem, no matter how limited our choices seem to be, we always have a choice.

* * *

IF VIKTOR FRANKL found choice and possibility while he was in a concentration camp, then we can certainly find choice and possibility in troubled times. If you're reading this, you have more options than he did.

"When we are no longer able to change a situation, we are challenged to change ourselves.

Everything can be taken from a man but one thing: the last of the human freedoms—to choose one's attitude in any given set of circumstances, to choose one's own way." - Viktor Frankl

In this chapter, I'm going to walk you through the steps you can choose to take, which will activate your Quantum Prosperity and Productivity. You really can make your Epic Dreams come true, no matter what's happening outside of you.

You always have power over your energy and your choices. No one can take that choice away from you.

Nelson Mandela exercised this power while he was in prison. Because he was open to possibility, he received the inspiration to write to the US from jail. He had no reason to believe it would make a difference, but he kept going anyways. So can you!

THE IMMENSE POWER OF THE QUANTUM FIELD

Our interaction with the Quantum Field is the most powerful relationship we have. We can use the field to shift and heal our past. We can use it to create the change we desire to see in the world.

In the Quantum Field, there is no past and future, and things exist only in the eternal now. We can use the energy of something in the future to heal things that happened in the past. We can also Timeline Hop and Instantly Manifest, if we invest the time and energy to master ourselves and become one with the field.

Everything is energy, and when you become more energy and less matter, you are one with the field.

When you start to play with the field, you will begin to see that by changing your energy, you can change your life. When your consciousness changes, the physical world changes, and you bring the unseen into the seen very quickly. This is called a quantum leap.

Let's find some potent ways to shift our energies so we can change our lives and the planet for the better. Let's get started.

STEP 1: TAKE RADICAL RESPONSIBILITY (AKA BE A KARMA YOGI)

If Viktor Frankl could have positive thoughts in a concentration camp, then you can certainly choose to espouse them now, even during a pandemic, even if you are struggling mightily with your external circumstances, even amidst rampant racism and abuse.

For the moment, ignore what is happening on the outside, and instead focus on what you'd like to have in your life instead.

How will you change your energy and change yourself to have that? What will you choose?

You have way more power than you realize! Take radical responsibility for your life and future; step out of your limited, conditioned self and into your Future Self right now.

Be a Karma Yogi: Whatever duties you have in life, you do them with full attention and joy, without focus on the results. That's advice from my very wise Dad. We fondly call these Dadism's.

Take responsibility for creating coherence and congruence in your energy field by:

- Eliminating behaviors and energies that are self-harming or that harm others
- Having higher standards, rules, and guidelines for yourself and others
- Having a high level of integrity; your word is law
- And, having lots more that we can explore together if you want to go deeper

The rest of these steps are going to support you to increase your energetic congruence and coherence so you can more easily magnetize your dreams.

Actions:

1. Identify and journal about:

a. Behaviors and energies you need to eliminate

b. What standards, rules, and guidelines you need to put in place

c. What a higher level of integrity means to you

2. Make commitments and set targets based on what you discovered in your journaling.

STEP 2: ACTIVATE THE FOUR PILLARS OF PROSPERITY

Now that we have established that you do have choices, even when it feels like you don't, how do you know what to choose?

This is where I turn to Feminine Form Vedanta and Ayurveda. Don't know what that is? Just think of it as where Yoga came from.

When I was little and we would sit down to pray at family Havan, my Dad would ask us what the four aims of our life are. I would excitedly yell them out: Dharma, Artha, Kama, and Moksha. Little did I know that these precious moments would turn into my lighthouse as I was navigating hurricane-level storms in my inner and outer world.

4 Pillars of Prosperity: When Divine Desire (Kama) Intersects With Divine Design (Dharma) that Is Where You Create True Wealth (Artha). And, big bonus, it's also the path towards spiritual liberation (Moksha) and elevating this reality.

1. *Dharma* – Purpose, your calling, the reason why you were born and the meaning of your life
2. *Artha* – Prosperity and wealth derived through following your soul's calling, the means to fulfill on your purpose and your desires.
3. *Kama* – Pleasure, play, delight, desire, and sensual gratification
4. *Moksha* – Paradise; peace that comes from spiritual liberation; and, freedom from pain and personal reincarnation.

* * *

So where, in the past, money, business, spirituality, sexuality were all split and compartmentalized, now they MUST come back together for true success.

* * *

ACTIONS TO TAKE:

1. Assess where you are right now with these 4 Pillars of Prosperity
2. Tune into where you desire to be
3. Be honest with yourself about the gap
4. Journal about what you discovered
5. Set targets based on what you discovered

STEP 3: CREATE YOUR DAILY NIRVANA PRACTICES

At the center of the diagram, you see Daily Nirvana. Your Daily Nirvana is the key to everything you want because it's the key to changing your energy, to releasing old traumas, and to deconditioning your mind. And, done right, it can also activate your extraordinary future, your epic dreams.

Daily Nirvana is your state of inner peace and flow. It's your state of energetic congruence and coherence. The more Daily Nirvana you experience, the less inner conflict you have and the more clear and confident you naturally are in the expression of your true self.

It activates Quantum Prosperity and Productivity by raising your frequency and vibration.

How do you create Daily Nirvana? The first key is custom designing a nourishing daily morning practice that ensures that you become the Vortex to your Destiny.

If you are just starting out and you don't have much time in the morning or you have huge resistance to doing a morning ritual, then just take 1-5 minutes to do any one of these:

1. Take 1 minute and just sit in silence with yourself.
2. Read a page in a book that inspires you
3. Pull an Oracle card or Tarot Card
4. Stretch your body

5. Ask yourself - how do I want to feel today? And, what will I do to create that feeling?
6. Do a round or two of sun salutations or some other quick exercise or stretching to get your blood moving.
7. Meditation of your choice (guided, focus on a candle, transcendental meditation, focus on your breath in and out, or chant)
8. Journal

It's also great to do a mid-afternoon 5-minute check-in to see how you're doing, and an evening practice to tune into how your day went. I don't want to overwhelm you, so I'm not going to share more about that now. Start with the morning practice, and when that becomes a part of you, add the evening practice and then the afternoon practice.

"You will never change your life until you change something you do daily. The secret of your success is found in your daily routine." - John C. Maxwell

For more information about creating your Daily Nirvana Practices, go to my web site at *www.epicdreamacademy.com* and download the Epic Dream Accelerator. It includes several great Daily Nirvana Practices and 2 inspiring meditations that help you to start your day off with the right energy.

Another piece that's key is to focus on changing your energy. Here's how you can do that instantly. In the Quantum Field, all energetic potentials already exist. This means that whatever you wish to activate in your life can be activated just by you tuning into it.

First, set an intention or a target for yourself.

Then, ask: What is an energetic potential that would uplift my life? Or, what is something that would contribute to this target?

Joy, Curiosity, Fun, Play – these are all good things that can amplify almost any target or intention.

Then, ask: What Emotional or Energetic Addiction would get in the way of me achieving this target or intention? Write about this pattern or set of emotions. If there's more than one, name it too.

Now, tune into the intention or target again, and have gratitude for it as though it's already here. Have gratitude for your life, just as it is right now.

Actions:

1. *Do the Energetic Shift Process outlined above*
2. *Download the Epic Dream Accelerator*
3. *Decide what your Daily Nirvana Morning Practice will be*
4. *Start tomorrow!*

STEP 4: WRITE YOUR EPIC DREAM VISION

In order to create your dream life, you must know where you are going! That's where the Epic Dream Vision comes in. It's essential to activating your Quantum Prosperity because it brings in the creative energy of the universe to support you.

Take at least 5 minutes and write down your Epic Dream Vision in the present tense, as though you already have it.

I'd suggest weaving in elements about Money (Artha), Your Great Work (Dharma), Your Epic Love (Kama), Your Vibrant Health (Kama) and your Spirituality (Moksha).

Did you write it in the present tense? Did you include all 5 senses as you wrote it down? Did you think big enough?

Navigating life without this piece in place is like taking your car out for a drive without knowing where you are going, but expecting still to arrive at a particular destination.

You wouldn't do that when going on a trip, so why are you doing that in your life?

Remember, you are an Infinite Being and the only limits that exist are the ones you place on yourself. And, oddly enough, not writing out your dream is a kind of limit. You are limited to your current consciousness and reality.

> *BONUS TIP: As you write, activate the Supernatural Goddess Energy within you: the highest, most magical, most miraculous, most divine version of yourself and become that in your life! A true merging of 3D and 5D.*

THERE'S a Supernatural Goddess in every woman! Your soul and body come from a Creator, from God, from Divinity, from a Sacred place, and even if you don't feel much connection to that place within you, it's always there. You have magical powers and gifts beyond what you've ever imagined.

Action: Write your Epic Dream! It will activate your future!

STEP 5: DESIGN YOUR MOST POTENT PERSONALITY

"Your personality creates your personal reality." - Dr. Joe Dispenza

This quote is one of my all-time favorites! We all have parts of our personality that are an amazing contribution to this world and that we want to keep. And, we all have parts that we know we'd like to release or improve. This is a vast topic, and I'm just going to get you started here.

Our aim is for you to become the Limitless You: Be unapologetically your True Self. Release limited parts of your personality and decondition yourself to act beyond shadow archetypes like people-pleasing and needing approval and validation, so you can feel truly safe inhabiting the vastness of creative energy that is your True Self, your Soul, your Atman.

For you to have your most Potent Personality: Design your new personality based on your truest, deepest self, infused with the potential of your Future Self you long to embody, so you can feel deeply fulfilled, manifest quickly, and be the lighthouse for your mission, weaving in the most powerful archetypal energies.

I LOVE doing this work with the women in my community. And, I'm excited to get it started with you.

A great place to look for parts of your personality you want to improve is some of the flaws your parents had, whether they exist in you or whether you reacted to those flaws and created some other version.

For parts of your personality you'd like to cultivate, look to people you admire.

ACTIONS:

1. *List three traits you'd like to release or evolve.*
2. *List three traits that you'd like to cultivate.*

3. *Remind yourself of these in your Daily Nirvana Morning Practice and assess how you did during your evening practice.*

STEP 6: ACCESS QUANTUM PROSPERITY & PRODUCTIVITY

We create this through:

1. *Blissipline:* a state inside, where all the actions you take feel fun, inspired, fulfilling, and blissful. Then discipline feels easy and natural. It doesn't require any forcing, prodding, or cracking of the whip to make it happen. It's a state of Infinite Flow.
2. *Planifesting:* is where manifesting, planning, and inspired action come together to make your epic dreams real.
3. *Wealth Alchemy:* Creating prosperity in a pleasurable way through your purpose and alchemizing all obstacles into fuel for your Divine Destiny.
4. *Soul-driven Success:* Combine Soul, Strategy, and Structure to create true Success your way and on your terms.

Blissipline and Planifesting lead to Wealth Alchemy and Soul-driven Success at the intersection of 3D and 5D.

When your actions are infused with purpose, even the most boring, mundane activity can be blissful. For instance, if you need to do a job you don't like in order to take care of your basic needs or the needs of your family, you can bring purpose and gratitude.

ACTIONS - REFLECT and journal on the following questions:

1. *Where could you use more blissipline in your life? A good place to look is where you are feeling negatively about things you need to do. There are some clues there, either regarding your attitude or in what you are choosing or not choosing to do.*
2. *Do you have a plan to make your epic dream real? If so, write about it. What are your next steps? Ask your intuition.*

3. What are your targets for this month? For the next 90 days? For the year?

STEP 7: LUMINARY LEADERSHIP & LEGACY

Create a legacy based in showing up in luminous leadership in your own unique way, integrating your intuition and intellect to create the solutions your community most deeply needs.

Your work and wisdom is your legacy. It can impact people for years to come. What would you like to pass down to future generations?

ACTIONS:

1. *Reflect upon what your Luminary Leadership & Legacy looks like.*
2. *Write about it in your journal.*

I HOPE that you have enjoyed this chapter and that it supports you in making your epic dreams real, no matter what is happening on the outside.

Here's to your Quantum Prosperity and Productivity! I'd love to stay connected at: *www.epicdreamacademy.com*

Infinite Love & Gratitude,
Kavita

ABOUT THE AUTHOR

Kavita Rani Arora, Esq. is the Founder of the Epic Dream Academy, where thought leaders, changemakers and visionary leaders come to express their most deep, true, powerful selves.

She's an Unconventional Business Strategist and Spiritual Catalyst who teaches Quantum Prosperity & Productivity Strategies to Visionary Women Leaders so they can make their epic dreams real -- and exceed their targets while taking exquisite care of themselves (Blissipline).

For more than a decade, she's worked with thousands of people, including leaders from UBS, Morgan Stanley, and Wells Fargo, as well as high-powered lawyers and visionary entrepreneurs worldwide through her transformational programs, workshops and retreats. She's spoken alongside luminaries such as Marianne Williamson, Lynne Twist and Gabrielle Bernstein. Kavita is living her dream in Southern California with her husband and son.

> **Website:** *www.EpicDreamAcademy.com*
> **Email:** *Kavita@EpicDreamAcademy.com*
> **Facebook:** *www.facebook.com/EpicDreamAcademy*
> *and www.facebook.com/*
> *groups/QuantumProsperityandProductivity*

KAYLEIGH O'KEEFE

SOUL EXCELLENCE LEADERSHIP - A NEW PARADIGM FOR HIGH-PERFORMING FEMALE LEADERS

To Women of Excellence

I had just earned a six-figure commission check, and I wanted to throw up. "How much longer can I do this?" I thought as I swallowed hard and forced a smile in front of my colleagues.

How much longer could I win results, but lose myself? I had experienced over a decade of win after win in both corporate and technology startups. I noticed that the higher I climbed, the more I was expected to conform and the less I felt able to lead as myself.

It took me a long time to realize that I had been overworking my excellence muscles while letting those of my soul atrophy. But what did this realization mean? And what to do about it?

I see that you are a woman of excellence. You are a leader who has stood out your entire life for the results that you work hard to create.

And I trust that you're here because you've realized that you've been playing by a set of rules you don't agree with anymore. You have recognized that there is a more magnificent expression of yourself to share with the world, but you aren't quite sure what that means or how to embrace this knowledge.

You desire growth. You love beauty and quality. You care deeply for your friends and family. You want to have an even bigger impact and leave a legacy. Your excellence in the world is undeniable. You are here to reclaim your soul.

My own desire for excellence was etched in my mind early on.

THE EXCELLENCE BOOK

As a child I couldn't wait for summer to end so I could go back to school. In elementary school, I would carefully lay out my outfit the night before, and set my radio alarm clock early enough to have time for a bowl of cereal and the chance to read the sports section of the newspaper, provided that my dad had already read it. I loved learning and, naturally, I loved all of my teachers. And yet, one stands out: Mr. Tomich.

Mr. Tomich was my fifth grade teacher. On the first day of school he presented us with *The Excellence Book*. I sat up a little straighter as he shared more about the large notebook and its empty pages. Our goal as students was to sign the book as many times as possible throughout the year.

To earn a chance at this award, we had to be excellent. We could earn As. We could deliver the best book report. We could help a fellow classmate with a math assignment. Or, we could be absorbed in a game of kickball against Mr. Segara's class and see Mr. Tomich walk toward the gym entrance. The first three students to sprint to the head of the line got to sign *The Excellence Book*. Mr. Tomich valued all-around excellence.

That year, I made it my mission to sign the book more than anyone else. I wanted to be the "most excellent." I toiled over a diorama of Harriet Tubman leading the way on the Underground Railroad.

I kept one eye on the kickball game and one eye on Mr. Tomich during recess, ready to bolt like a cheetah if I saw any sign of movement back toward the classroom. I used my talent for vocabulary to help my peers in our small reading groups. I was determined to win. And I did—by the end of the year, I had signed *The Excellence Book* the most times.

Signing my full name, Kayleigh Marie O'Keefe, in cursive into a book synonymous with excellence has stuck with me until this day. From that moment on I didn't want to just be great, I wanted to be excellent. This desire guided my choices throughout my education and career.

I didn't just want to graduate from Duke University, I wanted to graduate with distinction by completing a senior thesis. I didn't just want to earn my MBA, I wanted to be our schools' commencement speaker. And in corporate, I didn't just want to do the work, I wanted to be the leader. Excellence at all costs.

THE SEARCH FOR CONNECTION

Underneath the outward success, I was undertaking a parallel inward journey to cope with an ever-expanding sense of despair and disconnection. "Was this all there was?" I kept wondering.

I tried everything to reconnect with the person I thought I was, and to cope with an ever-present desire to drink myself into oblivion. You name it, I tried it. Therapy, Alcoholics Anonymous, antidepressants. New relationships, new cities, new workout routines. I would feel inspired to master a new modality, and then deflated when I couldn't sustain the sense of connection and confidence I desired.

The only times when I saw a glimmer of escape from the disconnect were when I traveled to Spanish-speaking countries. There was something about communicating in a different language, a Romance language, that opened up my heart and allowed me to express myself at a level inaccessible to me in English.

I lived with homestay families for weeks at a time in Spain, Nicaragua, Bolivia, and Argentina while volunteering on local projects. In our breakfast conversations over *cafe con leche*, I shared my desire to explore, to write, to create. Often I was laughed at for being "a dreamer" and advised to "just get married," but I shared my heart without caution.

In those experiences abroad, I felt the deep connection I desired, and then dropped back into the world of meetings, metrics, and milestones. I carried on in my career and achieved until suddenly, I hit a wall.

It was the summer of 2018, and I had just spent the last year working on a four-million-dollar annual contract, the first of its kind for the young tech company where I worked. Our customer finally signed the deal late on a Friday afternoon.

My colleagues blasted Lil Wayne's "A Milli" over the office speakers and cheered me on. It should have been a moment of celebration, but all I felt was depleted and exhausted. I couldn't imagine doing the work that lay on the other side of the contract.

I typed in the words "retreat," "women," and "Hawaii" into Google. I didn't quite know why I chose those words in that moment; I just knew that I wanted to get away. I discovered a Feminine Mastery Retreat on Maui led by Cyndie Silbert, an expert who has helped hundreds of women uncork their feminine expression.

I was intrigued by the juxtaposition of the words "mastering the feminine," and two weeks later stood on lush Maui with twelve other women.

My experience on the retreat cracked me open. I reconnected with my feminine nature. For the first time, I truly connected with my emotions. I felt my body and breath, and I learned how to express myself in a loving, grounded manner. I mourned my loss of innocence from past trauma. I forgave myself for years of suppressing my emotions and intuition.

I felt like I had just discovered an unknown planet, and I continued to explore the themes of embodiment, surrender, and attraction by connecting with thought leaders like Natalie Murray and her life-changing work on boundaries and releasing deep trauma, and Leigh Jane Woodgate and her intrepid community of Divine Feminine Leaders.

Through these amazing women and others like them, I learned that in order to create a more beautiful, connected world, I had to stop pushing and forcing and start allowing and attracting. I felt called to direct my desire for excellence inward toward my soul.

My decade-long gradual awakening was punctuated by the moment on Maui. I realized that I had been overly reliant on my masculine energy, attempting to force myself into a corporate structure designed for uniformity. I accepted, perhaps for the first time, that I was a woman, that I had deep desires, and that I wanted to be a source of light—not simply a source of productivity—in the world around me.

MY FEMININE AWAKENING

Years ago, I had cut myself off from my feminine nature. Heck, I didn't know what "feminine nature" was! My mind swirled in an endless loop of the same self-loathing thoughts. I could not access my emotions or articulate how I felt. I was either OK, good, or great, not far from the grunts and shoulder shrugs of teenage boys. I had no awareness of or access to the wide spectrum of emotions.

But after Maui, I noticed changes.

I started to notice my body. For the first time, I even liked my stomach, wide smile, and mismatched eyebrows. I wanted to nourish my body with healthier foods, strengthen it through yoga, and dance until three in the morning. I began adorning my body with beautiful, dangling earrings and vibrant purple and magenta blouses. I felt the world around me take notice.

I became more aware. I was aware of the masculine demands of the workplace—even in workplaces led by women. The late-night Slack messages. The early-morning meetings to sync with the team on something that could have been shared in an email. The setting of BHAGS, "big-hairy-audacious goals." The focus on results at the expense of morale and feelings. After the retreat, I instead began to organize my meetings differently and to highlight the feelings we wanted to create with the client.

I fell back in love with myself. I realized that my superpowers extended beyond the virtues of excellence, intelligence, and discipline—so valued in the corporate world—and into the feminine ones of intuition, expression, and creation. I reset my own expectations and goals for myself, focusing on the quality of my relationships and the integrity of my self-expression, instead of valuing myself based on my salary and bonuses.

I began creating results in a new way. Before, I plowed toward a revenue goal through sheer willpower. I worked harder, stayed up later. Now, I visualized the beachfront house with the orange tree and the amazing playroom I desired to create for my future children. From deep within I received my own internal wisdom, that of the concept of Soul Excellence.

Soul Excellence entered into my consciousness once I had reconnected with my feminine energy. It hit my head and heart simultaneously, a bolt of lightning that invigorated my body. And then I experienced what it meant to create in a deeply feminine way. Excellence had always lived within me, but now I was eager to reclaim the soul part.

I left San Francisco and moved to South Florida by the beach to create the space I desired for my soul's excellence to flow through me and out into the world. I didn't know what it was, exactly. I didn't have a clear path from the idea to how it would be expressed. I didn't have all the answers. What I did have was an intuitive hit, an awareness that there was a better way to be a leader.

I wrote, I blogged, I podcasted, I created videos. I *expressed*. Without attachment to a specific outcome and without a corporate filter, I shared myself. The process was deeply intuitive. I felt calm, confident, creative, and collaborative. The writings on my blog helped connect me to an essential oil expert, a local yogi, and the creator of a new political movement. Each person I met on the journey shared their desires to grow and create a better world, and then introduced me to other people yearning for a different, more enjoyable way to create results.

Soul Excellence flowed through me so naturally that I gave birth to the Soul Excellence Archetypes. The archetypes are a way for leaders who find themselves disillusioned by how work gets done in the corporate world. These leaders want to connect back into their soul, the source of their love and connection, and help guide others to do the same.

THE SOUL EXCELLENCE ARCHETYPES

An archetype is a perspective or lens through which to see yourself and your impact beyond your title and accomplishments. It is an encouragement to accept your invitation back to you.

Reconnecting with your Soul Excellence is a wake up call to shift into a new paradigm of leadership. It is a way to bring forth all parts of you to lead from a place that cannot be taught in the corporate training environment. It is about magnifying your power and your influence to create the beautiful, vibrant world in which you want to live.

The Soul Excellence Archetypes offer you the opportunity to move from analysis the strength of the masculine, and into embodiment, the strength of the feminine. This shift was a critical turning point for me on my journey.

I had taken all of the personality tests out there, and I had purchased and read all of the related profiles. I was structured in my approach to get to know myself; I had wanted definitive answers, not nuanced archetypes. Through the creation and expression of these archetypes, I moved beyond analysis and logical understanding and into full acceptance and embodiment.

The Soul Excellence Archetypes are described below. Each of these archetypes live within you, but one will call to you more as your first sign of focus for your Soul Excellence; this is your primary archetype.

It offers you a perspective into your leadership superpowers - the unique way that you create impact in the world. The other archetypes support you as you embrace the multi-dimensional leader within.

* * *

The Soul Excellence Archetypes are as follows:

1. *Integrator* – You are a harmonizer who brings people together to collaborate on big ideas by tapping into individual strengths. You believe deeply in the power of unlocking the individual greatness of your team and followers, and trust that you will manifest partnerships that multiply your individual brilliance and impact. Your presence is inviting, and you are motivated by *connection*. In nature, the giant Sequoia Tree integrates massive root systems to stand the test of time.
2. *Inspirer* – You are a communicator who lights up an audience and motivates people to take action through your words and ideals. You relish expressing yourself and sharing lessons learned along your journey. You share your ideas in a way that connects with the pure virtues stored within your followers' hearts to expand their view of what is possible. Your presence is uplifting, and you are motivated by *expression*. In nature, the stunning array of flowers inspire us all to embrace love and beauty.
3. *Initiator* – You are a trail-blazer who gets things done at lightning speeds, demonstrating the power of action. You take risks, trusting that you will learn and create impact along the way. You believe that taking action is the only way to contribute in a soul-inspired way. While others sit on the sidelines or share uninformed opinions, you live in the arena and are the first to blaze the path. Your presence is energetic, and you are motivated by *results*. In nature, a lightning bolt demands our attention and lights up the entire sky.
4. *Innovator* – You are an independent thinker who challenges the status quo and offers new ways of being into the world. You don't just wish things could be better, you make it happen. You are never satisfied until you've discovered an eternal truth. From that wisdom, you offer new frameworks, new technologies, new modalities, and new ways of being for the world. Your presence is fascinating, and you are motivated by *possibilities*. In nature, a volcano sits dormant and then explodes to create new landscapes.

BEFORE CONCEIVING of the Soul Excellence Archetypes, I relied on my drive, intensity, and focus. On this journey, as I allowed the Archetypes to enter my heart, I sensed that my primary archetype is the Inspirer. I love to use my vocabulary, research, and stories to lead through expression. Soul Excellence inspired me to embrace vulnerability to supercharge the superpowers of the Inspirer. I had to move from my intellect and into my heart and then into my entire body.

As we embrace the power of our archetypes, we move from a conscious understanding to a deeper expression that comes from breathing, creating space, opening up to possibilities, and gently releasing thoughts that divide us from our true, loving nature. Beyond communicating with my words, I live inspired. I act in alignment with my primary leadership archetype and I call forth the other archetypes to support me in living out my mission—to remind individuals to pursue greatness at the deepest level of their being.

YOUR INVITATION TO SOUL EXCELLENCE

You are a woman of excellence. You are a woman of soul.

I understand how conflicting it can feel to awaken your soul. It can be disorienting to consider that the work you've excelled at may have been at odds with your core values of connection, love, and integrity.

It can be scary to climb to the top of the mountain only to realize that you don't like the view. You may feel like the only way to express this growing inner desire is to abandon your career and ship off to Bali. Honor your accomplishments thus far and launch forward on a new soul-guided trajectory led by your Soul Excellence Archetype.

Awaken your feminine power and leadership potential by discovering your Soul Excellence Archetype. It's the first step to lead in a way that attracts all that you desire to achieve through growth, connection, meaning, and joy. You'll find me and the Soul Excellence Archetype quiz at *www.kayleighokeefe.com*.

ABOUT THE AUTHOR

Kayleigh O'Keefe is the creator of Soul Excellence.

    She is a leadership mentor who inspires individuals to chart a new course in life in order to bring more soul-defined success, fulfillment, and joy into the world.

    Kayleigh spent over a decade as a consultant for Fortune 500 companies and team builder at early-stage technology start-ups. She received her B.A. from Duke University and her M.B.A. on a full scholarship from the University of San Francisco.

    Kayleigh has walked over four hundred miles across two different routes of The Way of St. James pilgrimage through Spain and Portugal. After spending most of her career in Washington, D.C. and San Francisco, she now lives and creates by the beach in Ft. Lauderdale, FL.

    You are invited to shift into a new paradigm of leadership by participating in her signature program, The Soul Excellence Leadership Pilgrimage.

Website: www.kayleighokeefe.com
Instagram: www.instagram.com/KayleighOK_11
Facebook: www.facebook.com/kayleigh.okeefe
Email: kayleigh.okeefe@gmail.com

KRYSTAL ALEXANDER-HILLE

EXPANDING INTO GALACTIC EMBODIMENT

Conscious Leaders birthing the New Earth by expanding into their galactic wisdom and claiming their life force energy

I had just arrived at Australia's biggest Tantra Festival, Taste of Love, when the world went into a mad panic over toilet paper.

The stock market plummeted and the first restrictions came into place to supposedly contain the deadly strand of corona virus, COVID-19, on March 13, 2020.

International boarders were closing and participants of my Egypt Initiation Journey were asking for some kind of reassurance. Was the tour still going ahead? Would there be refunds? I took a deep breath and went into my divine masculine to find some answers. At that stage, there were none. We were asked to get comfortable with uncertainty.

I was reminded that our human will is so insignificant compared to divine will. As a child, I saw light beings from other realms beyond our human existence. However, I soon got engrossed in the fears and struggles of human existence, especially those imprinted by my parents, who grew up in post-war Germany, which caused my vision to close down.

Now once more, I was asked to align myself to divine will and release the resistance of denial, the first phase of any grieving process.

I went for a walk on the vast, empty beach to centre my nervous system and expand fully into my highest essence in preparation of facilitating the opening temple night of the festival. Three hundred people gathered in the tent to journey into a deeper connection with themselves, their bodies, their aliveness, others, earth and spirit.

Two nights later, when I guided the closing temple, I knew we had to postpone the Egypt Retreat till next year. I also knew that this was the last opportunity for many months to gather in community and create a powerful field of conscious intentions for the planet and the universe.

How could I best prepare these beautiful souls for what was to come? What experience could I give them to strengthen love and gratitude in their hearts and fully step into sovereignty to awaken and unplug from the matrix of illusions and lies?

I chose to work with the themes of sovereignty, gratitude, and celebration to counteract the collective contraction and fear created by the pandemic. Our souls were soaring, our hearts wide open, our bodies alive, and our minds at peace.

I closed the night with these words: May we remember this connection and aliveness in the months to come, for we have the freedom to choose our state of being, no matter what.

*　*　*

OVERVIEW

"As above so below, as within so without, as the universe so the soul."
Hermes Trismegistus – author of the sacred hermetic scriptures

THE CORONA VIRUS crisis has created a global pattern of disruption, a forced change, that has shocked humans out of their slumber, their comfort, and their complacency, and challenged every single man and woman on the planet to ask questions. Some are awakening to the deceptions, lies, and hidden agendas behind this crisis. Others are re-evaluating their priorities in life.

What is the sleep we are waking up from?

What awareness are we moving into?

What has galactic embodiment and the claiming of our life force got to do with our awakening?

What has it got to do with the evolution of human consciousness and our ability to birth a new paradigm in harmony with a galactic mission?

When we understand the bigger picture, of what is unfolding in our world, we can put into context our own individual journey, fine-tune our soul's purpose or mission, and inspire our clients and communities from a place of greater sovereignty and empowerment.

To fully implement this, we must create the best possible physical vessel in which to host this consciousness and there is no better way to do this than the exploration and expansion of our pure and potent erotic energy, which in essence is our life force energy.

* * *

THE BIGGER CONTEXT OF THIS NEW ERA

The evolution of human consciousness started over 500,000 years ago, when hunters and gatherers were living to merely survive. It was the age of maturing the base chakra, learning about safety and security and how to take care of our basic needs of survival.

Once that was mastered, humanity moved into the Golden Age of the Goddess, beginning as far back as the Upper Paleolithic cultures about 25,000 BC and reaching its peak through the Neolithic time around 7000 BC, when the feminine sacral chakra, dedicated to creativity and sexuality, was being matured.

A matriarchal, matrilineal, and polyandrous society was thus birthed, in and around ancient Egypt, Sumerian, and Mesopotamia. It was a time of thriving art, song, and dance, all centred around a strong temple culture. Temples were the economic centre of society where the Great Mother Goddess, Queen of Heaven, was revered as the serpent prophetess of great wisdom, the original Creatress and the patroness of sexual pleasures and reproduction.

Asset (Isis), Hathor, Ishtar, and Innana were among her many manifestations and known as the teachers of sexual practices.

The priestesses, who were aware that sexual energy is a sacred life-force energy, honoured these teachings and celebrated them through sacred sexual rituals in the temples and in many of these cultures, sexuality was widely understood as a pathway to spiritual ecstasy. It was the path to enlightenment. Shame did not exist.

This culture thrived until around 1500 BC and the rise of the power-hungry Amun Priests in Ancient Egypt. Shame was birthed, and around 1000 BC, when the then Nomadic Hebrew tribes invaded the Middle East and forcefully shut down the temples, history was rewritten and women in particular denied the opportunity to practice their temple rituals.

In order to gain control over a powerful people, the story of original sin was created, where Eve ate from the forbidden tree of knowledge. From that point on, it was said that women could not be trusted. Thus they became the property first of their fathers and then their husbands, and we still see women being 'given away' by their fathers during marriage ceremonies.

Women were publicly stoned in the market squares if they were seen going to their temples. This created the fear of death in relation to sexual expression and in relation to following inner guidance.

The persecutions continued into the Middle Ages, where witch hunts and crusades extinguished the priestess practices; the codes of the divine feminine went underground and became dormant within our cells. Today they are awakening again, but we still need to release these 'fear' codes from our DNA that have been genetically passed on for life times and generations.

The hidden blessing of the past four thousand years or so was the maturing of our solar plexus chakra. Power struggles had to be experienced in order to mature the power centre. Separation was created. The triangle of victim, perpetrator, and rescuer became a never-ending wheel of incarnations. We have been moving from one role to the other, always trying to break out of the cycle and back into pure power, not power *over* another, or suffering *from* another's power.

Right now, human evolution has reached the time of transitioning from maturing the solar plexus chakra into the heart or life-force chakra. Astrologically, we are moving from the Piscean Age into the Aquarian Age and are currently waking up to the deceptions, mass control, and mass hypnotism of the past four thousand years.

We are moving out of a wounded, male-dominated society that functions on hierarchy, control, intimidation, doubt, fear, separation, and scarcity, into one based on equivalence, acceptance, harmony, unity, connection, and abundance. We still have a long way to go, but we are ready to birth the new earth now.

Since we are leaving duality behind, I am convinced that this is why there is so much gender diversity popping into mainstream awareness.

In the heart, or life-force chakra, a new Golden Age can be birthed. We will embrace diversity, integrate the fragmented aspects back into wholeness, celebrate inclusivity, build partnerships and an inner union between our masculine and feminine aspects and everything in-between, to come into true unity consciousness.

As we release sexual trauma and shame, we embrace our wholeness and the wholeness of the planet. This is why erotic embodiment matters. This is why it is the pathway to the galactic wisdom and the birthing of a new paradigm. We do not reject, we do not judge, we embrace ALL that is and ALL that is yet to be.

* * *

THE GALACTIC AGENDA

"All the world's a stage and all the men and women merely players."
William Shakespeare

WHAT IS PLAYING itself out on this planet is the physical enactment of an agenda needing to be resolved in the higher dimensions. But to share the big picture and how all the dimensions interact would go far beyond the scope of this chapter, so I will just focus on the basics, what is most relevant to our evolution and awakening:

Everything in the universe is forever expanding: stars, galaxies, and consciousness. And so, around 40 Million years ago, the fifth-dimensional Lyran star consciousness, which includes the Pleiadians and Sirians, who aspired to ascend to seventh-dimensional consciousness, lived in harmony alongside each other in the third dimension, but each race was secretively thinking that their values and their way of operating were superior to the other races.

In order to flush these conflicts to the surface to be resolved, the ninth and seventh dimensional consciousnesses of Andromedans, Hathors, and Arcturians, directed the Dracos to attack the Lyrans. They are a Reptilian race, operating from a place of purpose and desiring to ascend to the fifth dimension, to Lyra. This was to expose the underlying separation that Lyran star races were running and resulted in a war between not only the Reptilians and the Lyrans, but between the Lyran races themselves.

It was for this purpose (amongst others) that the human race was genetically engineered with DNA from each of the conflicting star races. The intention was that this human being would create the template to resolve the inner conflicts and upload this template to the higher dimensions.

This is why we are so often plagued by inner conflicts and have to deny one part of us in order to let another feel validated. This is why our vision is often distorted.

In order to achieve inner union and stop reacting out of the fight, flight, or freeze response, our DNA is changing and our reptilian brain is currently being reprogrammed.

For the past year, I have been actively working with the Dracos and numerous star races and higher dimensional beings to assist in the unification and elevation of consciousness, both in channelled conversations and inner journeys. An extraordinary unfolding of events.

One more race that I will mention are the 'Blue Birds' - the 'Avians.' They are instrumental in this current shift and introduced themselves about four years ago. A highly advanced race from another universe, they arrived to bring codes of higher divine feminine frequencies to this universe. Some of us are the portals for these frequencies and codes needed to move into this next phase. Perhaps you are one of them?

We are the pillars of light, dotted around the planet, deeply centred in our body, nodes of the grid of consciousness, fully expanded and activated through the galactic connection, standing together in collective leadership.

We are integrating all fragmented aspects of self, and, in doing so, integrating the fragmented aspects on this planet and the galaxy in order to live with a new unity of consciousness, embracing diversity and being united from a place of love and acceptance.

We are birthing a new earth through our energetic or physical wombs.

* * *

WHAT DOES IT MEAN TO BE A CONSCIOUS LEADER OF THIS NEW ERA?

Being a conscious leader in these times means having a fierce courage to be ourselves.

It means living in alignment with our values and embodying our mission. It means releasing all doubts, all fears, and all comparisonitis, and claiming the knowledge that no one can do what you do the way you do it.

As I said, we are birthing a new earth through our energetic or physical wombs. Our wombs are the most magical and powerful force in the universe, filled with life force energy.

That's why patriarchy had to cripple and shame it: to control us, to silence us, to make us birth more fear and separation, instead of deep connection and abundance.

We can change this as we reclaim the power of our wombs and release shame and sexual trauma. We can change this as we embrace our wholeness and the wholeness of the planet. Claiming our life force and our erotic innocence matters. It can become the pathway to galactic wisdom and the birthing of a new earth.

***

WHAT IS GALACTIC EMBODIMENT?

Galactic embodiment brings the higher dimensional wisdom into the physical body so that it can be acted on from a powerful place of purpose.

It is the embodiment piece that is missing for many healers and lightworkers. Some are so empathic that they don't feel safe in their bodies and hover, without centre, somewhere in space, scared of the world and in their wounded feminine energy.

On the flip side, we have the high achievers who have always done it the hard way. This was the conditioning I inherited: stuck in the 3D, wounded-masculine, patriarchal way of pushing to make things happen, forgetting how to tap into the flow of the galactic higher guidance.

Galactic embodiment means that we can personify, realise, and manifest our multi-dimensional spirit self in the physical body, integrating the wounded masculine and feminine aspects back into their divinity, creating an inner partnership of divine feminine conception and visioning, and divine masculine action and realisation.

When we become skilled at embodying our multi-dimensional self in our body, we have the capacity to change, manipulate, and influence more and more of our reality and become master manifesters.

* * *

RETURNING TO THE TEMPLE

"In order to live a life of meaning we must go beyond a life of acquisitions and move into a life of devotion."
Carolyn Myss, Medical Intuitive

WHEN EVERYTHING in our lives is done with reverence, from a deeply conscious state of connection to the divine, we are in flow, in gratitude, in deep connection to the highest vibrational state of being. From this place, life is blissful, ecstatic, and deeply peaceful. From this place, synchronicities and instant manifestations occur.

When we remember that we are intergalactic beings, operating on multiple dimensions at once, when we are aware that our vibration creates energetic footprints on the earth and ripple effects throughout the whole universe, we become grateful and more mindful of the thoughts and feelings we cultivate.

It means listening deeply to the whispers of our body, our heart, and our soul, so that we can be in alignment with our highest truth at all times, and from that place, we can hold a powerful container for our clients and communities.

We know that a temple is not an external building we visit; our bodies are the temple, the living, breathing temple of our soul.

How are you treating your temple? Are you looking after it with loving care or are you hating parts of it?

How are you treating your inner sanctuary? The womb as the birthplace of all things? The cervix, as the altar of your temple? Are you numbing them out or cultivating sensation?

Many women have a numb cervix because they have allowed abuse to happen, either because their higher self has chosen to put them in a helpless situation, or because they consented to abuse, something I used to do over and over, when not listening to the whispers of my womb.

How do we reclaim the sanctity of our temple? I will share some ideas soon.

* * *

UNDERSTANDING THE EROTIC-GALACTIC CONNECTION

"We all taste God, taste Goddess, taste pure Spirit in those moments of sexual rapture, and wise men and women have always used that rapture to reveal Spirits innermost secrets."
Ken Wilber, Author of Sex, Ecology, Spirituality

THE CONSCIOUS CULTIVATION of our life-force energy brings us into harmony with our erotic power, the very centre of our magnetism and manifestation magic. This expands our essence to connect with our multi-dimensional self and can create heightened states of awareness, expanded consciousness and ecstatic states of bliss from which we can access inspiration and cosmic guidance for our life and business.

Erotic energy is the fertiliser of inspiration; it is pure creative energy. It is our life-force energy that has the potential to not only birth babies, but also a new era, a new earth, a new way of living and a new way of doing business. It pulls us out of our mental faculty into the world of the senses and into the galactic world of pure potential.

This is where sex magic comes in. "Consciousness, with Intent, Manifests." The higher our level of consciousness is, the faster we can manifest our intentions. Erotic energy expands us into these higher states of consciousness from where our pure intentions can manifest faster and more powerfully than in the normal waking human state of being.

* * *

TOOLS TO CULTIVATE YOUR INNER TEMPLE

I have created a magical guided journey that has the potential to bring you into loving acceptance of your whole body, to release stagnant energy, fear, and shame and to awaken the full potential of your life-force energy. In the second part of this journey, you are guided to activate the unity codes from your galactic, multi-dimensional self and bring them into your physical vessel.

Rather than writing it into this chapter, you can download the audio-recording from my website. This means that you go on a guided journey, instead of reading and meditating both at the same time.

Download the guided journey here: *www.krystalalexanderhille.com/awakening*

* * *

MAINTAINING YOUR GALACTIC EMBODIED CONNECTION

It is relatively easy to connect to heightened states of awareness during a guided meditation. The challenge lies in maintaining this high frequency consistently and over longer periods of time as we move throughout our day.

There are several ways to practice this.

Firstly, you can incorporate a version of the meditation I share into your daily morning practice. You can also set an alarm and connect to this frequency several times throughout your day. This strengthens the muscle of co-existing in the multiple dimensions at once.

Secondly, I am extending a sacred invitation to you to join my community of conscious leaders, spiritual entrepreneurs, and healers in the *Temple of Galactic Embodiment*.

Join us if you desire connection with your multi-dimensional Self more deeply and choose to embody your highest essence more consistently, so that you can channel your unique soul frequency into your work, create more magnetism, joy, and financial abundance from a place of true sovereignty.

Thank you for shining your light in this world. Thank you for being one who awakens at this time. Your light matters. Your love matters. Your being matters.

Your soul has chosen to be here at this extraordinary time, and I honour you for answering the call, for courageously stepping into the fullness of who you are.

With love,
   Krystal

ABOUT THE AUTHOR

Krystal Alexander-Hille is a Soul Leadership Coach, Tantra Teacher and Spiritual Mentor. She enables conscious leaders, business people and light workers to embody their soul essence by guiding them to amplify their intuition, magnify their power and expand their vision so that they can birth the next evolution of their multi-dimensional self, create more meaningful connections, deeper intimacy and greater financial abundance from a place of embodied sovereignty, joy and grace.

Aware of her galactic origins, Krystal comes from a soul lineage of ancient high priestesses, embodying divine feminine codes. She offers initiation journeys to Egypt & Mexico, facilitates tantric in-person and online workshops, and is particularly proud of her latest creation: *The Temple of Galactic Embodiment*, a membership platform for conscious leaders, birthing a new era.

Krystal holds a BA in English Literature & Theatre, a diploma in Life Coaching and TimeLine Therapy and is a certified Tantra Teacher and Reiki Master. With 30 years in leadership and personal development, over the past 12 years, Krystal has contributed her wisdom to numerous international summits and podcasts, and is the author of 'She Who Would Be Queen', 'In the Womb of the Goddess', and contributing author to 'Reclaiming Lilith, Reclaiming Ourselves', with two other book contributions to be released later in 2020.

Originally from Germany, Krystal lives with her young family in county Victoria, Australia.

> **Website:** www.KrystalAlexanderHille.com
> **Facebook:** www.facebook.com/pg/krystalalexanderhilletemple
> **LinkedIn:** www.linkedin.com/in/krystal-alexander-hille
> **Email:** info@krystalalexanderhille.com

LACHELLE AMOS

JOURNEY TO THE HEART WISDOM LEADER: CONFLICT RESOLUTION IN A NEW WORLD

Many paths lead up to the same mountaintop. So too are there many ways to fully understand the transformational power of the heart.

My path, forged through hard work and giving too much of myself, led me by the age of 27 to my first international, non-governmental organization, Country Director position.

As a young woman holding senior management positions for nearly a decade in a variety of global contexts, I faced a plethora of challenges that my Master of Arts in International Peace & Conflict Resolution didn't prepare me for. I quickly moved up the professional, international service ladder, managing multi-million Dollar/Euro/Pound projects across the Middle East, East Africa, and South Asia at the community, state, regional, and international levels.

Throughout, my ability to tune into my "Heart Wisdom" served as an unconscious survival trait.

Life in some of these countries layered another component of stress. Mobility, and the subsequent exposure, was limited for our safety. In Iraq, this was intended to reduce exposure to car bombs and targeted kidnappings.

Embassy and partner meetings aside, we only traveled between the house and office by car in Baghdad, separated by only a couple of city blocks in a guarded area.

In South Sudan, our guarded walls fortified us against prevalent break-ins and carjackings.

With comparatively eased mobility, I escaped to the limited number of restaurants and friends' compounds during daylight hours. Mostly, I self-imposed a curfew, feeling it was too risky to drive myself around much after sunset. (Working with a small organization meant a small budget and no night and weekend driver.)

In my first year of working in South Sudan as Deputy Head of Mission, the management team very quickly realized that if they wanted action on their program requests, it was best to speak with me, rather than the Head of Mission.

That year, at 30 years old, I managed the resolution of 6 different death threats made against various members of my team. I organized 6 separate medical evacuations. In one intense moment of conflict, I steadily and calmly stood my ground and made my point clear without ever raising my voice when one of my team members screamed so close to my face that I could feel the heat of his breath, his hand heatedly waving nearby my head. I then promptly and compassionately terminated him.

Along my journey, I fine-tuned the efficacy of my budding "Heart Wisdom Leadership," consciously claiming and honing it as a pathway for everyday life. After multiple burnouts, I committed to better prioritize my health and well-being. With my Yoga Alliance Registered Yoga Teacher 500-hour certification in hand, I founded Silence of Sound Yoga, leading yoga and sound healing teacher trainings, retreats, workshops, classes, private sessions, and Heart Wisdom coaching sessions around the world for 4 years.

HEART WISDOM

My journey has taught me that in tuning into your Heart Wisdom – the intuitive voice, loving whispers, and powerfully compassionate commands – you embody and radiate all that you are.

Physically, our hearts are power houses! The scientific research of the Heart Math Institute, Dr. Joe Dispenza, and others reveals that our hearts are comprised of some 40,000 sensory neurites, making it a command center – a gateway to non-local knowing.

These heart neurites allow us to tune into the happenings of the environment around us before our physical body and mental awareness even realize it. The heart neurites are at work when we begin to have an emotional response to something (like an image) seconds before it even visibly appears.

Recall in your body how it felt the last time you were fully relaxed versus highly stressed. How did your breath differ? Did your thoughts flow at the same speed? Which emotions were more prevalent?

When we lead from this knowing in our hearts, allowing it to be like our body's Chief Executive Officer, the rhythm of our heart rate appears smooth and fluid on an electrocardiogram. In this state, our hearts compassionately command our brains (the body's Chief Operational Officer) how and what to communicate out to the rest of our body's vital orans via our nervous system.

When, however, we allow our brains to run the show, the heartbeat's rhythm becomes short and jagged. This happens when we're stressed or thinking too much. Essentially, in this overly stimulated state, our Sympathetic Nervous System, responsible for our Fight-Flight-Freeze mechanism, disconnects our physical body from consciously responding to its very source of life-pumping energy.

Consider that in our current global situation, the very virus which has caused so much fear targets the heart and the lungs, which together distribute and nourish the body with life-force energy, *prana* as we call it in yoga. Instead, it stagnates, coagulating as mucus in the lungs. What can we do about this?

As a yoga teacher I enjoy understanding the heart from a subtle energy perspective. Our hearts are a place of balance, bridging our lower energy centers - responsible for governing our physical needs and earthly state of being - with our upper *chakras*, which connect us more subtly into our spiritual and interconnected state of being.

Our hearts also bridge the different layers of our being: physical, mental, emotional, spiritual, and bliss bodies. From a place of unconditional love – without expectation, conditions, and attachment – our hands are physical extensions of our hearts, energetically bringing balance through equal giving and receiving.

FEAR

Coming to the heart of the matter of our current global dynamics, fear levels are astoundingly high. As an emotional state with an important evolutionary function, fear is a vital force of protection and certainly needs to be honored. Too much or prolonged states of fear, however, produce a *granthi*, psychic knot.

This keeps our Sympathetic Nervous System in overdrive, inviting our brain to overrule the healthy balance of our hearts. In this state of fear – this disconnection from our hearts – we begin to physically disconnect ourselves from others, avoiding in-person human connection and physical touch.

After a break-up, for example, many of us tend to build some sort of emotional wall around our hearts out of fear of getting hurt again. Our bodies may even begin to physically create a protective barrier with shoulders rising towards the ears and rounding forward. Guarding our hearts, we may withdraw ourselves from potentially intimate situations, until we've processed the hurt from the previous relationship.

Under current "stay-at-home" orders around the world, social distancing measures remove much of the physical human contact our hearts desire. Without some of the subsequent practices, that imbalance of the heart enables higher stress levels, emotional explosions, etc. The outbursts, threats, and health issues I encountered amongst my team in South Sudan may seem extreme. Yet, how often over the last few months have you or those you're in place with snapped, broken down, or withdrawn while attempting to balance the different values and needs of everyone confined in your immediate space?

Yes, it's important to take precautionary measures. However, when these measures are designed and implemented from a place of fear, they run the risk of stripping away even more human connection and/or exacerbating or prolonging the conflict. It's like placing a bandage on a hemorrhage, hoping it will stop, rather than actually investigating and directly addressing the root cause to stop the bleed at its source.

Fear-based withdrawal begins to perpetuate a "me" vs "you", "us" vs "them" mentality. This dehumanization has been at the root of many conflicts – and even world wars! – throughout human history.

It also fuels the xenophobia and racism exacerbated by remarks of those holding positions of power and influence that point fingers of blame and place certain groups of people at greater risk of discrimination and even violence because of their identity – including elements of which they were born into and have no control over.

PRACTICES TO EMPOWER YOU AS A HEART WISDOM LEADER

Conflict Transformation

The beauty of conflicts is that they hold amazing potential for transformation, whether at a systemic institutional level, regarding tension with your partner, or because of a deep inner conflict. Our deep-rooted thoughts and beliefs – individually and collectively – are reflected in the types of conflict and our reactions or responses (there is a difference!) to them.

Transformation at any level requires vulnerably courageous trust. This is difficult to embody when stress levels run high and we fear the safety, livelihood, and survival of ourselves and our families. Have you ever held yourself back (consciously or not) from pursuing your dreams because you didn't know how you would still be able to pay your bills? Similarly, it's challenging to resolve a conflict without first addressing the concerns of one group that feels, for example, that their access to drinking and agricultural water is threatened.

Thoughts together with feelings form the basis of our beliefs. Changing these beliefs that inform our decisions and actions requires a certain amount of vulnerable trust. Fear is considered a psychic knot that sits at the base of the spine.

Imagine for a moment that each of your 60,000-75,000 thoughts per day could be placed on the energy center that the emotion associated with the thought corresponds to. Now imagine that each of these thoughts could be physically weighed. If we're ruminating in worries and fears, we'll be weighted down at our base, unable to stand up, unable to fully grasp the trust required to initiate the change process.

Grounding

A fundamental step towards greater balance of your Heart Wisdom is to invite some of the fear that may be driving you to take a back seat. We can do this through grounding practices. Feel into practices that bring you back into your physical body. Perhaps that's practicing yoga, dancing to your favorite song, walking in nature, etc.

Bringing your focus back into your body is equally about acknowledging and honoring your feelings, as emotions are energy moving through the body. When we choose – and it is indeed a choice, albeit not always an easy one! – to spin our gears in fear, we risk that energy getting stuck in the emotional body. Over time, if not released, it physically manifests as "dis-ease" in the body.

Breath

Focusing on the deep flow of the breath is one of the best practices to release what no longer serves the body and ground us back in the present moment. This was pivotal in my ability to remain calm and take steady action in managing the death threats and medical evacuations in South Sudan.

As it relates to fear specifically, I invite you to find a quiet place to sit comfortably for a few minutes, either cross-legged or in a chair with the soles of your feet on the ground. Ensure your spine is tall. Relax your shoulders and draw the fronts of them slightly back, opening across the front of your chest.

With your gaze soft or eyes closed, begin to focus on the flow of your breath in and out through your nose, allowing each inhale to be equal and even to your exhale; your breath steady and full. On your next inhale, scan your body head-to-toe, compassionately observing any thoughts, fears, or other contracting emotions or physical tension in your body that you're ready and willing to release.

Visualize it leaving your body as you exhale. With your next inhale, direct all the life force energy to those areas, replacing that bit of released space with nourishing light. Inhale to where your body needs it and exhale, releasing through an open-mouth sigh, connecting with sound.

Repeat this process as many times as feels necessary to calm yourself, drawing focus and energy into your physical body. The slow, deep breath, as well as the audible open-mouth exhale, helps release fear by activating the Parasympathetic Nervous System, controlling the Rest & Digest mechanism. This tells your body, "I'm safe. I'm ok. I can relax."

ATTRIBUTES OF THE HEART WISDOM LEADER

Becoming the Mindful Observer

Releasing some of your fear and worries alone isn't going to transform the thoughts and inherent beliefs that perpetuate conflict at all levels. Tuning into your Heart Wisdom also requires becoming your own mindful observer.

Just as with meditation, *asana* (physical yoga postures), and life in general, mindfully increasing awareness to your own patterns is a practice. One that requires compassion, a key quality of the heart.

Compassion

As you notice yourself slipping back towards or into the thought pattern you desire to change, self-compassion is vital. Here the mindful observer – almost as if you were outside yourself looking in – notices without comparison, evaluation, attachment, or judgment. This objectivity already has an element of compassion embedded within it. Yet self-compassion takes it a bit further.

In the space of desiring my work to make a difference in the lives of our beneficiaries, as well as knowing that my managerial decisions impacted the safety and well-being of my team, I strived for years to be "perfect." Being compassionate towards myself was crucial to transforming this pattern.

In those moments when you become aware of your inner critic and the stories you've created, compassion is reminding yourself that it's ok to give it another go. To give yourself a smile and a hug and to honor that awareness is the first step in the process. The practice over time is to observe the pattern slightly quicker than the time before, even if only inestimably sooner.

Gratitude

As Wayne Dyer once said, "When you change the way you look at things, the things you look at change." Cultivating a gratitude practice is an immensely powerful way to embody compassion. Invite yourself to journal 3 things daily – big or small – for which you are grateful about that day.

When I began this practice, the first week was easy. As the days progressed, I struggled to find new "gratefuls" each day. My list even superficially included the color of my eyes. At that point, my teacher challenged me to dig deeper, vulnerably asking friends and family what they appreciated about me.

The greatest challenge of that exercise for me at the time was to then openly receive and fully accept the compliments. Equal giving AND receiving is another key quality of Heart Wisdom.

Empathy

Embedded within compassion is also empathy – the practice of imagining yourself in someone else's shoes. Visualizing and feeling the details of another person's circumstances, as if they were your own, helps you understand a little bit where along the other person's life path they may be.

In doing this with mindful awareness, we're able to relate a little more to the other person(s) by noticing any shared circumstances and qualities. This practice essentially serves as a humanizing technique that works at the personal, community, or larger group levels, including internationally.

As mentioned before, our beliefs are formed by the combination of our thoughts and feelings. This exercise is most powerful when we feel the visualization of their experience. Which emotions did they express or appear to exhibit?

Imagine for a moment those are your own emotions. This is also important because the way we perceive the world around us reflects our own personal reality, shaped by the beliefs of our childhood caretaker(s), education, societal norms, etc. Embodying the mindful observer is a life-long practice that eases over time.

As my colleague aggressively invaded my space in South Sudan, in addition to slowing my own breath, I empathetically connected to where he was: stressed, frustrated, and trying to implement programming under challenging circumstances. In no way did that condone his behavior towards me. (I did terminate him, in part, for the repeated outbursts.) Yet, it allowed me to better understand his perspective, helping me level out the conversational tone.

Initially, this empathy practice can be quite challenging to visualize with a stranger. Often it can be equally as challenging to swap places and imagine how you would feel if someone expressed those same sentiments to you, especially if your pattern is one of a strong inner critic.

Begin by visualizing someone you love or hold dear. How might they react if you said those same words toward them? How would it make you feel as those words left your mouth, directed their way? What could you say – and over time begin to think – differently?

JOURNEY TO THE HEART WISDOM LEADER

The word *yoga* is based on the Sanskrit root *yuj*, which translates as union, oneness, and to integrate. Numerous other traditions and philosophies teach this same principle, or some version thereof. Your heart is a place of unity.

Whether fear, love, or any other feeling, the flowing emotional states we honor and then ultimately choose to stay in are felt by and impact those immediately around us. They ripple out into your community and contribute to a collective emotional state.

Empty supermarket shelves bought out in a panic are one example of this. We are each individually responsible to family, friends, and the larger community to ground regularly, calm the nervous system, and increasingly choose to stay in the higher frequency emotions of gratitude, appreciation, kindness, excitement, joy, and love.

With mindful awareness, the practice of observing your thought and communication patterns without criticism, comparison, evaluation, and judgement allows you to more objectively see your personal reality and its impact on others. With empathy and child-like wonder, observe how your thoughts, feelings, beliefs, intentions, and actions shape your external reality as a direct reflection of your own inner landscape.

From this grounded place of trust, you can more easily transform the patterns that detour you on your journey to becoming a Heart Wisdom Leader. One that invites you to tune into the majestic subtleties of the heart: *Anahata Naad*, the "unstruck sound" of the cosmos.

A journey that invites you to tune into the intuitive, courageously compassionate, balanced, powerful embodiment of unconditional love required to birth a new world.

ABOUT THE AUTHOR

LaChelle Amos is an International Peace & Conflict Resolution Expert with experience leading teams in the Middle East, East Africa, and South Asia. As the Founder of Silence of Sound Yoga, she blends this experience together with her Yoga Alliance 500-hour Registered Yoga Teacher certification as an international teacher and sound healing practitioner.

LaChelle guides women to tune into their own intuitive Heart Wisdom by teaching them how to resolve their external conflicts and holding a safe space for their own inner healing work. She intuitively blends the wisdom and tools of peace & conflict resolution, yoga, sound healing, and heart-centered coaching, so that they fully embody (inner) and radiate (outer) peace.

Wherever around the world her yoga mat may be, LaChelle joyfully transforms Happy Baby Pose into a Laughing Baby. Off the mat, you can find her adventuring up mountains.

Website: www.silenceofsoundyoga.com
Email: info@silenceofsoundyoga.com
Facebook: www.facebook.com/silenceofsoundyoga
Instagram: www.instagram.com/silenceofsoundyoga

LEIGH JANE WOODGATE

THE RISE OF DIVINE FEMININE LEADERSHIP & SUSTAINABLE BUSINESS GROWTH

I never wanted to be an entrepreneur. I was quite happy as an employee, propping male CEOs up by supporting them from the wings and backstage to look good. And as much as I loved enabling them to realise their visions, I found it extremely challenging to witness the lack of integrity that many of them seemed to have.

As a strategic thinker and deeply intuitive woman who has built successful global businesses alongside influential entrepreneurs and CEOs for more than 20 years, what I have come to learn overtime is that these men did not lack integrity. What they lacked was the desire to engage all parts of their human operating systems - their mental, emotional, physical, energetic and spiritual bodies - whilst integrating the cycles of nature in alignment with individually tailored business strategy, in order to optimise their performance and contribute to creating reputable organisational cultures to support sustainable business growth with simplicity and flow.

Throughout the past two decades I have witnessed the destruction that is caused within organisations when people in power do not know themselves intimately, nor choose to accept all parts of themselves unconditionally, or desire to learn how to balance their masculine and feminine energies; the energies that support the creation of structure, ability to focus, and the art of connecting meaningfully through humility, gentleness, and sensitivity.

The truth is that business strategy will only get you so far. Without tuning into your intuition, integrating the cycles of nature with your humanity, and aligning tailored business strategy to each individual, life and business will feel clunky.

As a human being, you are nature. You are made up of all of the elements; earth, air, fire, water, and ether, all of which play a fundamental role in your capacity to lead with integrity and sustainably grow your business in order to effectively contribute to the evolution of humanity and the planet. Your whole entire existence is supported by Earth, the first element. Without it, you would literally have no place to live. The second element, air, enables you to breathe. Without it, you would die. The third element, fire, ignites your passion and reminds you just how quickly things can be destroyed. The fourth element, water, cleanses you, and supports you to surrender. The fifth element, ether, is conscious awareness - the container for everything in manifested reality. These five elements are recognised in Mother nature. You cannot ignore what she's made of, and you most certainly cannot ignore her seasonal, planetary and universal cycles, as we are all connected to each of her elements, the planets, the cosmos and beyond.

No matter how smart you are. No matter how many letters you have behind your name. No matter how many influential human beings you know. Unless you know yourself intimately, accept all parts of yourself unconditionally, and choose to commit to learning how to integrate your mental, emotional, physical, energetic and spiritual bodies, in alignment with the cycles of nature, and an effective business strategy, tailored to who you are as a human being, there is no possibility of building and growing a sustainable business without burning out.

IT'S TIME FOR CHANGE.

The patriarchy doesn't work, neither does the matriarchy. It's time for Divine Feminine Leadership; creation, intuition, community, sensuality, love, empathy, compassion, understanding, gentleness, humility, sensitivity, integrity, structure, focus.

You are Divine, a creator being, made of stardust, and to it you shall return. Connect, focus, commit. No-one is getting out of this human experience alive, so you might as well choose the way in which you would like to experience this human adventure.

Balance your masculine and feminine energy, integrate the highest version of yourself with the cycles of nature, feel the support of the elements, learn how to listen to your inner whispers, and take courageous action so that you can realise your dreams with grace, simplicity and flow.

Align, integrate, feel, listen. How do you feel? What can you hear? What are you ready for? Pause, reflect, be present and self-assess. You may be on top of the world, you may be in transition to the next evolution of self, or in this moment, business and life may be feeling clunky. Wherever you're at is perfect. And if you're unsure of where to next, go back to the starting point and build solid foundations so that you can grow your business to be the force for good that you so deeply yearn for.

Your values, principles, mission, purpose and vision for your life and the world, matter. This is your personal and ethical framework that supports you, your clients, your team, your family, your community, your business, and the planet to thrive. Without them you have no foundation, and without solid foundations, you're on a road to nowhere.

INTUITION. NATURE. STRATEGY.

The three pillars of Inategy Business School, a leadership collective and online business school for conscious leaders who want to build and grow sustainable businesses without hustling or compromising who they are to achieve their wildest dreams. The days of adrenal fatigue, anxiety, depression and revolving doors are coming to an end. It's time to do life and business differently. It's time to BE more.

IT'S TIME TO BIRTH A NEW EARTH.

The human race is being invited to integrate naturally advanced technologies; conscious awareness, heart intelligence, and womb wisdom. The question is...are you ready to accept the invitation?

The reality is that people are impoverished. Some are starving. Too many don't have access to health and well-being, quality education, clean water, sanitisation or electricity. Women and children are forced to do horrific things to survive. There are inequalities everywhere. Climate change is real. Modern day slavery is a thing. Life below water and above land is slowly dying. There are injustices everywhere, and it's time for the world to wake up. Less fear, more love. Less separation, more togetherness. Less judgement, more acceptance. All basic concepts and ways of being that contribute to a world where everyone makes it.

ANYTHING IS POSSIBLE.

Know that the moment that you decide that you are no longer available for anything that is out of alignment with that which is important to you, you make changes, and they happen fast.

I never wanted to be an entrepreneur. What I wanted was freedom. The freedom to pick my son up from school at 15:00 everyday, be there for him every afternoon and evening, and have the energy to be truly present. What I desired was to be authentic. To have the possibility to be myself, trust myself, feel safe to trust others, and express all parts of myself without any censoring. To be respected for who I am, feel a deep sense of connection with each and every being who crossed my path, and be surrounded by people of integrity.

At the time, in my final role as an employee, I was driven by the FARC.IT model; freedom, authenticity, respect, connection, integrity and trust - otherwise known as the values that influenced my personal decision-making framework. And before becoming an entrepreneur, every single one of these values (and principles) were challenged. For three and a half years my values and principles aligned with those of the organisation by which I was employed, until they no longer were. I got to a point where freedom, authenticity, respect, connection, integrity and trust were no longer accessible. At the time, I thought to myself, *"If we can't get the culture "right" in an organisation focused on supporting other organisations to improve their culture, then there is no hope of me finding an organisation that has the kind of culture that aligns with that which is important to me."*

And so I jumped ship and had 11 weeks to build and grow a business sustainably from the ground up. With two thousand Australian dollars in my bank account (enough to cover my living expenses for one week), a totally shattered nervous system, and a lack of self-worth that almost brought me to my knees in 2018 I made it happen. Overnight, I went from EA to CEO.

> *"Leigh, you are like an air traffic controller, which is by the way one of the most stressful jobs in the world. You can see all the planes on your screen, you have every pilot talking into your earpiece, and your job is to ensure that everyone takes off, lands safely and on schedule, without crashing into one another"* ~ Executive General Manager, The Ethics Centre

In my past life I was an EA. And overnight I went from Executive Assistant to Chief Executive Officer. How? I remembered who I was, what I was on this planet for, and why it was important. And what I realised, was that there is no perfect job. You have to create it for yourself.

No matter how aligned or inspired you are by the mission, purpose and vision of an organisation. Unless you feel like you have the freedom to express all parts of yourself, be recognised and rewarded for your contributions, and feel supported to grow within the organisation, you will feel dissatisfied.

There comes a time in your life when you realise enough is enough, and instead of waiting for someone to light up your world, you set your world on fire yourself (metaphorically speaking that is). The question is, do you give yourself permission to own all parts of yourself? Do you give yourself permission to own your superpowers?

Me? I help conscious leaders to build and grow sustainable purpose-driven businesses so that they can experience more pleasure, build substantial wealth and create greater impact with grace, simplicity and flow. I help visionaries - who have a deep desire to contribute to the sustainability of humanity and the planet - to transform their big dreams into sustainable businesses. I see them for who they truly are, enable them to own all parts of themselves, and support them to do only that which sets their soul's on fire. That's my superpower. I'm an anything-is-possible-make-it-happen kind of woman. What's yours?

From EA to CEO, nothing much has changed. I'm still making sure that everyone who crosses my path, takes off and lands without hurting themselves. The only difference is, that I no longer hurt myself in the process. The days of burnout are over, and martyrdom is nothing but a distant memory. These days, inner peace is the driver of all that which I choose, and by putting myself first, I create greater capacity to serve others more powerfully.

Making money is easy. Business can be simple. Doing what sets your soul on fire is your birthright. Get clear on your niche. Position yourself as an expert. Share valuable content that transforms the lives of others. And learn how to care less about what others think of you, and care more about bridging the gap between power and leadership.

In 2018, if you had told me that by 2020 I would have a 6-figure business, on the path to generating half a million in revenue, be in partnership with over 20 successful female entrepreneurs, supported by a team of incredibly aligned individuals with integrity, and have helped hundreds of high-achieving female entrepreneurs to build and grow their purpose-driven businesses sustainably, in order to bring more harmony to the world and bridge the gap between suffering and self-actualisation, I would have laughed.

CHANGE HAPPENS FAST.

The moment that you own who you truly are, get clear on what deeply matters to you and why, you're able to make decisions that support you to realise your deepest desires at an accelerated pace. The question is...are you willing to own all parts of yourself? Or do you continue to invest your energy worrying about how you may be judged by others?

WHAT'S NEXT?

To increase your income, impact and influence with grace, simplicity and flow so that you can experience more pleasure, build substantial wealth and create greater impact, you are required to do three things:-

1. Listen to your inner whispers and take courageous action.
2. Integrate your human nature with the cycles of Mother nature; seasonal, planetary, universal, and beyond.
3. Align your business strategy to your personal operating system; your mental, emotional, physical, energetic and spiritual bodies.

INTUITION. NATURE. STRATEGY.

Otherwise known as the art of divine feminine leadership and sustainable business growth. The opportunity to experience more pleasure, build substantial wealth, and create greater impact with grace, simplicity and flow. It's all up to you, and you are being invited to live from a place of curiosity and possibility.

When you know who you are, who you are here to help, how you can help them, and why you choose to help them, nothing can get in your way. Not even a global pandemic. Do what you love daily. And let everything else go. Surround yourself with people who inspire you, and stay clear of the people that don't - it's a waste of energetic real estate.

A healthy mind, body and soul. Sustainable energy levels. Deep and meaningful relationships built on trust, unconditional love, conscious communication. Unwavering kindness, generosity, honesty, integrity and respect. Financial abundance generated with ease, and re-invested without fear of loss. The ability to live life on purpose, and express all parts of yourself without fear of rejection, judgement, or abandonment. Health, relationships, financial education, self-expression. These are the pillars to your success.

Know that you matter, that what you have to share with the world matters, that your presence on this planet, matters, and that not everyone is going to agree with what you have to share. And that's OK. We are not here to agree with one another.

We are here to enjoy our individual and collective experiences without making one another wrong.

There is no right or wrong. There are merely different perspectives. And all of them are valid. There are awful things that happen in the world, and this is the evolution of humanity. It's a work in progress. As are you. And you have the capacity to make a meaningful difference. Continue on your journey to find the courage to live true to yourself, unbound by the rules and regulations of a system that clearly doesn't work. Continue on this journey of being human, one that requires a deep level of integrity with self; a commitment to live true to oneself, meet all parts of oneself, and create the space to love, accept and forgive oneself - by far, one of the most challenging, yet deliciously nurturing journey's any human being on this planet can ever embark on. A journey that most human beings are not courageous enough to go on.

You are perfect as you are. All parts of you. The mother, the father, the slut, the male whore, the self-righteous b*tch, the nurturer, the little girl, the empowered woman, the goddess, the king, the prince, the addict, the protector, the fool, the hermit, the warrior, the narcissist, the high-priestess, the trickster, the shadow, the tyrant, the sadist, the detached manipulator, the addicted lover, the weakling, the masochist, the denying "innocent" one, the impotent lover, the bully, the know-it-all, the momma's boy, the coward, the dummy, the dreamer, the innocent, the orphan, the hero, the caregiver, the explorer, the rebel. Your shadows, your light. And everything in between. The conscious. The subconscious. The unconscious. All is welcome.

> "Carl Jung theorized that human beings have a set of shared unconscious, instinctual psychological ideas that are passed down from generation to generation regardless of the culture. Called the collective unconscious, these thoughts and instincts are expressed as archetypes and can influence a person's behavior without his or her conscious knowledge. An example is the shadow archetype. The shadow archetype is supposedly the reservoir of repressed urges and emotions that are expressed outwardly in the conscious mind as the very aspects a person dislikes about himself or herself. As the word shadow implies, this archetype is often seen to be a dark force. When a person looks inward and glimpses emotions or behavioral tendencies that are frowned upon by society, he or she may choose not to recognize the behavior as a natural part of the personality. Anger, selfishness, violent

tendencies, the quest for unbridled power, and some sexual impulses are examples of the type of behavior a person may choose not to acknowledge..."
www.wisegeek.com/what-is-the-shadow-archetype

Oh so many archetypes to embrace. And as my trauma therapist once so poignantly reminded me, *"Leigh, we are all the ar*sehole in someone's story."*

Remember, you are not going to be everyone's cup of tea or tasty meal. And that's OK. Not everyone is invited to your dinner party. There are close to eight billion people on planet Earth and there is most certainly not enough space at your dinner table for all of them. Speak to those who enjoy what you have to serve. Stay in your lane. Follow your path. And live in alignment with your truth, without making anyone else wrong for theirs.

Being human is as complex as it is simple. And until we build the capacity to embrace all of our archetypes, the world will continue to be in turmoil, driven by power, lacking effective leadership.

Quite simply, it all starts with self. And it all ends with self. The moment that you choose to operate from a place of love, empathy, compassion, respect, understanding, gentleness, humility, integrity, structure and focus...life and business becomes simple, purpose-driven and pleasurable. Being human becomes a much more decadent experience. And the art of self-leadership and inner healing become the new normal. So the next time that you feel judged by self or another, I invite you to ask yourself the question, *"is there for me to learn from this?"*

For the conscious leaders who care about contributing to the sustainability of humanity and the planet, remember to tune into the three fundamental elements that powerfully support your meaningful intentions.

+ INTUITION: Listen to your inner whispers - tune into
your wisdom, have faith, trust yourself - and take courageous action.

+ NATURE: Integrate your human nature - your personal cycles - with the cycles of Mother nature; seasonal, planetary, universal, and beyond.

+ STRATEGY: Align your business strategy - planning, organisation, financial management, sales, marketing and communications - to your personal operating system; your mental, emotional, physical, energetic and spiritual bodies.

Life's too short to be afraid of all the things that can possibly go "wrong". Own your super powers, listen to your inner whispers, and take courageous action. The world needs you.

Thank you for all that are and all that you do. You are magnificent.

Love always,
   Leigh

ABOUT THE AUTHOR

Leigh Jane Woodgate is a Business Growth Advisor, Leadership Mentor, Author of two international number 1 bestselling books *"Trailblazers"* and *"Awakening"*, and the Founder of Inategy Business School, a Leadership Collective and Online Business School that enables conscious leaders to build and grow sustainable businesses without having to compromise who they are to achieve their wildest dreams.

For over 20 years Leigh has built successful global businesses alongside influential entrepreneurs & CEO's. She understands the power of balancing masculine and feminine energy, integrating nature's cycles and aligning tailored business strategy to each individual to support sustainable business growth. Her clients work with her to learn how to do less and earn more so that they can experience more pleasure, build substantial wealth, and create greater impact with grace, simplicity & flow.

Born in Johannesburg. Raised by one of the first men in South Africa to gain custody of a child in the 1980s. She lives in Sydney with her 11 year son, Noah the Kid.

Connect with her here:

> *Website:* www.leighjanewoodgate.com
> *Facebook:* www.facebook.com/Leigh.J.Woodgate
> and www.facebook.com/leighjanewoodgate
> *LinkedIn:* www.linkedin.com/in/business-growth-strategy
> *Email:* leigh@leighjanewoodgate.com

LEONIE LAUKKANEN

OVERCOMING FEAR & RETURNING TO WHOLENESS

In moments of intense darkness, we can see elements of our soul that lead us to discover our truth. So many of us live in our darkness and we use our fear like a heavy curtain.

We shut out our light. In a room full of darkness, we can always see the light, shining through the cracks. If we embrace our light, our light grows and the darkness fades. We all have a light inside us. I am not afraid of my darkness anymore.

Honestly, there have been times when I have been more afraid of my light. It shines like a diamond and it is overwhelmingly beautiful. Our darkness makes us appreciate our light, and our light gives us gratitude for our darkness. It shows us our true potential is limitless.

Those words are from the final reflection of my book *Mother Om - Connect with yourself and your child in one mindful moment a day*. I birthed my book into the world 6 years ago today, on Mother's Day. I wrote my book when I was a single mum to my eldest during a heartbreaking divorce as I transitioned into a new life. I left the corporate world of sales advertising and became an entrepreneur, teaching yoga and mindfulness to kids, and then their mothers and families.

The breakdown before the breakthrough. My awakening from mother to mystic.

Eight years later, I am re-married and now have 3 beautiful children: Lael (11), Luna (5), and Phoenix (2). I have a multi-award-winning business and a global podcast, and I am a professional speaker and a luminous teacher. For the past 10 years, I have been teaching yogic principles, mindfulness, intuition, and the art of living life using the divine guidance from our heart's intelligence.

I teach spiritually awake women how to consciously co-create their life with the universe. This is my intention for our time together, to share with you this ancient knowledge: the laws of the Universe. Written in secret for wise sages in the past, this is now available for everyone to embody. I guide women to overcome fear and return to wholeness.

Life is full of transitions and unexpected changes.

I had committed to a year-long program to train as an Intuitive Guide with the Institute of Intuitive Intelligence. I got married and Phoenix was our beautiful, surprise wedding gift. This time was challenging as I was once again engulfed in darkness with postnatal depletion from intense sleep deprivation. This time, instead of being consumed by my shadows, I called in my support network of mentors and teachers. I deepened my spiritual practices, and I transformed my fear into faith, re-emerging as an intuitive Mentor.

And then the world as we had known it ended.

A deadly virus came to lock us down. One that feeds on our deepest fears. Threatening our existence. Unimaginable grief for those directly affected. We retract. The media frenzy grips us in a panic.

And then the earth starts healing right before our eyes. A voice inside us whispers: this is what we have been asking for, the end of the old paradigm. And even though it will be our political leaders that will make decisions for our future generations, which leave us feeling powerless due to hidden agendas, we start to question our existence, our purpose for our time here on earth.

This pandemic threw us from our comfort zone, bringing intense challenges and chaos. We rapidly go from denial to anger to acceptance as we witness an unfolding. A new way of living, an awakening. An invitation for us to birth a new paradigm. United as one. A world that holds deep-rooted principles woven together that promote connection, compassion, community, and commitment. We witness random acts of kindness, we connect with old friends online, we care for the vulnerable. We take back our power. The transition begins. For our earth to shift into a new era, we must all be in this together.

I wrote about these values in *Mother Om*. I continue to stand by these powerful words that ignite our inner knowledge and I have added one more: contribution. Radical acceptance and responsibility. For our earth. For ourselves. For our loved ones.

There has never been a better time to embrace change. The emergence of the Kybalion, sharing the Universal Laws, is a sign of these times.

Now, we can begin to govern these laws. To consciously co-create our lives with the Universe, connecting to our intuition and our heart's intelligence. There is without question a higher power, an unseen truth that has created these unprecedented times. Instead of retreating into fear and uncertainty, let us create a partnership and collaborate with the Cosmos, changing our limited perception of what living in our physical reality means and "waking up" by cultivating a life-long relationship with Universal Consciousness. Intuition is the bridge between worlds. Heaven and earth. Our God nature, our true state.

We start taking ownership of our thoughts, feelings, and emotions.

We must overcome this feeling of being disconnected from our roots. From the stories we tell ourselves that are not true we lose parts of ourselves as our journey evolves with motherhood, relationship breakdowns, and our human suffering. We get lost in the mundane mayhem of life. We suffocate in the prison of our minds, the thought wars and our shadows. We gasp for air as our soul screams: there has to be a better way of being in the world.

Feeling isolated, misunderstood, unworthy, that we don't belong and are incomplete. That we are not enough. We fear control, failure, perfectionism, safety, death, the list goes on. Fear is the condition that keeps us separate from ourselves, our deepest knowing. It's time to create a new normal. We simply cannot thrive under the old paradigm. A study reported in the Global Burden of Disease in 2017 estimates 792 million people lived with a mental health disorder. That is one in 10 people. Mental Illness is a global pandemic.

Why would we want to return to that "normal" way of living?

Our mind is our best friend or our worst enemy.

This is our path, our sacred contract, our purpose. Our evolution. The dance between our head and heart. Yoyoing between fear and love in each moment. We begin our descent as we meet, release, and clear our fear. We practice forgiveness to ourselves and others. We reunite with our soul.

I have always believed we can create a life full of abundance, one filled with magic and miracles. Everything we need is inside of us. As we have all collectively been in a global lockdown, what an incredible opportunity has presented itself. To ascend, together. To return to our holiness.

When we can't go outside, we are forced to go inside.

To sit with ourselves. To connect with our partners, our children. To look after our neighbours. To spread compassion in our communities, which is the elixir we need to fill our emptiness. To cook together, to plant seeds and watch them grow. To sit in the sunshine and feel her magnificent energy overflowing into our cup so we can give that warmth to others. To look at the faces in the clouds, the children in the stars. To be in awe of the thousands of butterflies that send us signs of hope and courage. To feel wrapped in the arms of Mother Nature as we see her transform in a matter of weeks.

Nothing has external power over us.

Not the full moon, our crystals, or our superstitions. We have a choice. We can change our emotional state. We can create rituals that promote connection and compassion with ourselves and our loved ones. We commit to using spiritual tools and practices as we double our daily devotion.

Everyone has access to their intuition, no one is unique; we all have this special gift. Like a muscle, it takes time to activate into a clear channel for such heartfelt wisdom. There are different types of intuition. We can see, feel, hear, or simply know when the divine speaks to us.

We contribute to the collective by understanding we are energetic beings. We prioritise our health and our energy, we nourish our bodies, we rest, and we follow our light. This sends healing sparks of joy that connect and encircle the globe with each deep conscious breath we take.

We understand we have the whole universe inside of us. That we are never alone. Archetypal patterns of energies flow through us as we commune with our spirit guides. Synchronicities are everywhere as we awaken the wisdom of our third eye, which is the periscope to our heart. We change our perception of who we are. Our spiritual stamina and self-esteem are at the core of our daily decisions.

We meditate. We journal. We ask for guidance. We connect to our womb, our creative power centre. We heal our sister wounds. We balance our masculine and feminine energies. We honour the authentic men in our lives that support us. We embrace all parts of who we are.

Our inner wild women, our innocent maiden, our fearless queen, our strong warrior, our eternal student, our fierce teacher, our wise crone, our creative goddess, our peacemaker wife, our loving mother, our unstoppable maga, our healing alchemist, and we step into our Priestess power. These sacred feminine archetypes scaffold our awakening, holding us, guiding us, while we serve what is right in front of us.

We feel our monthly cycles unite with the moon and the tide. We tune into our energy bodies, our chakras, and we choose to live with mindful intentions to be a clear vessel for the Infinite to commune with us, so we heal ourselves, and then, heal others. We crave human connection and rejoice in sacred, orgasmic intimacy with our chosen life partner or smile at a stranger or engage in an elbow pump of gratitude for the barista that makes us a cup of coffee. We hug our children tightly and open ourselves up to effortlessly give and receive love. We don't reject or sabotage our joy.

We are overwhelmed with tears of gratitude and unconditional love when our soul comforts us, that we are all intricately connected. Like a gigantic spider web of invisible threads of energy.

Enter the Hermetic Laws.

1: THE LAW OF MENTALISM

We are all one. There is no you and I, only we. We are with the one mind of God. Spirit. Source. This law tells us all of creation exists in the mind of God, and that our lives exist in our minds. Our perception is our reality; things are how we think they are. Our world is how we choose to see it.

Suddenly we understand our fear is guiding us home to our truth. To show us what needs to be cleared so we can create the life we desire. The opening of the door to the basement of our subconscious mind, which controls 90% of our lives as it instructs our reasoning, conscious mind into action.

Our beliefs, our stories, our habits, driving us to manifest chaos, and we are not even aware that we are doing it. Until we change our mind. We privilege our intuitive intelligence. If all is one, then there is no separation. We have always been a part of the benevolent Universe. We are not broken; we don't need to be fixed.

We simply need to return to our holiness.

And, then through our quest to go deeper, with a compassionate, fearless gaze, to find the answers we seek, we discover it is our heart that holds the key to our awakening. The gateway to our intuition, where we receive our divine guidance, is through our heart's intelligence. The Heart Math Institute teaches us about the heart and brain proving that we make our decisions from our intuitive heart. We often feel conflicted as our mind thinks one thing, but our heart feels another. As humanity starts to practice heart-based living, it will bring us into the next level of consciousness.

2: THE LAW OF CORRESPONDENCE

As within, so without. As above, so below. This is the second law of the Universe. Finding congruence in the chaos. Taking inspired action. Our inner world is a complete reflection of our external world. The thoughts and images in our mind create the exact likeness in our reality.

Upon self-reflection of our life journey, we see how we have awakened from our suffering and can see the lessons and blessings. I see I created my divorce, which led me to my divinity. That gave me my sensitive son with ADHD, who remains one of my greatest teachers. That turned my adversity into opportunity, which has helped and healed thousands of mothers around the world.

After opening my heart again and writing my book, I met my husband and instantly found a love so profound I am lost for words. We conceived our two children without even trying. I had two natural, drug-free births after having a traumatic, emergency c-section that led to a profound healing experience. This has taught me that we can also awaken through our joy. It is our choice. We are incredibly powerful beings.

How do our feelings become our words that become our actions that become our reality?

Using our symbolic sight. Surrendering and trusting the process. Letting go of our attachments to outcomes. Our need for external approval. Meeting our fear in each moment, which blocks our intuition so we can hold the vibration of the one mind. This is not an easy path to take. It is not for the faint-hearted. It is confronting. It takes courageous action. We do not believe; we are not God-enough. To me, the word God means love. Love is the highest vibration. Where there is love, there cannot be fear.

We don't need to be protected. Even when a global pandemic strikes. It will be our fear that kills us in the end. When we do not release emotional stress and trauma in our physical body, it becomes toxic and makes us sick. It plays havoc with our lives. So, together we focus on what we can control. We sing songs of positive affirmations with our kids as we wash our hands. We spray our homes and we pray. We surrender to our path, not our plan. We embrace the third law.

3: THE LAW OF VIBRATION

We embody our energy, that we are energy first, physical second, that we are nothing but a vibration. When we are stressed and anxious, we feel dense and we cannot receive our intuition. When we are full of bliss and joy, we are a clear vessel for guidance. Consciousness creates. The universe feels us. It is our vibration, our feeling state, not our thoughts that are creating our reality.

Our feelings are our prayers.

As I have personally embodied these teachings, my journey has evolved from teaching mindfulness to heartfulness. I see so much magic in my clients as they create and launch successful businesses that serve humanity. Birthing books, programs, and partnerships as they step into their Priestess power. Calling in their deepest heart's desire. Creating babies, attracting their soul mate. Overcoming illness to wellness.

These women are not afraid of their light.

They are magnificent and their presence is in their power. They emulate ancient magic and wisdom and they move mountains with their joy. They are committed to their path of service. To mindfully raising the next generation. To protect and heal

Mother Earth. To make conscious daily choices from a place of love, not fear. To continue to find congruence and take inspired action even during the most challenging times. To rise from the ashes.

I invite you to connect with all the women in this book. Surround yourself with great spiritual teachers. Devour the works of my personal favourites: Caroline Myss, Marianne Williamson, Gabby Bernstein, Dr. Joe Dispenza, Elizabeth Gilbert, Brene Brown, Russell Brand, and my teacher Dr. Ricci Jane Adams.

After 20 years of being an eternal student, learning many practices to enhance our self-awareness, the most powerful practice I have found is Intuitive Intelligence Tapping. I use this process with my clients, on myself, and with my kids. Tapping on parts of our body releases stuck energy and emotions. Bringing us from fear to love. In a heartbeat.

Plus, it enables us to practice self-forgiveness, self-compassion, and gratitude. Every day. Like magic, gratitude turns what we have into enough. It takes us from our busy minds, into our hearts. I practice Heart Congruence, developed by the Institute of Intuitive Intelligence, based on the work of the Heart Math Institute.

I invite you to continue our sacred journey together and join my free, 4-part Heartfulness masterclass series on my website so you can learn these powerful tools, understand how to access your intuition, embody the Hermetic laws, and meet, clear, and release your fear.

In truth, what we have been taught about our intuition is wrong.

Be alone in stillness. Clarity does not come in the chaos. This may present itself differently each day as you show up, powerful, to awaken our world. It could be dancing with your kids, cooking for your family, walking in nature, lighting a candle for a loved one, saying a prayer, asking for guidance, journaling your feelings, and using your spiritual tool kit.

And finally, beautiful soul, I have a channelled message to share from the Great Mother. Mother Gaia. Mother Earth.

"Hand over your weariness to me, your exhaustion, your dis-ease. Sit with me. Take off your shoes, place your feet on the ground. Feel my unwavering support pulsating from the earth's core. I invite you to allow me to hold you in my arms, while you hold space for your loved ones.

We are all one. One heartbeat. We breathe together. When we heal, we heal the collective."

I look forward to connecting with you.

Love and light,
　Leonie xx

ABOUT THE AUTHOR

Leonie Laukkanen is an Intuitive Mentor, Teacher of the Intuitive Intelligence Method. Speaker, Podcaster, Author of the award-winning international bestselling book, *Mother Om*, and the creator of Luna Phoenix Designs.

For over 10 years Leonie has been teaching yogic principles, mindfulness, intuition and the art of living life using the divine guidance from our heart's intelligence. Leonie teaches spiritually awakened women how to consciously co-create their life with the Universe by guiding them to overcome fear and return to wholeness.

Her clients work with her to embark on a sacred journey to clear lifetimes of old beliefs and trauma so they can serve the planet from an empowered place, gracefully align with their soul's calling, and live life with ease and grace.

Leonie lives in Brisbane, Australia with her husband and 3 young children.

Website: www.leonielaukkanen.com
Heartfulness Training: www.leonielaukkanen.com/heartfulness
Facebook: www.facebook.com/magneticmama
Instagram: www.instagram.com/leonielaukkanenintuitivementor
and www.instagram.com/lunaphoenixdesigns
Email: leonie@leonielaukkanen.com

LINDSAY CROWTHER

THE CHAKRA SYSTEM: YOUR ENERGETIC ROADMAP TO WORTH & WELLNESS

I magine if every woman you knew was able to show up for herself, each day, unapologetic and fully embracing all that she is. Imagine if you could show up for yourself that way.

What types of things would you create within your home, your relationships, your career, and your life? What would you be able to create for the world if you had an eternal flame of confidence burning brightly within you?

I have been the woman that hated what I saw in the mirror. I have been the woman that bullied herself relentlessly with violent thoughts about my body, my abilities, my intellect, and my choices. I have felt the searing pain of self-loathing, and I know that it seems like an impossible place to pull yourself out of.

We have waffling support when it comes to building high-octane self-esteem. We have mothers living familial beliefs about women and their roles; we have fashion magazines, Instagram models, a billion-dollar diet industry, uneven pay grades, and unequal representation in politics, company management, engineering, IT professions, the sciences, and healthcare professions. We are constantly being bombarded with messages that we are not enough, not worthy, and not at all lovable as we are.

I have spent the last decade working to unravel the lies created to keep women small and less significant than they have the potential to be. Chain by chain, I have released this body from the bondage of societal expectations along with self-doubt, criticism, and hatred. As a registered yoga and meditation teacher, I guide women through their own journeys of igniting and maintaining a resilient self-esteem.

I did not have a guidebook on my journey; it took a lot of trial and error. I often had to teach my teachers how to work with me, especially in the yoga world. I have a big, beautiful body and it is different than bodies they are used to. I had to learn about my body in order to move, stretch, and heal it. Through yoga I gained an awareness of the stories my body was holding onto, the trauma we had not yet released, and the patterns we were seemingly stuck in. While moving through yoga teacher training, I discovered a system that would change the trajectory of my life. I discovered a way to heal my body, mind, and my spirit - the roadmap I always wished was available had appeared.

The Chakra System is an energy system within the body. Sanskrit for "wheel," the word *chakra* can be visualized as a series of energetic wheels. Our seven major chakras sit along the spine, starting at the tailbone and ascending to the top of the head. This system, its philosophy, and its integration into my daily life and practice is what allows me to show up for myself, day after day, embracing all that I am.

I use this system with my clients and students as a road map to healing each dynamic body: emotional, mental, physical, and spiritual. It can be used to deconstruct belief systems, cultivate emotional resilience, diagnose limiting stories, and heal different areas of the physical body.

As we walk through the chakras one by one, and explore each theme in relationships to esteem, you may see where you experience disruption and low self-regard in your own body. I have included exploratory questions for each chakra so you can begin to heal where you need it.

MULHADARA (ROOT CHAKRA)

Sitting at the base of the spine, the root chakra is the first to develop and its major themes are *safety* and *deservingness*. As the first chakra, Mulhadara is the foundation for our lives; it stores important information and beliefs about our safety, deservingness, and sense of community. Disruption in this chakra will throw the entire energetic body off-balance. We cannot cultivate upper chakra health when our foundation is shaky.

Because the root chakra starts developing at birth, we have little to do with its programming. Essentially, our beliefs about safety and deservingness were never ours to begin with. As infants, we did not have the self-awareness to choose how our needs were met - or even what our needs were. We relied entirely on our caretakers to handle every need of our tiny lives. The caretakers ability (or non-ability) to meet those needs is where we start developing our sense of safety and deservingness.

A healthy Root Chakra cultivates a sense of safety and deservingness from within.

A misaligned Root Chakra will create chaos in our lives as we search to feel secure, wanted, and taken care of.

Even the most dedicated and aware caretakers cannot anticipate the needs of every child they care for. We cannot change the past, but we can heal it.

Root Chakra explorations:

Do I have a healthy sense of safety? What does safety look like to me? Were my needs met by my caretakers? If not, where did I feel unsafe or undeserving of attention or love? Is the foundation of my life built from safety and deservingness or am I allowing myself to feel unworthy of care?

SVADHISTHANA (SACRAL CHAKRA)

Within the sacrum of the hips, Svadhisthana joins Mulhadara in developing in early childhood; it is here we begin to develop a sense of self. "Svadhisthana" means "one's own seat."

I like to imagine this as our seat at the family or tribal table. It is how we were allowed to show up in our tribe, and how we continue to show up in our community now. The major themes of the Sacral Chakra are *relationships* and *creativity*. Both integral to the development of a secure sense of self.

As we grow, we begin to see ourselves separate from our caretakers. We become daughter, sister, granddaughter, etc. We notice how our caretakers interact with us and each other. While some programming and beliefs about relationships are actively taught, many of the themes we adapt to are passively shown to us through the actions of others.

We learn our role here, and the roles of those around us. Roles are not always healthy. Toddlers are often criticized, silenced, ignored, or at extremes, punished for their curiosity and exploration of independence and sovereignty. The way our caretakers handled our behaviors is what solidified our beliefs about our roles in relationships. Were we criticized? Discouraged from being loud or speaking out? Was playfulness frowned up on? Were we idolized with an inflated sense of importance? All of these things can lead to disruption in the theme of relationships in Sacral Chakra.

Creativity and imagination are also developing during this stage of life. How our caretakers and family received our creative abilities will absolutely influence the way we show up for ourselves as adults. Being ridiculed will lead to fear of embarrassment. Being told to stop or be quiet will lead to the fear of expression. Being ignored will lead to the fear of having nothing of importance to contribute.

When we see these themes running in the Sacral Chakra it becomes obvious why so many people have a hard time developing lasting interpersonal relationships, expressing creativity, and showing up as their whole self.

Sacral Chakra Explorations:

What does a healthy relationship look like to you? Were you modeled healthy relationships or unhealthy relationships? Explore what you were taught about relationships. Were they mean, sarcastic, or unsupportive? Was there competition for attention in relationships? Abuse? How did your caretakers handle your curiosity and creativity? Do you limit your creative expression for any reason?

MANIPURA (SOLAR PLEXUS CHAKRA)

Meaning "the jewel of the city," Manipura is where self-esteem lives in our energy body. The personal power center can be a roaring fire sitting just above the naval, though misalignment can cause MAJOR disruption in your mental, physical, emotional, and energetic bodies.

Manipura, just like the other chakras, has multiple facets and themes. For our exploration of the chakras and self-esteem, I want to expand into the themes of *identity* and *worth*.

Developing in early childhood through adolescence, Solar Plexus Chakra is where our true sense of self and identity begins to bloom. We are increasing in independence and in our ability to care for ourselves and, if given the opportunities to explore those things in a supportive environment, the self-esteem will flourish. If we do not feel safe in our exploration of independence, if we are criticized for choices or preferences, or if we are coddled and not allowed to be independent, we are robbed of our ability to create a strong sense of self.

People-pleasing behaviors often start here in the development of Manipura; going to college for a profession your parent chose, eating foods your partner prefers, remaining in unhealthy relationships or jobs, etc. These are all behaviors that exist when we lack a strong sense of self and worthiness.

Worthiness can be explored in the same way we talked about deservingness. Support and acceptance of our tribal members and families are integral here; the self-esteem develops and is reliant on the feedback of others. If we feel unaccepted, we begin to feel unworthy. When we feel unworthy, we will shy away from our true nature and develop a personality that is built off other's expectations.

Solar Plexus Chakra Explorations:

Were you supported and encouraged to explore who you are? Were you allowed to make small (or big) decisions for yourself? Did you experience consequences (good or bad) for your choices? Were you loved and accepted regardless of opposing tastes, preferences, or opinions? Explore these questions as deeply as you need to.

ANAHATA (HEART CHAKRA)

Love means so many things in our modern cultures. We "love" a favorite pair of jeans or personable celebrity. We "love" cheesecake or our mom's signature spaghetti, but when it comes to loving others, we experience difficulty cultivating lasting relationships. Why is this?

The short answer can come from the meaning of the Sanskrit word "anahata," translating to "unstruck." Imagine your heart as a delicate vase. When whole you can fill it with love and pour love from within it.

When hearts get struck, or broken, our heart vessel may experience problems with both giving and receiving love. Love can neither be poured from nor poured into a broken vessel and so we search for others to mend our broken hearts, a selfish and never-ending search for understanding love.

Within the Heart Chakra we explore love and *compassion*. I often ask my students: *can love exist without compassion, or can compassion exist without love? Are they the same thing? How often are we "loving" without compassion?*

Compassion is the root of love. Compassion doesn't seek to understand or to commiserate. It doesn't have anything to gain from its presence in a relationship with others or with ourselves. As the Heart Chakra develops in adolescence, we have many, many examples of love - some of them healthy, others' not so much.

Much like Svadhisthana Chakra, our ideas, beliefs, and values of love come from modeled behaviors. We continue to watch our fathers, mothers, extended family, authority figures, and peers to understand love and compassion. We observe kindnesses and offenses and we begin to craft a story of what "love" looks like in our minds.

The love we are capable of accepting comes from within these stories. If we are looking outside of our own heart spaces for love and compassion, we will be disappointed every time. No one's story about love will fully align with our own. Love is an inside job.

Anahata Explorations:

What do you believe about love? Have you experienced loving relationships with others? If yes, were they obligation and judgement free or did they come with expectation? What love are you most comfortable receiving? Is it a self-serving love or one of freedom and compassion? Does your own "love" come with a price? For example, you expect someone to heal you, take care of you, or make your life whole?

VISHUDDHA (THROAT CHAKRA)

"Especially pure," is the Sanskrit translation of "Vishuddha." I teach a special workshop that bridges the Throat Chakra and the Sacral Chakra. This is because our ability to express ourselves is developing along with our creativity and relationships with others.

Expression and *boundaries* are two main themes of the Throat Chakra. Our ability to express ourselves as adults is highly influenced by the way our caretakers handled our personal expression.

If it was sloughed off, pushed away, or relatively ignored, we develop weakness and anxiety in our Throat Chakras. We become unable to express and communicate clearly due to fear of judgement, ridicule, or outright rejection.

"Essentially pure" communications and expressions are built of honesty and truthfulness. We are able to express our needs without being apologetic or worried about how others will receive them.

In order for us to create healthy and sustainable boundaries here in the throat chakra, a fully seated self-esteem is essential. Without our lower chakras healthy and aligned, our ability to express our needs, boundaries, desires, dreams, and ambitions is greatly minimized and, in extreme cases, blocked completely.

A healthy Throat Chakra keeps communication lines open and objective. When exploring honest and objective communication, it is apparent why compassion is essential.

Throat Chakra Explorations:

Are you truthful in your communications with yourself and others? Do you find yourself censoring thoughts and feelings to accommodate the feelings and comfort of those around you? Are you over-stepping other's boundaries with your need to be "right?" Are there any areas where self-expression becomes difficult?

AJNA (THIRD EYE CHAKRA) & SAHASRARA (CROWN CHAKRA)

These two chakras are so connected in themes and programs, exploring them together is a strong strategy for identifying blocks and misalignments that can prevent high self-esteem. These upper chakras are about *vision* and *interconnectedness*, particularly to a Divine power.

Tribal and cultural systems will often have their own belief systems of a higher power, all varying to different degrees. We are born into these belief systems and, because spirituality and religion carry so much weight in a culture's identity, many of us adopt these belief systems without a deep exploration of what they actually mean for us.

An adopted belief of a judgmental, higher consciousness can be dangerous and may put our psyche in a state of fear, even if we felt supported within our own family systems. It is important to explore what we believe about God, Spirit, The Universe,

Source, or whatever name you are comfortable with - or if you believe in something greater than you at all.

When our vision (Third Eye Chakra) is clear, we are open to Divine inspiration and can move fluidly through the challenges of life. As we learn to trust our intuition and think outside of the constructs of our belief systems, our self-esteem is reinforced and cultivated within the upper chakras. I like to put the theme of *trust* here in Ajna because, as we learn to trust in a power working for us, it is much easier to trust ourselves.

The Crown Chakra is what connects us to God and to each other. If we are able to dissolve the illusion of separation and duality, we begin to identify with all beautiful things in creation, and see ourselves as simply one of them.

A night of gazing at stars, or viewing a sunset from your back porch, comes with awe and wonder and, most importantly, comes *detached and judgement free.* Have you ever stared at the stars and picked their position or luminosity apart? Maybe felt you could have picked a better pallet for a sunset? In Divine creation and connectedness there is gratitude and the ability to honor things just as they are.

Third Eye Chakra and Crown Chakra Explorations:

What do you believe about God? Do you believe in God? Is your idea of God different from that of your culture? Do you believe in a power that is for you or against you? Are you afraid of judgement? What are some experiences in your life where you felt divinely guided or inspired?

This exploration of the chakras and self-esteem is a very short version of what I do within the space of my classes, courses, and coaching programs. Working on building a strong sense of self does not come easily or quickly. By committing to exploring how the theme of each chakra affects your ability to show up for yourself, you are peeling back layers of beliefs that keep your true self hidden.

Our programming is so intense sometimes, that *many of us don't even know who we are* to begin with. Of course our self-esteem and worthiness is suffering over the lost sense of personal identity. If you are feeling lost and unsure about who you are under all of these layers, please know you are not alone and there is still plenty of time and opportunities for you to build a lasting flame of self-esteem and worth. It is never too late to start expressing love and gratitude for yourself.

The chakra system is a dynamic tool and roadmap to healing within the mental, emotional, physical, and spiritual bodies, and I want to remind you that you have all of the answers to your questions, challenges, and sufferings inside of you - available at any time. I believe that for myself and I believe that for you.

You are wild, wonderful, worthy, and worth it.

Namaste,
   Lindsay

ABOUT THE AUTHOR

Lindsay Crowther is a sage of spirit and science. She couples metaphysical healing systems with modern research-backed science to identify misalignment in the mind, body, and spirit. As a registered yoga and meditation teacher and experienced Akashic record reader, Lindsay's courses and programs create a nurturing space to discover the whole self.

As the founder of *Buddha Body Yoga*, Lindsay creates space for women of all sizes to form deep, meaningful connections to their bodies. Her small group and 1:1 online programs use modern science and ancient energetic philosophy to heal limiting beliefs, past trauma, and negative karmas, while cultivating a deep and unwavering sense of self.

Lindsay uses the Chakra system as a roadmap to both deep healing and intentional creation. She believes that it is within the energetic body that all things are created or not created.

Lindsay lives in Boise, Idaho with her family and extensive crystal collection.

Website: www.lindsaycrowther.com
Facebook: www.facebook.com/lindsaycrowthercoaching
Instagram: www.instagram.com/theblondeguru

LISA FARRINGTON

PINTEREST MARKETING

Before my divorce in 2012, I would pin things to my 'Bucket List' board on Pinterest. Little did I know back then that I would turn my love of Pinterest into a business.

I have such a passion for Pinterest because it's where I collect my ideas, get inspiration, and have my eyes opened to endless possibilities. It's why, globally, 367 million active Pinterest users also use the platform.

It's a (visual) search engine, the third largest behind Google and YouTube, so Pinners (as Pinterest users are known) are on the platform actively searching for inspiration, how to learn something, and planning their purchases. In fact, 93% of Pinners plan their purchases on the platform!

Traditionally Pinterest was once thought of as a platform for women planning weddings, looking for recipes, or crafting. That has changed drastically. For a start, 50% of new sign-ups are now from men. Anything and everything can be searched for on Pinterest.

For me, Pinterest is a form of escapism. It's not picture-perfect like Instagram. It feels very real, no fakeness involved and no need to engage with other users. It's a place to daydream and plan for the future.

In these times of Coronavirus, searches for 'stress relief' have tripled, which does not surprise me at all. Decluttering and cleaning is huge, as is virtual learning. With stay-at-home orders in place, searches are up 55% year on year and new sign ups to Pinterest are up 30%.

People are using Pinterest to plan, for the immediate future, and more distant future. Yet, only 28% of marketers globally are capitalising on it to help people find their businesses or products.

Pinterest marketing basically means you create clickable pins. They can be a photo, a graphic designed image with text overlay, or even a video. A whole strategy behind how to get your pins found, and we'll cover that.

I'm guessing 95% of people reading this book will never have even considered Pinterest marketing. You probably didn't buy this book to read about Pinterest marketing, unless you already follow me! Maybe you have already tried and given up.

The reason I believe that so many brands and businesses either don't try, or give up, is because they simply don't understand how the platform works. Since Pinterest went public in April 2019, more of the big brands have started to get onboard and it's certainly become more mainstream.

However, there's so many businesses still doing it badly, or not at all. The mistake they make is that they treat Pinterest like it's a social media platform, when it's not. It's a search engine. In Pinterest's own words, it describes itself as "the world's catalog of ideas."

If you have a business, chances are you already have curated content that is either perfect or could be repurposed for Pinterest. Pinterest can drive traffic to any URL you have. For the majority, that's a product for sale or a blog post.

But it doesn't have to be; it can be a podcast episode, YouTube video, Instagram post, Facebook group, lead page, freebie opt-in to join your email list, or your product listing on the likes of Etsy, eBay, or Creative Market.

So what can you actually do with Pinterest for your business? There's so much! Including selling a physical product or digital product, driving brand awareness and purchase intent to an upcoming product or service, or getting people on your email list. You can send people to your blog, vlog, or freebie opt in order to start warming up your new audience with the know, like and trust factor.

Then you can show your expertise and sell high ticket items, such as a one-to-one coaching programme. You can even carry out affiliate marketing to make money on Pinterest. It's so versatile. The main thing to remember is that, used effectively, it drives traffic. You still have to strategically make the sale or conversion.

I haven't introduced myself yet, so who am I to teach you about strategic Pinterest marketing?

A bit about me - I'm a Pinterest Marketing Strategist, founder of Pinterest Marketing Agency, Lisa Farrington & Co. We work with clients globally and I'm proud to say that Pinterest is the number 1 traffic driver for our clients. Prior to starting my own business, I worked in strategic Government, within the UK and Australia.

In 2015, just before my 31st birthday, I left the UK to travel and work in Australia. I finally got to tick those pins off my Pinterest Bucket List board! Including things I never thought I would get to do (the divorce had hit me hard financially), like flying over Heart Reef in the Great Barrier Reef and seeing the sky lantern festival, Yi Peng in Thailand.

I started in Singapore, before heading on to Australia, then the USA, Denmark, and Thailand, before returning to Australia, where I had a working holiday visa and found a job in Project Management; it lead to a 4 year visa. I had the dream city centre apartment in Sydney CBD, with a gorgeous 50 metre indoor and outdoor pool with a part glass floor, which showed the waterfall feature at the entrance.

But something still wasn't right. The job came to an end, and with my 3 months notice, I set up my virtual assisting website, knowing that in the future I wanted to be able to work and travel. But my heart wasn't really in it and I found another job in a prestige team instead. Eventually I knew it was time to leave Australia; there was something in me that wasn't happy.

It was around that time that I found out you could become a Pinterest Virtual Assistant. I just knew! I didn't want to do regular admin work. I'd done that in my teenage years. This was my thing! I loved Pinterest.

As I did training course after training course, I learnt that I had something that many on the courses did not. The ability to think outside the box. My years of strategy gave me the edge to not just look outside the box, but as if there were no box.

I've worked with a variety of niches, a variety of companies - some large, some small. I've presented at virtual summits, given guest expert presentations and hosted masterclasses to train many entrepreneurs. Some entrepreneurs have had great Pinterest success just from talking to me for 30 minutes.

So this is why I wanted to be part of this book, to get my message out there further about how wonderful Pinterest marketing is when done effectively and how you can start doing it too, especially in the challenges of 2020. I see business owners giving up, women stressed out home-schooling during lockdown and not feeling supported to do more, like own the successful businesses they have the desire to build.

The saddest thing I see is that the majority of them (and this is true even for bigger brands) already have the perfect curated content. It's just that their understanding of Pinterest and strategies are lacking.

I believe that for women, COVID-19 is offering them the opportunity that I already had:

- to see what they really want in life
- to awaken to possibility
- to see what they don't want and determine what is possible

Even general Social Media Marketers and marketing teams have been slow on the uptake of providing Pinterest marketing as a service. It's like this magical, mystical unicorn that no one really seems to understand well. It pains me when I see a big company putting money into paid Pinterest marketing (Promoted Pins), only for their organic efforts to be lacking.

There are over 200 billion pins saved on Pinterest, with over 2 billion searches performed every month. Pinners come to Pinterest to discover, plan, and then act. "The best ideas come from brands and businesses."

So, why not take the time to properly understand it? So that you can utilise it in all it's glory and drive mass traffic to develop and grow the business you crave and use the money for good.

Whether you want to end world hunger, campaign against animal cruelty, or ensure that the earth is sustainable for future generations. I love that a business can give each individual CEO the tools for their vision.

So why exactly should you use Pinterest for business? I'm sure you want to know what the benefits are! Well for a start, it brings mass traffic when used effectively (I'll talk about that later on). Pinterest is the number 1 traffic driver for myself and my clients. Even organically you can get millions of eyes on your pins and so many people to your website.

"How many people exactly?", is one of the regular questions I get asked. It's hard to say, because it differs for every niche. For one person with a very small niche, that may be 2,000 people per month. For another it could be in excess of 100,000.

What matters is that you convert that traffic. Let's say you are in that very small niche group, only getting 2,000 people per month, and you sell a $10,000 coaching package; you might only need three of those people per month to sign up with you.

That's very different to being a blogger who uses affiliate marketing and advertising (rather than selling a service or product themselves) and needs 100,000 people to create anywhere near the same

$30,000. Swings and roundabouts; each individual case is different. The good news is that, although Pinterest marketing can start slow and steady, it has a snowball effect. It grows and with dedicated work, the possibilities are limitless.

At this point, it's probably best to tell you that it's a great long term strategy, and that's because it's evergreen. That pin that you pin today could potentially still bring you traffic in five years' time.

If you're using Facebook or Instagram for marketing, you've probably noticed that after a day or two, you're no longer getting engagement on your post, unless the rare event happens that the post goes viral. That's because a Facebook post has a lifespan of 3.2 hours and an Instagram post 13.2 hours.

When you compare that to Pinterest, it's 3 months plus. So a great benefit is that you are still getting traffic on your content in the future.

An example to explain this: before I started taking on paying clients, I tested my skills on my sister's hairdressing salon. I created a pin with her logo for balayage hair and, whilst it did well at the time, seven months later it went viral. At this stage I hadn't even pinned on her account for months, as I was now working with paid clients. It literally just started driving her mass traffic.

A lesser know thing about Pinterest marketing is that it can also increase your Google rankings, even without paying for expensive ads or having to be up on Google SEO. Many of my clients reach the first page of Google without paying for ads at all. For one client, that was first page on Google out of over 8 million search results, for a blog post

that was written 2 years ago. It doesn't even need to be current. Do you know how much companies pay to get to the first page of Google? Let that sink in. She got to the first page of Google without spending a penny on advertising.

Yet, if you do want to invest in ads, known as Promoted Pins, a company called

Neustar found that retail brands saw a 2x higher return on ad spend from Pinterest than from social media and a 1.3x higher return than from traditional search.

That's because Pinners are looking on the platform to buy, which you just don't get so much on social media. Pinners are 130% more likely to purchase products than from social media. 83% of active weekly Pinners have made a purchase based on content they saw from brands on Pinterest and 97% of searches are unbranded, so it's a great way to get found! Neustar found that because people come to Pinterest to seek inspiration early in their shopping journey, it has a lasting impact on their final purchase decision.

There are many different types of companies who can benefit from Pinterest marketing. They include online businesses who aren't limited to a particular country or area, or who offer digital products, in addition to businesses who ship worldwide.

Where it becomes more difficult is a bricks and mortar business, especially outside of the USA. It's not to say that those businesses cannot find success with Pinterest, but they need to utilise strategic measures to ensure that they are getting the right traffic. This means using the location in SEO keywording and in a hashtag strategy, alongside paying for Promoted Pins, so that they specifically target the location.

For example, a hair salon in Manchester, UK may want to target only that specific area, just for women aged 18-50. To do this, Promoted Pins would be essential, as there would be no point in getting traffic from the USA or Australia, unless the salon sold an online course or shipped products worldwide. But if global brand awareness is what your business wants, then Pinterest is definitely for you!

Pinterest is perfect for entrepreneurs who don't want to spend their time doing daily Facebook lives and getting on video. Who don't want to spend their time engaging with other people's content on the likes of Facebook, Instagram, Twitter, or LinkedIn. Who want to grow their email list on a daily basis. Who want to drive traffic to their products or into their funnel, without having to cold message. Pinterest is for businesses who want it streamlined and automated.

Pinterest is for all sorts of businesses. This includes product based businesses, service based entrepreneurs, consultants, coaches, those selling digital products and online courses, plus bloggers.

You name it I see people on Pinterest marketing it. From the likes of real estate agents, to mindset coaches, to immigration lawyers, to web designers. I've even given a Pinterest consultation to a charity to discuss increasing brand awareness and increasing donations.

Even if a person doesn't buy straight away, it's great for getting them into your funnel to grow the know, like, and trust factor.

The first step you can take to determining if your ideal customer or client is on Pinterest is to start typing what you think they are searching for in the search box and see what comes up. If Pinterest suggests it, then you know your audience is searching for it on Pinterest. This is what is called Pinterest SEO (search engine optimisation) or keywording. This keywording is the backbone of your Pinterest strategy and using it effectively is what gets your business found.

So Pinterest is a search engine, right? So next you'll want to compile a list of the search terms that you want to rank for when your audience is searching Pinterest. You'll need to spend a while researching this. You can literally just search in the search bar.

When you click on what it suggests, underneath will be coloured boxes with more words. Click these coloured boxes and drill down, until there are no more coloured boxes. These terms are what are known as 'long tail keywords'. You'll want a list of at least 100, a mix of short and long tail keywords. You can also utilise the Ads Manager function to see what keywords Pinterest suggests there.

Now it's time to develop your profile. You'll need a business account and I suggest setting up 10 boards to start with, based on the keyword research that you have carried out and the content you already have (blog posts etc).

You can always add more boards, but this is a good starting point. When utilising your keywords, make sure that you use the space Pinterest provides in full, and no keyword stuffing; Pinterest doesn't like that. They want a user-friendly experience.

You'll want to use the keywords you have found, in 7 different places:

1. Pinterest profile name
2. Profile description
3. Board titles
4. Board descriptions
5. Pin titles
6. Pin descriptions
7. Text overlay on your pins — yes, Pinterest can "read"!

Once your setup is complete, it's time to start adding pins. This means creating your own pins to link to your blog posts, products etc. You can use Photoshop, but if you don't know how to use it, Canva is a great, easy option to start designing.

Once you've got some pins it's time to start a pinning routine. You'll want to pin between 10-30 high quality pins each day; you can use other people's content too. I suggest using a Pinterest approved scheduler like Tailwind to assist you, so that you have a consistent pinning schedule. Pinterest likes consistency and new content, so keep creating!

There you go; those are the basics to Pinterest marketing. It's too much to cover everything in this chapter alone, so come find me on my social media channels and blog for some great, free content.

Or if you'd like me to teach you, or you just want to offload and outsource, I'd love to help you. Check out my bio for my contact details and where you can find me.

ABOUT THE AUTHOR

Lisa Farrington is a Pinterest Marketing Strategist, who enables businesses to get noticed and drive purchase intent through strategic Pinterest marketing. She runs a Pinterest Marketing Agency, Lisa Farrington & Co, working with clients across the globe.

During her 18 year career in housing and regeneration, high-level strategy and project management were the focus. She translates a strategic approach in client work and focuses on getting results by using high quality Pinterest SEO and attractive pin design to maximise brand awareness for her clients.

In 2015 she quit her job, rented her apartment and sold her car and possessions to escape regular life in the UK. During this 3 year journey of travelling the world and living in Australia, she experienced her own awakening and her business was born. She travels when she can and works to educate businesses and brands to the wonders of the mystical unicorn that is Pinterest.

Website: *www.lisafarringtonco.com*
Email: *lisa@lisafarringtonco.com*
Facebook: *www.facebook.com/lisafarringtonco*

MARY GOODEN

DISCOVERING YOUR SOUL'S PURPOSE
THROUGH YOGA, MEDITATION & REIKI

I have spent the last 20 years learning, practicing, researching, and mastering the art of living soulfully on purpose!

What does it mean to live soulfully? Living from a place of inner balance and harmony — aligning what you think, feel, say, and do.

Through my committed effort, along with the practice of yoga, meditation, and reiki energy harmonizing/healing, I have fully embraced soulful living and discovered my soul's purpose. I am willing to share my experience, guidance, and love to support and serve you in the most sufficient and fulfilling way, so that you too can live soulfully, on purpose.

It all starts with a great mantra, a short statement that echoes in your mind, especially when you start to feel a decline in your energy or vibration. The mantra that I hold close to my heart is, "I am open to receive all that the universe has for me."

With faith, hope, and love as my super powers, my journey has encompassed first-hand experience and research on the benefits of yoga, meditation, and reiki energy harmonizing/healing.

These modalities have led me to self-trust, authenticity, enlightenment, and purpose. I have been guided to share my experience and support you in discovering, living, and sharing yours. Several times a year I offer private and semi-private spiritual retreats to support clients in connecting with their deepest desires and embodying their soul's purpose.

I invite you to open your heart and your mind during this season of transformation. Let's take a deeper look at these modalities and how they are used to reshape your inner world, as well as some of my experiences and enlightening moments.

It all started with a yearning for something different. I loved a tough physical work-out; I was a runner and weight lifter, a real cardio junkie.

As I write this now it was more than likely the insatiable need to be enough, high-anxiety, and coffee provided me with an endless amount of energy. I was a mother, workaholic, and a work-out addict. I managed a fast-paced, highly profitable business and taught several fitness classes a week.

I was delighted to share my knowledge, expertise, and energy with anyone who was willing to listen and try new things. My friend Stacey came in to work one day super excited to share her discovery of a new yoga studio, and I was all ears! I was always eager to try new experiences and was somewhat familiar with the movement of yoga, so I decided to give it a try.

It was truly love-at-first feel; the energy that filled the space was calm, peaceful, and compassionate. Beautiful words of love and encouragement lined the walls and were a positive reminder to always speak softly.

Almost immediately, this become the most desirable part of my week. On Sunday night I would take the "Sacred Music" class; it was a 90-minute candlelight flow, the perfect way to prepare for the week ahead. The instructor, Kasia, is a treasure who will live in my heart forever.

I mention this class specifically because this is where I first received the calling to become a yoga instructor. I remember it like it was yesterday: as I began to awaken from savasana, coming back to consciousness, I knew in that moment that I absolutely wanted to make others feel exactly as I felt: pure, content, and at peace with all things. The very next day I sought out a yoga teacher training program that felt right and my journey of self-study was about to blossom.

It is true what you have heard: life is a journey, not a destination. In fact, the darkest moments and experiences in our life bring us the most profound growth. I am certainly not suggesting that you seek the dark moments, nor am I saying that if you haven't experienced the darkness that you are not growing.

Honestly, I wasn't exposed to what felt like my darkest moment until 2014, however looking back now it was the brightest experience on my path. Awakening feels awkward most of the time, an instant where the light breaks through the darkness.

It is about getting out of your comfort zone and inviting a positive change in the way you perceive your experiences. What I hope to share with you in the practice of yoga, meditation, and reiki energy harmonizing/healing is that you are the creator of your perception, your experiences, and your life, regardless of external circumstance and limiting beliefs. We are all here to discover and serve a purpose, a personal mission to expose the light, not only within ourselves, but in those around us.

YOGA, MEDITATION, AND SELF-REALIZATION

The practice of yoga is certainly not a new tradition. Hatha yoga has been shown in ancient texts to date as far back as 800 years. In what we call the Western World, the first school of Hatha was established in 1918. Yoga is defined as the uniting of the mind, body, and spirit to your higher consciousness, God, Divine, or Source.

It has been noted as a healing science, as regular practice will increase awareness and decrease disease. Yoga is a practice of self-study or self-realization. I like to think of it as a coming home to yourself.

Practicing yoga and meditation regularly will lead to health benefits and help:

- Decrease anxiety and release you from "fight or flight" mode, creating more time spent in a clam state of peace.
- Encourage a cultivation of non-judgement, self-trust, balanced ego, and genuine kindness.
- Increase flexibility, muscle strength, respiration, and circulatory health, along with energy and vitality.

Yoga offers eight limbs or basic guidelines on how to live a meaningful or soulful life. The first four aspects lean in a more practical direction and are designed to prepare you for the second half of the journey, the pathway to Samadhi, described as a pure state of ecstasy.

The last four aspects relate to meditation and creating a space for you to hear the whispers of your soul. This part of the journey requires that you fully embody your authenticity.

1. *Yamas* - which follow the golden rule of "treat others as you wish to be treated," drawing focus to your own behavior, nonviolence, truthfulness, non-stealing, and non-possessiveness, refining your personality.
2. *Niyamas* - which deal with self-discipline and spiritual practices, purity, contentment, self-study, and surrender to your God, Divine, or Source.
3. *Asana* - which relates to the physical practice of postures, developing a relationship with your body and energetic awareness of yourself. The practice involves moving the body seamlessly with the breath, learning self-discipline, compassion, and acceptance as you meet the body where it is, concentrating, and being present, which will be useful in meditation.
4. *Pranayama* - which relates to gaining mastery and full awareness of your breath. This is the life force within. The breath is the largest healing system in the body and possibly the one that we take for granted the most. In my experience it isn't unlikely for a doctor, psychologist, or psychiatrist to suggest that you take deep breaths to calm yourself down. I give yoga a standing ovation for teaching me how to breathe! Breath-work can be practiced as an isolated technique, however it is integral to the physical practice of yoga posture.
5. *Pratyahara* - meaning detachment from external distraction or sensory transcendence.
6. *Dharana* - concentration and focus on stilling the internal distractions of the mind.
7. *Dhyana* - meditation or contemplation, becoming fully aware without any focus.
8. *Samadhi* - union of self and a connection to a higher consciousness, to God, Divine, or your Source.

In my opinion, Samadhi is achieved through living authentically and in alignment with your soul's purpose. A blissful experience of being one with the Universe and fully aware of all the abundance that surrounds you.

Through consistent, daily practice, patience, self-love, and self-acceptance anyone is capable of this experience or enlightenment. I support clients fully on this journey with seminars, on-site and online class offerings for both yoga and meditation, as well as a comprehensive yoga teacher training/self-study program.

Listed below are a few of my offering:

AWAKENING

- Yoga Teacher Training Program. This course is approximately 4-6 month in duration and is designed to help you create a deeper connection to self. Additionally, you will learn everything necessary to deliver yoga privately or in a class setting.
- Mindfully living and loving the journey is a meditation-based course. Discover your innate ability to create harmony in all areas of your life. Learn the benefits of breath, mantra, and meditation as you embark upon your journey toward mindfulness.
- Energy empowering and clearing meditations based on the lunar energy. These offerings are reiki inspired and include connecting to a higher self, breath-work, chanting, mantra, emotional freedom tapping, fire ceremonies, meditation, and yoga nidra.
- Refreshing retreats in Sedona, Arizona. This offering is a mindful journey of the heart! A time for reflection, relaxation, and rejuvenation for your spirit. This all-inclusive retreat will invite you to find clarity, purpose, and freedom. A space to fully immerse in your heart's desire. Itinerary includes yoga and meditation, reflection and release activities, day trips to Sedona with Vortex visit, outdoor adventures, and personal loving support!

REIKI AND CHAKRA ENERGY SYSTEMS

Reiki energy harmonizing/healing is an amazing gift that was shared with me during an interesting time in my journey. I hold a master level in this modality, which has been a vital skill that serves to guide and support clients in discovering their inner light and purpose successfully.

I offer on-site and online seminars, workshops, harmonizing/healing sessions, and spiritual attunement sessions that are loaded with information on energy harmonizing/healing, including:

- *Reiki level 1, 2, and 3 Attunement:* Attunement is the process of transferring the power of universal life force energy to the student by a reiki master.
- *Chakra 101:* Exploring energetic anatomy. Clients are provided a complete guide on the chakra system and an open discussion about how

chakras impact your life, as well as how to create inner balance and harmony.

Reiki is a "spiritually guided life force energy." This modality takes a holistic approach to harmonizing/healing the body.

The technique aids in the reduction of stress and promotes relaxation and healing. It is administered by "laying on hands" and is based on the idea that an unseen "life force energy" flows through us and is what causes us to be alive. If one's "life force energy" is low, then we are more likely to get sick or feel stress, and if it is high, we are more capable of being joyful and healthy.

I have thoroughly studied reiki energy, along with the chakra energy system, for the last decade. A chakra is literally a vortex of energy, connecting our physical existence to higher and deeper non-physical realms.

These seven, energetic set points in the body act as filters for the experiences that we encounter from past lives all the way to the present moment. What we generate determines much of what we receive, hence the idea of karma. A blockage or imbalance in one or several of the chakras can initiate mental, emotional, physical, and spiritual ailments.

When properly balanced, the seven chakras work together to create the optimal life. I personally use reiki, yoga, crystals, sound healing vibration, and mantra mediation to heal and restore chakra balance. I have a daily practice of praying, visualizing, and aligning my mind, body, and spirit so that I may present as the very best version of myself.

Each one of the seven chakras is responsible for the emotional and physical energy within a certain point of your body.

The following is a map of the chakra location and purpose:

1. *The root chakra "Muladhara"* is located at the base of the spine and manages your security, stability, and assurance.
2. *The sacral chakra "Svadhishthana,"* located above the root and below the belly button, manages your emotional resilience, including guilt, shame, and co-dependency, along with being a center for creativity and sexuality.
3. *The solar plexus chakra "Manipura"* is known as the "fire of desire," just

above the belly button. This super powered chakra manages self/ego, confidence, acceptance, and self-belief.
4. *The heart chakra "Anahata"* is located above the solar plexus in the center of the chest. This amazing space of energy, light, and soul expression manages, love, compassion, forgiveness, and gratitude. I believe the space of the heart chakra is where your voice of purpose lives. Every morning before I get out of bed, I pause in stillness with both palms on my heart space and listen for the whisper of my soul.
5. *The throat chakra "Vishudda"* is located in the center of the throat space. This is where we enliven self-expression, courage, and authenticity.
6. *The third-eye "Ajna"* is our connection to clear thinking, imagination, self-reflection, and intuition. It is nestled in the center of the brain near the pineal gland.
7. *The crown chakra "Sahasrara"* is your spiritual connection to a higher consciousness, God, Divine, or Source. A balanced crown chakra allows you to feel freedom, unity, and complete harmony!

Combining the knowledge and practices of yoga, meditation, reiki, and chakra energy allows you to truly know yourself and in the knowing self-love, self-trust, and self-acceptance ignite the light of the soul.

BEGINNING THE JOURNEY

Treat this journey the same as you would a new friendship, get excited about it, prepare for new adventures, surrender to the unknown, and have fun! When I was running one morning, I was thinking of ways I could encourage clients to embrace this way of life and this is what I heard:

S.I.M.P.L.E. – Seriously Imagine More Positive Life Experiences!

What is pulling on your heart strings right now? What in your life is screaming for your attention and transformation? Honor everything that you hear and write it down. On the same piece of paper write down your dreams, your wishes, and your desired outcome.

Now, let's pick a mantra to help you eliminate distraction. A mantra encourages you to practice activation of free will, no longer ruled by the seeds of your mind. Practicing a mantra will reduce the mental fluctuations of your mind quickly. If the mind is steady, your body will follow. Allow me to share a few that I have used to embody soulful living:

- "Everything I need is already within me."
- "I am open to receive all that the universe has for me."
- "I can achieve anything I desire."
- "I am present in this moment, accepting who I am where I am."
- "I love myself, I trust myself, I am enough."
- "My life is filled with abundance and prosperity."

Is there a mantra that resonates with you here? Maybe something is already entering your mind that is perfect for you in this moment. Use your mantra as often as possible to bring yourself back to present-moment awareness.

Meditate with your mantra. Meditation is not a practice of sitting in a dark room as still as possible; I tried that for a minute and all I could feel was chest pain. Look for guided meditation, offerings that take you on a journey.

I have developed specific meditations for my clients based on their individual needs; I would be honored to do this for you too. You can also find some great offerings on YouTube. Yoga nidra specifically works with mantra meditation. This practice is referred to as "yogic sleep." How can you go wrong with that!

Make yourself a yoga date and take your mantra with you! Research some local yoga studios or try a few online if that feels better. If you're a beginner, find a basic class and remember the guidelines of yoga: this practice is a judgement free zone.

In my yoga classes I constantly remind my clients that the mind tells the body and the body responds. I remember my early days on the yoga mat; this energy of force to get my body to look a certain way, it was my ego's need to look like my mat neighbor, who had been practicing yoga forever.

What I learned is that force is not necessary, everybody is designed different, everybody will look different and feel different, so I started embracing my differences. My yoga still teaches me self-love, compassion, and trust. What I learn on my mat, I live off my mat.

If you start to feel distracted or frustrated, inwardly repeat your mantra. I make it a point to try everything twice, just in case I missed something the first time. Success lies in your ability to love and accept yourself exactly where you are!

Finally, schedule yourself a reiki or energy harmonizing/healing session. This is a holistic modality that is purely designed to create inner harmony. I understand the dis-ease that is created by unfortunate life circumstances, anxiety infused lifestyles, hopelessness, and the need to be free from limiting beliefs. Allow yourself to experience this amazing, energetic tune-up.

During the 2020 pandemic when this book was published, we were all gifted with an opportunity to awaken. Some of us have spent our lifetime living in a state of dis-ease.

Open your heart, your mind, and your soul to receive the gift of a new life. Allow yourself to transform, to release from cultural conditioning, and to live fully! It is a daily practice of making the choice to live in your truth, your light, and your purpose.

The universe is here to guide you, love you, and support your destiny toward soulful living. I am here to support you in whatever form you need me.

This is the year the universe, mother earth, your God is calling you to awaken; the stage has been set, the mind, body, and spirit are designed to unite and deliver the path to your soul's purpose.

Be brave and move wholeheartedly into what lights you up.

ABOUT THE AUTHOR

Mary Gooden is the founder of Yoga Etc. and Divine Reiki Love. She believes that abundance thrives in your ability to remain aligned and authentic, which is a daily practice.

Mary has studied and practiced Yoga, Meditation, and Reiki Energy Harmonizing for almost 20 years. By taking an intuitive approach, she focuses on creating a space for clients to embody spiritual wellness for soul discovery.

As a limitless source of God's Love and Light, she coaches and empowers clients to discover their unique gifts so they may live and serve on purpose. Mary's intention is to restore inner harmony, authenticity, and freedom to as many individuals as possible.

Several times a year, Mary shares her love of sacred Sedona, Arizona through private and small group spiritual, soul-satisfying retreats. She currently resides in New Orleans, Louisiana with her husband and beautiful teenage daughters.

Website: www.yogaetcboutte.com
Email: yogaetc.boutte@yahoo.com
Facebook: www.facebook.com/Yoga-Etc-1626488234322170
and www.facebook.com/GodlyReikiLove
Youtube: www.youtube.com/channel/UCMIm_7kmeQuVhGD-QcqAyXQ

MICHELLE ASPINWALL

FASTING OVER 40 FOR BEAUTY, VITALITY & LONGEVITY

Aging is a gift.

Having the gift of gathering 48 years of memories, experience, suffering, and love is my human experience.

The thing I tell myself in the deep parts of my heart is that this aging process is uniquely mine and is not anything to fight, defy, or turn back, nor am I broken, or need fixing as a result of my aging.

One has a rare opportunity to inhabit a human vessel; it's been said that souls line up for a human body.

A valuable aspect of aging is learning what you can alter, and using the mind and your free will to mold the experience of aging. The past 15 years have been my waking-up period. I had the unique opportunity of healing through suffering. Thinking that aging was happening *to me*, not *for me*. Lately I have felt fortunate to see the process as *happening for me* because it changes how I do life. And it's altogether a better quality of life.

This all began with my practice of fasting.

I have worked with a body of women, who all want a different experience with their body. Some with aging, some with specific health conditions, and some who want more energy and clarity. But as the vast majority of my clients are women (although I have worked with men and enjoyed it) not a single one of them suffered from learning how to intermittent fast.

This practice is a gift for women in mid-life especially. As you will understand later, it's not just the process of fasting, but the process of eating that is crucial to our particular stage in life. And this chapter is devoted to each of these women, as their journey was forever changed. And here is why.

What I have come to know (because this includes me) is women tend to fill their plates in the same way that they live their lives. And most women have a relationship with food that they describe as tumultuous and started very young.

What you put on your plate, how you perceive what you put on your plate, how you enjoy what's on your plate (and I'm talking fats, carbohydrates, vegetables, meat, fish, plants, berries, tubers, herbs, spices, sugar, honey, all of it, all of the beautiful enjoyment and the things that bring us mouth-gasms) it starts here, because it becomes us. When it's time, you see things differently; you put food in front of you that you've never eaten before.

The women I work with learn to see food as nourishment, eating a colorful plate not to excess and not as a reward for pushing, exercising, or accomplishing a goal, and certainly not for numbing. Then you tend to live a full life filled of purpose and fulfillment.

You can fill your plate with music, you can fill your plate with orgasms, you can fill your plate with love, you can fill your plate with people around you that expect and only want the best of you. Or you can see life metaphorically as, 'If I do this, then I need to work out tomorrow', or 'If I eat this, then I need to NOT eat that tomorrow.'

This way of viewing your plate informs your cells; it tells your body via your thoughts, and via your hormones, because we are connected through lots of different areas in our brain, and then it hits our nervous system and travels through energetic channels to our organs. So what you tell yourself about everything you eat, what all the people you surround yourself with say, the art you take in, or the aspects of life you deny yourself all inform your internal environment.

The vessel doesn't just exist in the mind. We are not just what we think, we're not just our emotions. We get to have a life where you can thrive and flourish and do profound good.

Do you want to live a life where you have boundless energy? Where your skin glows? Where your voice sings? Do you want your life to be an expansive adventure of love and joy and wealth?

The way to get to this incredible place is deciding right now, for yourself that it's time.

But in order to feel differently one must do or see things in a different way.

Start by saying this to yourself: What we put in our mouths becomes our eyes, our brains, our organs, our blood, our thoughts, our emotions, and our hearts.

If that's what you want, it all begins with how you eat for your constitution.

It's not only what you eat, but how you combine your food, in conjunction with when you eat. Make no mistake, intermittent fasting is a lifestyle, not a diet. And I think most women will say dieting is hard in practice, but easy to imagine. Fasting is hard to think about, but quite satisfying in practice.

Below I have separated intermittent fasting into a few sections: eating for your constitution, eating windows, and food combining.

Here is where I tie aging, specifically women over 40 and the unique cascade of hormones, with fasting. Prior to 40, women have the beauty of estrogen and hormones on our side, but after 40 this shifts.

Our hormones are not doomed after 40 to perpetual imbalance. Taking responsibility for your habits, and creating rituals to support this portal is a necessity for vitality. Aging and the menopausal transition is not a medical condition. It's nothing to fear and certainly not solved by medical intervention.

Hormonal suffering near 50 is customary, but not normal.

This is the time to take that radical responsibility and mix it with delight.

So learning how to eat for your constitution, which includes eating for your current age, is where to start.

Next learning to fill your plate with the beautiful bounty of nature, and combine food in a way that satiates and nourishes your hormones and delighting the senses.

It is essential to think of Fasting as eating, not NOT EATING.

Now the fasting side of it, which is what everyone fixates on.

Do you want to know the secret of fasting?

Eat in a distinct window of time, and then don't eat outside of that window.

It's really that simple.

EATING FOR YOUR CONSTITUTION

Now, what does that mean?

Constitution is part age, part genetics, and part physiology.

After 40, estrogen is beginning to lower, so preserving it is key.

So when a woman fasts during her cycle — whether that be menstrual or moon — it's crucial to work with your estrogen and progesterone so as not to further diminish estrogen.

Constitution is also recognizing when your digestive fire burns hottest and this determines the quantity of raw food you can eat, the best time to eat raw food vs cooked food, and usually the best time of day to eat your largest meal. It is essential to consider both time of day and seasons.

Our constitution resides in our frame, meaning how we are built does have a say in how and where we carry our mass and how we process estrogen.

It's all unique and specific to you.

FOOD COMBINING

Filling our plate is more than just macronutrients. Nourishment is understanding how to fill your plate with beauty, the essence of beauty and joy. How can your plate be beautiful? How can you fill your plate with edible flowers, with herbs sprinkled on top, with colors that you love because the colors you love are the colors you need in your body? It all goes back to the earth. Balancing our chakras, keeping our energy strong, and nourishing ourselves with the bounty of nature.

Food groups that nourish women over 40 are the dark leafy greens especially stinging nettles, dandelion greens, and watercress — the foods that are bitter, the foods that grow in the most adverse conditions, the foods that have a distinct and protective mechanism built into them.

I encourage you to eat them because they're chock full of nutrients that balance hormones and that fortify the blood because when our blood is rich and fortified, our blood is what goes around, it's what keeps us juicy, it's what keeps us oxygenated. Some facts about eating leafy greens, for example, they need fat to assimilate the nutrients and are easier to digest if cooked briefly so they are brilliant green.

Another group is sea vegetables like kelp, dulse, hijiki, and nori, as they are iodine-rich sources and help our thyroids. These can be eaten dried or reconstituted.

Combining sea vegetables with proteins and fats enhances the body's assimilation of nutrients.

Another group is nuts and seeds, like flax seeds and pumpkin seeds. They're going to provide iron and calcium. They're going to provide all the minerals that a woman in peri-menopause needs.

And by eating these powerhouses, the body knows exactly where to send them versus just supplementing. When you chew the food, you get the fiber, you get all of the amazing minerals and the vitamin D from the sun. Some might be asking about blended or juiced drinks.

Over 40, these methods of preparation can tend to raise blood sugar. I am not a fan of drinking smoothies regularly, especially combined with fruit. Blended food is a 21st century invention and for women over 40 tends to do more damage than good.

Finally, fats are our friends. Healthy fats include seeds, nuts, extra virgin olive oil, avocado and walnut oils, olives, avocados, and coconut products. Women's bodies need healthy fats especially for stabilizing hormones and rebuilding cells especially closer to and over 50.

EATING WINDOWS

Eating windows and fasting windows are what most people think of when they begin fasting. As you have read above, fasting is so much more than just when you eat.

And if you've never done this before, I'm going to tell you right now, the healthiest way to start is not to starve yourself, because as soon as you starve yourself of nutrients, you're going to crave everything or overeat inside your eating window.

When I work with women in groups or privately, I have everyone begin with an eating window of 10-12 hours, beginning with breakfast at 7-8am and dinner finishing by 8pm. And only after this becomes effortless do we then narrow the eating window because sleep, exercise, and digestive fire all play a part in establishing the ideal window, long term. For some a nine hour window is best and for others 5 hours is best.

The vast majority of women, after having mastered eating real food combined with the ideal proportion of fat to protein to carbohydrate for their age and frame, feel more alert, feel little to no bloating, and eat only when they are hungry, thereby maintaining a healthy weight well beyond 50.

Everybody's different. Finding your ideal window takes a few weeks. This is the beauty of who we are. We are bio-individual souls living in a human Earth suit, trying to figure out how to do this life.

I would like to sum up the past sections with this thought: Our habits and practices of eating, dieting, exercising for the sake of weight and stress are a whole new ball game after 40. As I have said often by 45, women's estrogen/progesterone levels begin to really shift and, for most, significantly decline.

This is not bad, it just is. Aligning with time, understanding when to fast in your cycle, is key to not disrupting your particular estrogen cascade. As women near 50, carrying an extra 5-8lbs is normal, but 20-30 pounds very well may not be and may be due to insulin resistance, blood sugar balance, and fat storage, which means added estrogen, as fat cells produce estrogen.

MYTHS AROUND FASTING

Will I mess up my hormones?

No, as long as you eat nourishing food of all colors, including protein and complex carbohydrates like beets, root vegetables, and occasional small amount of rice.

Will I slow down my metabolism?

Creating eating windows daily to include full meals will not slow down your metabolism. One would have to fast for more like 60 hours straight to reduce your resting metabolic rate.

Will I be hungry constantly?

The first 4-5 days is an adjustment, similar to bringing in a new workout. The body will likely need time to acclimate, but then after 7 days, cravings often decrease and your eating window becomes more of a way of life.

Will I be foggy or unfocused when waiting a few hours to eat?

Intermittent fasting has the opposite effect by the second week. The body tends to self-regulate and the benefits include enhanced focus and mental clarity.

Intermittent fasting has the ability to radically benefit the brain, especially for women. There is a clarity that tends to come after four weeks of consistent eating windows. Removing food addiction or food numbing clears space in the brain.

This shift makes it so much easier to analyze habits that may not be serving women as we age, which has the ability to drastically improve our lives. The outlook that comes with clarity has the ability to bring incongruences to the forefront.

Food has become the most socially acceptable and readily available drug on the planet. And somewhere along the way we have given up health and vitality for convenience. I deeply believe in a world where women master nourishing their bodies as they age and not feeding their emotions.

Aging is an internal game that pays dividends externally. Aging is also recognizing that what you do for your body in your 40's and 50's impacts how your health unfolds at 70+. This includes your aura, including how you radiate and how you manifest. Here we are, this is the new normal, and you are a part of the awakening.

And I'm going to tell you what the awakening is: The awakening is taking radical responsibility for your health with delight, not living in fear and panic, but with delight that you know how to nourish your body, your mind and your soul.

THIS is how women take back their power, aging with grace and longevity.

ABOUT THE AUTHOR

Michelle Aspinwall is an international bestselling author, and Age Alchemist, working with women over 40 hormonally, spiritually and emotionally.

Her unique approach combines cutting edge Western Science like integrative bio-hacking and specific hormonal testing with traditional Eastern healing like targeted intermittent fasting and plant medicine. Additionally, she is the creator of the bespoke skincare line A SKIN which is formulated to work with the seasons and made exclusively from oils, herbs, botanicals and butters.

Michelle and her family reside in New York City.

Website: www.michelleaspinwall.com
Instagram: www.instagram.com/michellepaspinwall
Facebook: www.facebook.com/a.skin.care
LinkedIn: www.linkedin.com/in/michelle-aspinwall-628789103/
Pinterest: www.id.pinterest.com/furrybabinga

NATALIE ANNE MURRAY

CREATING AUTHENTIC, DEEP & MEANINGFUL RELATIONSHIPS

What if you could transform your relationships just by transforming yourself?

I'm a Relationship Makeover Expert and I help soulful, high-achieving women, who struggle to feel empowered and authentic in relationships, to confidently be themselves, and communicate lovingly and powerfully, so that they can create deep and meaningful connections in their lives.

For the past 20 years I've helped 100's of women to fully recover from dysfunctional childhood and adult relationships, and I've witnessed the profound results that are achieved by women who *choose* to make the conscious decision to step out of fear, insecurity, and frustration into unconditional love, unshakeable confidence, and true, inner peace.

I am one of those women.

Despite being highly educated, and working in mental health, I suffered with low self-worth and an obsessive need for external approval and validation that blocked me from truly connecting with others in a healthy way.

I had a pattern of getting involved with men with addictions (that I felt compelled to save) and struggled to make friends or feel a part of my family.

My turning point came when my beloved first husband, Greg, died from the effects of alcoholism at the tender age of 42.

I nursed him at home for 6 months and losing him was my 'wake-up' call to start truly living my life, instead of staying stuck in anxiety, shame, and hopelessness.

So, I sent a prayer to the universe that said, 'I just want to love myself, be myself, and be happy.'

At the time I had no idea *how* I was going to do that, but I was 100% committed to finding out.

Fast forward to 14 years later and, with the help of many people, I have achieved all that and more.

I whole-heartedly love myself without self-consciousness, have an intimate marriage with my darling second husband, Alan, and a close, drama-free relationships with my children, my family, and my friends.

I now freely share my authentic gifts and talents to help other women find peace much faster than I did. And I know that every woman who is brave enough to 'Just Be Herself' is raising the vibration of the planet and creating a much-needed state of equality between men and women.

What I now know for sure is it's impossible to enjoy authentic, deep, and meaningful relationships if you don't feel whole, complete, and connected with yourself. But sadly, despite all the personal development tools used on the planet, many women still struggle to feel 'at home' in their own skin and are too vulnerable to share their true thoughts and feelings with others.

They give their power away by over-giving, approval-seeking, and avoiding conflict. They don't trust their intuition, tend to be controlling of themselves and others, and mistakenly take on all the responsibility for making a relationship work.

It feels difficult to let their guard down and be vulnerable, and yet vulnerability is the birthplace of the connection they desire.

It's sad because women are naturally hard-wired to create love and belonging, and when we feel cut off from these innate gifts, we feel empty, frustrated, resentful, and painfully disconnected from others.

This unhelpful pattern of relating is soul-destroying and exhausting, however, it's common and there's two clear reasons for it.

Firstly, for centuries women have been *conditioned* to hide who they are, put themselves last, suppress their voice and emotions, be afraid of men, and to keep the peace at all costs.

Millions of our ancestors have even been burnt at the stake for expressing feminine traits of emotion, intuition, healing, and creativity and, to survive, they were forced to conform and submit to a patriarchal society.

And, even though women in the Western world enjoy many more freedoms than our ancestors did, we are *still affected* by their traumas.

We know this to be true because the science of epigenetics has now *proven* that we can inherit emotional trauma and mental automatic responses to stress from our ancestors.

That means we carry in the very cells of our being recorded patterns and beliefs of pain, struggle, and suffering and we unconsciously play it out again in our own life.

The anxiety, sense of powerlessness, and feeling of 'not being good enough' that many women think is 'normal,' is *not normal.* It's a generational pattern repeating.

And we need to break this cycle to feel free, be authentic, and connect deeply with others.

Also, there is a second important fact to consider.

Women who desire to fully express themselves have already tried to heal with traditional, well-known psychological and therapeutic methods; however, these methods have usually been created by men, and *don't take into account the unique biological, mental and emotional differences between males and females*, so therefore, they often don't have a lasting effect for females.

I personally found it shocking to realise that the uniqueness of females has not yet been fully acknowledged by science.

For example, did you know that most medical research for medications has not even been tested on females, but on male castrated rats instead?

Yes, the patriarchal scientific world deemed that male castrated rats are 'close enough' to the biological make-up of females.

That's crazy when you consider that females born with a uterus have something that males don't and will *never* have.

The ability to create life.

Yes, females have a miraculous power to grow a baby and science has yet to comprehend the magic energy of creation that sparks that to happens.

So, because this mystery has not yet been scientifically qualified and quantified, it has simply been eliminated from the research equation!

But a uterus carries immensely powerful wisdom and knows how to pass it on for generations through our genes. Our uterus is the incubator of creation, so is it not therefore possible that there exists a *female unconscious mind* that males don't have access to and cannot comprehend?

Also, there are differences in the wiring of a male and female's brain, and females have hormones that give us a cyclical nature, rather than the steady experience of a man. We literally see and experience the world differently from males, so it makes perfect sense that we need a *female-specific transformation tool* to help us heal our deepest issues and blocks to connection at the core.

Thankfully that tool now exists on the planet and it's called Creatrix®.

As far as I know this is the world's only completely female-formulated methodology, that was created by a female for females, and that addresses epigenetics and the female-factor differences.

It's one tool to resolve <u>all issues</u>, without the need to know where they came from; so, you don't have to analyse yourself anymore.

And because there's no need to 'revisit' trauma or 'process emotions,' it's safe and can be used effectively for females who mistakenly believe they are 'broken' and 'unfixable.'

This is a holistic mind, body, and spirit process that effectively 're-sets' a female's programming back to a natural, whole, and complete state so they feel as if they've 'come home to themselves' for the first time.

Triggers dissolve and emotional intelligence increases ten-fold, so you feel joy, have more compassion for yourself and others, stop caring so much what others think, and trust your own inner guidance.

Relationships improve without having to 'try so hard' because you naturally find it easier to be yourself, accept others for who they are, and speak your truth lovingly, so you can create the opportunity for genuine connection to develop.

Creatrix® underpins the transformation I facilitate for females; however, it is supported by two other important steps.

Here is the three-fold approach that I guide my private clients through to help them successfully transform their relationship with themselves and others for good.

STEP ONE – CHOOSE TO BECOME A 'WOMAN OF INTEGRITY'

For your transformation to be complete and lasting it requires you to make a *conscious decision* to take full responsibility for your life and happiness.

That means being completely honest about all the ways your inherited, unconscious programming and behaviour has caused suffering for you, hurt other people, and damaged your relationships.

It also requires a willingness to recognise how you have benefited from staying the same and if you are truly willing to change. For example, how has your behaviour unconsciously helped you gain pleasure or avoid pain in the past? Are you ready to let that unconscious payoff go to create authentic relationships?

Yes, it takes real courage to 'own' your part in relationship drama and it's a powerful choice to stop blaming others and claim your power to create positive change instead. You don't have to know *how* you're going to make the change, but you do have to be 100% willing and vow to do the right thing by yourself and others, so you can truly 'walk your talk' and feel like you're living in integrity with yourself.

This is a humbling, confronting step, however, those who are ready to hold themselves 100% accountable are rewarded by the chance to experience true personal freedom.

STEP TWO – TRANSFORM WITH CREATRIX®

Make the powerful choice to put your logical, rational mind aside, and surrender to the mystery of your female unconscious mind with the Creatrix® methodology, so you can resolve your deepest mental and emotional blocks at their core.

I meet my clients weekly online and promise they will finally break the pattern of feeling unworthy, move on from their painful past, and learn to be true to themselves without the fear of being alone within 6 weeks and with guaranteed results.

STEP THREE – ALIGN YOUR LIFE TO YOUR TRUTH

After transforming yourself inside, it's vital to take inspired action to make practical changes in your life to live true to yourself.

That might mean making a change in your lifestyle, career, friendships or intimate relationships that you know in your heart you need to make.

It's not easy at first, but no one else can make those changes for you and, if you don't, you will create new problems for yourself.

These three key areas are supportive to your ongoing transformation into a 'Woman of Integrity':

1. Learn new relationship skills such as how to set healthy boundaries, manage conflict wisely, re-wire co-dependency patterns, and respect the differences between males and females, so you can create new ways of relating and experience authentic connection.
2. Reconnect with your body, emotions, and feminine energy and live in alignment with your feminine cycle, so you can stay grounded, honour your needs, and continue to take responsibility for your happiness.
3. Understand the energetic nature you were naturally born to express and create a personal dress style that reflects the 'real you,' so you can increase your presence, energy, and happiness, and appreciate more deeply the uniqueness of the people you love.

CURIOUS AND WANT TO KNOW MORE?

My work best suits soulful, high-achieving women who are ready to break the pattern of feeling disempowered and inauthentic, are driven to be the best version of themselves, value integrity, authenticity, and connection, and are committed to do whatever it takes to create a lasting, positive transformation in themselves and their relationships.

Here are 3 examples of past clients who chose to be inspiring, change-makers in their families:

1. Sarah was 55 years old and had been unhappily married for 35 years. She had always wondered if she loved her husband and had tried hard to be a 'Good Girl' and a 'Good Wife' by stuffing down her voice and her big personality to avoid conflict. She was filled with frustration, anger, and resentment and thought she had to leave the marriage so she could be happy. After choosing to become a 'Woman of Integrity,' Sarah felt true peace, self-love, and happiness for the first time in her life. She accepted and understood her husband's differences and spoke up to set boundaries and to renegotiate their marriage so they could create a positive, new way of relating to each other.
2. Alyse was a single, 60-year-old counsellor who, despite being a therapy client herself for decades, still felt like a scared, broken little girl inside and believed she would be alone for the rest of her life. She was an only

child who still felt unloved by her mother and she'd experienced multiple broken marriages that had hurt her children. Filled with guilt, shame, and low self-worth, she chose to become a 'Woman of Integrity' and finally felt like a 'grown woman' inside. Soon afterwards, she met a kind, loving man to whom she is now happily engaged. She also made peace with her mother before her mother died and now feels close with her adult children and grandchildren.

3. Chris was a 50-year-old single woman who recognised she had a pattern of choosing relationships with men with addictions. She also owned that she had major rejection issues after being abandoned as a baby, living with several foster families, and losing custody of her teenage children. She felt stuck in hurt, loneliness, and grief and chose to become a 'Woman of Integrity' so she could be a good role model to her children, despite having little contact with them. Chris bravely freed her heart and found herself again. She broke the pattern of 'rescuing' men and courageously reconnected with her children and now has a loving relationship with them.

Feeling inspired by these brave ladies?

If you know in your gut you want to become a 'Woman of Integrity' so you can finally feel joyful, confident, and authentic, and want to create deep and meaningful relationships, I invite you to take this first step.

JOURNAL QUESTIONS

Take out a journal and spend time honestly answering these ten questions:

1. Who or what am I still blaming for my unhappiness or sense of powerlessness?
2. What is my behavioural pattern of giving my power away in relationships (e.g. what do I regularly do, say, or think that's unhelpful)?
3. Has anyone in previous generations of my family experienced these patterns too?

4. What has this pattern of giving my power away cost me so far (mentally, emotionally, financially, physically, and spiritually)?
5. What will it cost me in the future if I don't change this pattern now?
6. Is there any reason I might be unconsciously holding on to this pattern because I'm getting a payoff? If so, what is the payoff?
7. Am I truly willing to create change in myself, even if it feels uncomfortable?
8. What do I truly desire to experience in my relationship/s?
9. How willing am I to fully own my power as a woman and to lead by example?
10. How willing am I to be happy?

Congratulations! It takes courage to honestly answer these questions and I'm inspired by you!

If you want to take the next step please know I work online 1:1 with women from around the world and my mission is to set 1000 women's hearts free. I would love you to be one of them!

Please feel free to connect with me via any of the links below and I look forward to meeting you soon.

You do have the power to just be *you*.

Love,
    Nat x

ABOUT THE AUTHOR

Natalie Anne Murray is a Relationship Makeover Expert who empowers soulful, high-achieving ladies to become 'Women of Integrity', so that they can be joyful, confident and authentic, communicate lovingly & powerfully, and create deep and meaningful connections in their lives.

Her specialist, online 1:1 service is underpinned by the revolutionary female-specific Creatrix® Breakthrough process and gives women a complete, lasting, inner transformation (within six weeks and with guaranteed results) so that they can break their pattern of feeling unworthy, move on completely from their past, and be true to themselves without fear of being alone.

Natalie has a 20 year career in mental health and is known for her online course, *"Boundary Queen – How to Create Meaningful Connections Without 'Losing Yourself' Again,"* and her refreshingly honest blog, *'Recover The Woman In You.'*

She is happily married to her second husband and lives in Newcastle, Australia with their spoilt rescue dogs.

> **Website:** www.natalieannemurray.com
> **Facebook:** www.facebook.com/natalieannemurray
> and www.facebook.com/groups/shawoi
> **Email:** nat@natalieannemurray.com

PETA PANOS

THE ART OF ASCENSION ALCHEMY – FINDING YOUR WAY BACK INTO THE LIGHT OF LOVE

Humanity has been at a crossroads through the Corona pandemic and the most powerful question we can ask ourselves is: What reality am I choosing to resurrect myself in, in the post Corona world?

A fear or Love based reality?

Because that is the real choice when it all comes down to it. Will I love myself enough to focus on keeping my vibration high and sovereign, letting go of the pain and struggle of the past, layer by layer, or will I allow my fears (which show up as fight, flight, freeze or people pleasing) to overwhelm me into lack & scarcity and compliance consciousness?

Now that more truth is surfacing and the world reels in economic crisis, please re-member that this crisis is not bigger than God/Goddess or our highest destinies. Every one of us contributes to the mass consciousness with our light or our darkness. This is the time we chose to come here for, so choose wisely.

Never before has there been a better time to raise your vibration, take back your power, find your authentic expression and say YES to a Love-based reality. The world has woken up to the fact that, despite borders, we are one and together; we can find new solutions, combining ancient ways and modern means.

And even if you have consciously chosen Love, know that fear and resistance will always come up, especially when you take new action. We are navigating unknown territory. The only way is through, and what you resist persists. So allow all the e-motions (energy in motion), feel every last bit of it and you will find that they move through you and dissipate fairly quickly. Focus on your breath and on being in your body, which makes you present and, instead of asking why you feel this way, accept that it is what it is and allow it (asking why, trying to work out who is to blame or how to control the outcome puts you in victim space)

Often, the emotions you feel are not even yours. We pick up energy from all around us and if you are highly sensitive, you can even pick up your neighbours feelings & thoughts. If you don't let them move through you into the Earth, you end up having to process them through your physical body.

The past IS gone, however, we do have the opportunity to start again and influence our realities to create the world that we want to live in. A New Earth that is kinder, more humane, honours sovereignty, with the Divine Feminine taking her rightful place. We have preparing for this time through the fast track of Ascension we have been on since 2000 and there is a growing, collective desire to re-invent ourselves through a re-connection to self and Gaia.

The best thing we can do right now is to rise above the stories we tell ourselves and re-member we live in an energetic universe and everything is energy. The more empowered you are, the more access you have to the awareness of your personal free will. The more you can come from a place of choice, the less issue you will have with moving forward.

We have moved out of the age of Pisces and the Patriarchal era, where power-over, competition, and lack & scarcity consciousness dominated the mass consciousness. We are currently ushering in the Aquarian age, the Golden era of collaboration, where unique gifts are honoured and sacred prosperity, harmony, and ease & flow are possible.

I don't say any of this lightly; I have dedicated many years to practicing, mastering and embodying the art of Ascension Alchemy AKA deep inner transformation and healing. I now hold sacred space to guide and support other wounded healers, leaders and Light warriors, as they journey within to find their own answers and heal past wounds.

I know what it is like to feel lost, overwhelmed and disconnected. I have been out of alignment with my truth, my soul, my Divine purpose and my personal power. I have been manipulated and I have manipulated in my quest to know who I am.

I have shrunk and held myself back to make others more comfortable, given away my power in order to receive love. I have compromised my dreams, taken care of others before myself and self sacrificed when my inner critic told me I wasn't good enough.

I have also had the courage to say NO MORE and have transformed toxic relationships, filled with co-dependency, expectation and obligation. I have broken through layer upon layer of distortion and Patriarchal conditioning to heal my wounds of Love. I have retrieved and integrated traumatised soul fragments stuck in abuse and betrayal from this and past lives. I have stood my ground before psychic attacks and healed ancestral programs. It's an ongoing journey for all of us as we venture into the unknown.

So how can we, as inter-dependant, sovereign individuals flow with the Universal energies consciously to raise our vibrations, let go of the past and become part of the solution?

Here are some of my key realisations from my journey with an invitation to take what resonates with you and leave the rest:

1. SOMETHING GREATER THAN US IS GUIDING OUR LIVES

Perhaps the greatest distortion we have been taught is that God is outside of us. We are sparks of the Divine, privileged to be experiencing an Earth-Walk at this time. The truth is "God resides in me, as me." Our god-self can be found in our hearts and is the real Source of our prosperity. After all, everything outside of us begins from within.

Be aware that your choices have consequences for others and our Planet, so make your decisions responsibly.

Be congruent with your spoken word too. Our bodies and The Universe hears everything we say, out loud and to ourselves.

2. WE CANNOT CONTROL WHAT HAPPENS, ONLY HOW WE PERCEIVE, EXPERIENCE, AND RESPOND TO IT

As we spiral through the polishing wheel of Ascension, we remember and then fall back asleep. It takes conscious awareness and curiosity to lean into the unknown, do the clearing & healing work and then anchor into higher dimensions until it becomes your new normal.

3. YOUR DESIRES LIVE WITHIN YOU FOR A REASON AND ARE POSSIBLE

They stem from your blueprint and you already have everything you need within you to live the life you know you are meant for. Trust and surrender to Divine Timing. Allow your hope and your faith in your highest potential destiny to draw you forward.

4. ONLY YOU CAN SHIFT YOUR INNER WORLD AND THEREFORE YOUR PROJECTION

So many fear going within, yet inner work is profoundly liberating. Having done hundreds of Inner Alchemy healing sessions (my own and for clients), I can share that the things we fear the most, come from being wounded and underneath all fear, is the fear of death.

I encourage you to do something daily to build prosperity consciousness and energetic strength. For me, its daily Kundalini yoga, energy clearing and listening to high vibrational podcasts. Dancing, shaking, singing and, replenishing yourself in nature work a treat too.

5. KEEP YOUR EYES ON YOUR OWN PATH OR YOU WILL BE WALKING SOMEONE ELSE'S

You have to take ownership of your path by taking a stand for your life and your dreams, especially as women in the post Patriarchal society. No more blaming and shaming others for how they make you feel or how they treat you. Stand firm in your Yeses and No's and you will find that when you respect yourself, others respect you too.

6. THE OLD WAYS ARE CRUMBLING & ARE NO LONGER SUPPORTED

We have been brought up in the Patriarchy, which replaced intuition and discernment with imprints of competition, judgement, separation and control. These are the key wounds that we are healing from. The Divine Feminine principles are being re-established and we are called to look at our personal relationships, what we really value, and who we are becoming on the New Earth.

Consciously or unconsciously, we all have imprinted distortions and wounds of love. These are all the spiritual bypassing, abandonment, denial, betrayal and persecution issues we have all experienced to a greater or lesser degree.

For a comparison chart on navigating the New Earth energetics, see the 1st link in my BIO.

7. MAKE PEACE WITH DEATH

We go through many cycles of birth, death and rebirth during our lives. We come in with a blueprint of our purpose & mission under a veil of forgetfulness. As we grow, social conditioning and our experience of the world are imprinted onto us, often subconsciously.

When we recognise we are experiencing this Earth Walk as a chapter of our soul's journey and accept death as a transition where we drop these physical bodies, it helps us keep the game of life in perspective and live more fully. See death is a door, rather than a wall.

8. HEALING IS AN INSIDE JOB AND BEST DONE WITH SACRED SUPPORT

It's almost impossible to see our own blind spots and we all need support to build our energetic calibre and boundaries. Working with trusted, empowered healers to hold safe & sacred space for us, allows us to process our wounds of Love and heal to wholeness.

There always needs to be an energy exchange, so get paid support. There is only so much we can process ourselves and eventually your friends will avoid you if you are constantly taking your drama to them in the hopes they will have your answers. We all need a safe port in a spiritual storm, some-one you can trust to hold Sacred space for you that is pure enough to not let their stuff get in the way of your process.

The whole point of the healing journey is to remember who you are and, when you free yourself from the fear matrix, you are able to experience your personal Heaven on Earth.

Be aware that as you move from the shadows into the Light of Love, the dark will try to bring you down and hold you back. It will show up in your family and friends, often within your intimate partnership, as resistance.

There may come a time when you have to go it alone by keeping your desires and plans to yourself until they are fully energised and becoming manifest.

This is when your energetic boundaries and healing energy work is most important. All of this is happening so that you STAND YOUR GROUND and align to the higher frequencies of Love, and so that your projection is one of love, freedom & sacred sovereignty.

9. LOVE IS NOT WHAT WE THINK IT IS

As we rise out of the lower frequencies of blame, shame, guilt & disappointment, we must move through the gateway of self-love and acceptance to align with the higher frequencies of joy, pleasure, bliss and prosperity. Make self-love your priority by filling your own cup first and taking care of others from the overflow.

I discovered that the all encompassing, unconditional Love that many of us are searching for, is not found in a romantic partner or another. It is found in our Divinity. It is our direct connection to the Source of all that is. If you think about it, we come from Love and we go back to Love. That is the love we have disconnected from when we feel isolated and alone. When you are connected to your inner Godself and filled with pure, unconditional Love, it radiates from you as a glow of joyful bliss. As a bonus, you are connected to your inner GPS and look and feel ageless.

10. WE GET WHAT WE FOCUS ON

With so many of our beliefs stemming from our cultural conditioning, it pays to re-evaluate everything and make new choices as you awaken.

Habits become patterns. Patterns become programs. Programs control us.

The easiest way to upgrade your life is to disrupt and then delete old programs that no longer serve. Replace old, harmful addictions with new good habits that reach a tipping point at 40 days and become your new normal.

One of the best shifts I made a few years ago was to change the measure of my success from money to joy. Because Joy is the most magnetic force in the Universe, and, when you are blissfully magnetic, you cannot avoid your highest potential destiny or your purpose for being here. The good news is, it is always something you love to do.

When you find joy in what you do, the money will always follow. This allows you to find harmony in your sacred square of prosperity (the 4 most important things to us – health, wealth, love/relationships and fulfilment)

On the New Earth, our unique gifts are needed now more than ever and, in a love-based reality, we get to live the life we are meant for.

* * *

THREE THINGS you can do right now to up-level your life:

1. THE MAGIC IS IN THE SUBTLETIES

When you quieten your mind, you discover that you can trust yourself and your body to know what to do in the moment.

Your immediate home space is a direct reflection of your inner landscape and visa versa. Keep it clean, organised and uncluttered. Bring in beauty and luxury wherever possible, even if all you can afford is a few flowers from the garden or a great smelling soap.

My beloved Mum always said that you can only do what you can do. You have to start with where you are and with what you have right now. And it is true; how you do one thing is how you do everything. If you take care of the little things with presence, the big things take care of themselves.

Focus on bringing calm and presence to everyday activities. I learned how to be present in the shower many years ago, washing my body with gratitude that I had arms to hug people and legs to move me around. It allowed me to move from meeting to meeting with full presence in my corporate CEO era. To this day, every time I step into the shower, I imagine the water is white gold pouring into my Crown chakra cleansing me internally and externally.

Find magic in day-to-day activities. For example: when I put laundry into the washing machine, I think about how the water swishing around is cleansing the energy on that side of the house; the family corner if you follow Feng Shui. Then, I put on a high vibrational audio, often Eckhart Tolle, sit on the bed and fold the laundry, imagining rainbow light coming out of my hands energising the clothes.

If I have a tricky situation where I feel blocked or stuck. I'll stop what I am busy with and go and do something mundane like vacuum a room or clean out a drawer. That action in the physical shifts your energy field and more times than not, by the end of the task, I know exactly what to do next.

2. RECONNECT TO SELF

Make time to connect to the deepest part of you and your inner guidance. All of your answers are already within you. Be unafraid to discover the depths of your own Being coming to life.

Spend some time working out what values you hold dear. What is important to you? Then, love yourself enough to be firm on your Yeses, what feels right and remember, *'No!'* is a full sentence.

Ask yourself powerful questions and journal the answers. Here are a few examples to get you started:

Who would I BE if I trusted that life was happening FOR me and not TO me?

If time and money wasn't a consideration, what are my grandest secret desires?

If I loved and accepted who I am, free from guilt, shame or judgement, how would I craft my life?

What would happen to my personal magnetism if I could trust that my life was moving in the direction of positive personal evolution and I got out of my own way?

If every hardship and wound of Love I have ever experienced, has brought me to this exact moment, what and who do I need to forgive so that I can give myself permission to move forward and THRIVE?

What does the most empowered, courageous, version of me look like?

3. RECONNECT TO GAIA

Remember that we are all Gaian and are affected by the Galactic progressions.

Make a positive contribution to Gaia and all of her creatures by recycling, making your own compost to feed the soil and growing organic food.

The signs and symbols are everywhere and everything in your space is a reflection of you and your energy. Get out into the natural world as often as possible and slow things down so you can notice the birds, animals & vegetation. They all have messages for you. Gaia will show you all you need to know about your current circumstances if you take the time to notice.

In closing, I'll leave you with the inspired words of Mike Heron:

May the Long-time Sun shine upon you,
   All Love surround you,
   And the pure light within you,
   Guide your way on.

ABOUT THE AUTHOR

Taste the nectar of life again.

Peta Panos is an Ascension Alchemist & Multi-dimensional Healing Journeys expert. She spent 21 years in the South African tourism industry where she successfully turned around 2 businesses and amalgamated 13 businesses into one, using soulful Conscious Creation and her gift of being able to see into the core of energetic blocks.

Founder of Spiritual Quest Journeys and Crafted Coaching, she now helps Highly Sensitive Empaths on their Divine Feminine healing journey to sovereignty through private deep-healing sessions, various programs and multi-dimensional healing journeys & retreats.

Amongst other qualifications, Peta is a Reiki Master; certified Intuitive alignment Coach; Divine Living Academy Alumnus, and is devoted to the mystical Priestess of the Rose path. She has been featured in many publications, including Soul & Spirit; The Mystic Way; Dujour; and Trekity. She is also a regular guest speaker on Transformational Travel and Ascension Alchemy.

Website: *www.spiritualquestjourneys.com*
and *www.craftedcoaching.com*
Facebook: *www.facebook.com/peta.panos*
Instagram: *www.instagram.com/petapanos*
Further Reading: *www.spiritualquestjourneys.com/blog/ascending-to-the-new-earth-navigating-these-times-of-change*

RACHE MOORE

ELEMENTAL ALCHEMY & INTUITIVE WISDOM

You are an exquisitely elemental being, grounded by earth, moved by water, empowered by fire, inspired by air and connected beyond your wildest dreams by the fifth element of ether.

Imagine you could glimpse into the future without ever leaving the present moment, and consequently make wise and wonderful life decisions with conviction and clarity to best serve yourself and the planet. You'd gain precious time and the ability to discern; you'd conserve vital energy, and save valuable resources and possibly heartache as well.

I have good news, we human beings have the sensitivity to do exactly this, to awaken our elementality, to strengthen our intuition, and hold unwavering faith in our senses' abilities (sensibility) to inform our choices so we can create greater impact based on our core values.

My name is Rache Moore, and I'm here to remind you of your exquisite true nature, awaken your innate wisdom, and arouse your senses so you can connect more deeply to your internal compass and your divine guidance, to ultimately create the life of your dreams.

We live in wild and wonderful times of boundless possibilities and endless choice. As a result, one of our greatest challenges is making wise decisions with clarity and confidence, we find ourselves overwhelmed and confused by the infinite array of options.

The cliché is true: the answers are right there in front of you, awaiting within, not just within yourself but within the elements of nature, who have become my greatest allies on the path to living my purpose with passion, grace, and ease.

As a spiritual mentor and empowerment coach, I've devoted the past twelve years to studying and teaching elemental alchemy, strengthening intuitive guidance and cultivating unshakable love, influenced by modern mysticism, contemporary ritual, yoga, dance, and holistic wellness to help thousands of men and women celebrate the beauty of being an equanimous human.

Now more than ever we, as individuals and a collective, need tools and practices to empower our choices and keep us inspired, discerning, grounded, and adaptable. So what can we do to strengthen our faculties? We can learn how to feel our intuition, fortify our senses, and reconnect to the wonder and wisdom of the natural world for greater perspective, and a renewed sense of belonging and direction.

THE GIFT OF ADVERSITY IS GROWTH

Spiritual awakening is not usually a choice, but rather the result of circumstance. Like many others, my awakening was triggered by great adversity; I developed an autoimmune disease at age 33, and in my struggle and search for guidance it was inner strength, intuition, and the wisdom of nature that saved me, by exposing myself and examining life under a new lens, revealing new ways to perceive my situation and make informed, empowered choices with clarity and courage.

Those empowered choices were the catalyst for me becoming the woman I am today, living my dream with courage and passion to help others fall madly in love with life, reclaim a sense of belonging, and return to wholeness. But before I could teach it, I had to learn it and live it myself.

It was winter 2009 in New York City when I was diagnosed with the autoimmune disease, rheumatoid arthritis. I was managing a fantastic cocktail bar at NYC's Ace Hotel, a sensational whiskey-infused hipster haven, and like most New Yorkers, I was burning the candle at both ends, working until sunrise, partying in warehouses, and pushing my body beyond its means.

I didn't realise it, but this diagnosis would lead to a radical and inspirational reinvention of myself and also catalyse my greatest love affair, with life and myself. I won't go on about the first 18 months of trauma, pain, insane amounts of meditation and painkillers or monthly tests for blindness and other side effects of the pharmaceuticals.

What I will share is how I became my first successful client by returning to nature, listening to the subtle messages of my body, turning inward to consult my intuition, and thus shifting my perspective from victim to visionary.

DISCOVERING THE WILL TO THRIVE

In my time of need I began seeking guidance from the only religion I'd ever known, nature. I'd always viewed the universe as the ultimate expression of divinity, so I began observing the flow of nature, how the elements of earth, water, fire, air, and ether exist in balance and harmony with life.

Nature puts life into perspective and simplifies our human trivialities and self imposed stress by reminding us we are magnificent, and part of something exquisite, grand and divine.

As I studied the elements I began to see how they relate to the five senses and subtle bodies, playing within the human body in similar ways as they did in nature. I realised that the beauty, wisdom, and qualities within the elements also resided within myself, and thus began the effortless reinvention of myself in the most magnificent ways.

Through our greatest challenges we discover our strengths and each test in this life is an opportunity to re-evaluate our personal trajectory and evolve by making choices that empower us.

Turning to the elements for guidance in these pivotal and challenging moments is simply tuning into ourselves:

- Our earth qualities strengthen us within.
- Our water qualities remind us to trust, let go, and flow.
- Our fire qualities empower us to discern and set boundaries.
- Our air qualities inspire us to open our heart and clearly speak our truth.

- Our ether qualities invite us to open to our higher, creative intelligence and intuitive wisdom.

When we understand this, we actually begin to see the hurdles of life as golden opportunities to accept what is with grace, to grow from the experience, and to continue to move with the ebb and flow of life.

One does not need to suffer or experience tragedy in order to spiritually awaken or strengthen intuition, however one does need the will, not only to survive, but to thrive in this lifetime, and, as I discovered, this is a driving force like no other.

Initially the doctors implied I'd eventually be crippled and there was nothing I could do aside from medicate, so naturally, I trusted their opinions, surrendered my characteristic lust for life, and went about becoming this new version of myself.

Very quickly I found myself losing connection with myself, aside from resentment and despair there was very little communication between my mental, emotional and physical body.

I felt disempowered, uncertain, anxious, and relying on my pharmaceutical pills for any hope of remission. Instead of cultivating my vital energy, I had given my power away and faith was replaced by fear because I didn't think there was an alternative.

It was 18 months into my journey when I became aware of my true relationship to the disease and its symptoms, realizing my unhealthy and unconscious attachment to victimhood and the resulting energetic depletion.

I decided to change my relationship with my body and learn how to listen again, to love and accept my disease as part of my whole being. I observed the thoughts and words I used, rewriting my story and reclaiming my power by taking full responsibility for the situation.

The biggest shift occurred when thoughts were calm and intuitive guidance came through, which told me to try a more holistic approach to treatment. This decision immediately shifted my perspective from the fear driven backseat to the faith driven front seat, taking hold of the wheel to lovingly steer my life back on track.

By acknowledging I was creating my reality with every thought and word that passed my lips, I realised I had to change the narrative, trust in myself and begin a new chapter!

INTUITION IS THE UNIVERSE WHISPERING TO OUR SOUL

My reinvention began with researching and commencing herbal medicine, followed by an inspired self care regime of meditating and practicing yoga daily, studying mysticism, and practicing daily personal rituals for healing, love, and empowerment, all guided by the cycles of nature and ancient earth wisdom.

It is now more than ten years since I was diagnosed and I am more fulfilled and joyful than ever, and now teach the very same healing arts and holistic practices to enable my clients to wake up grateful, joyful and grounded every day, trusting in the wisdom of nature and intuitive guidance from within.

As a species, we have lost our sensibility. We no longer rely on our intuition and senses to survive; we have become soft in this sense, detached from our acute ability to perceive the world around us with extra sensory ability.

However, the tides are changing and there is an awakening. We are hearing the cries of the natural world and coming to our senses, remembering our true nature, and reclaiming our sense of belonging.

I believe intuition is the universe whispering to our soul, guiding us home so we can be of the greatest service to ourselves, our communities and our planet so we might restore harmony and balance. It all starts within.

Self-awareness is the key to unlocking intuition and consulting our internal compass before making decisions; it mitigates the risk of blindly following the influence of others without discernment or careful consideration.

I encourage everyone to invite the wisdom of their body to rise and be heard, to question everything, and confer with yourself as a priority in times of great challenge and, most importantly, never abandon the will to heal and drive to thrive, for these are the most powerful medicines on earth.

We don't see the world the way it is.
We see it the way we are, so let's be enchanted.

Embarking on the journey of self-discovery is incredibly rewarding, however it is not for the faint of heart, or weak of character.

It is for the courageous, who recognize there is more to life than day-to-day doldrums and doctrines; it is for the curious, who yearn for enchantment to amplify their senses and know life more intimately; and it is for the modern mystics, who are awakening to the wonder, wariness, and wisdom within themselves and the waking world.

We don't see the world the way it is, we see it the way we are, and this understanding forms the basis of my psychology, teachings, and life philosophy. It's simply a matter of perspective. To see, feel, and trust the magic of life as a true reflection of oneself is to replace the judgemental and limiting self with one of potential and possibility.

It's no secret that humans tend to forget that, in our essence, we are nature, and remembering this truth helps us reclaim a sense of belonging to something mysterious, magnificent, and divine. This knowledge strengthens intuitive wisdom, because we can scientifically grasp that we are connected to something so much greater than our earth-bound body and it's limitations.

Whilst not everyone is ready to redefine themselves and pull back the veils of comfortable complacency, we can all benefit from activating our senses to enhance our ability to perceive life and its endless challenges in new and insightful ways. Intuition enables us to be moved by life.

This divine guidance can be referred to as our higher selves, that part of us that is not separate from others, but unified with clarity and purpose. Those with strong intuition gain the insight to discern and determine the higher path, one that will best serve themselves, their loved ones, their community, and the planet.

Let's face it, as a race we've collectively passed the point of irresponsible consumption and now realise we need to be of service... if not now, then when? If not us, then who? For some people, tuning into the higher self for guidance can be done intuitively without effort, however for most, it is achieved best through meditation, mindfulness, and stillness so we can sense intuitive wisdom.

So let's briefly explore what intuition is and look at ways we might come to know it better. Firstly, it is a body sensation, from a subtle feeling in the tummy to an overwhelming impulse washing the entire body, and like anything we choose to exercise, it strengthens the more we use it.

Intuition is felt and heard rather than thought and cognised in the brain. It is awakened not by thinking, but by activating our senses to perceive the world around us, then creating stillness and space to receive and comprehend with an expanded, universal awareness.

Working with the elements of earth, water, fire, air, and ether is an effective and accessible way to strengthen intuition because it awakens wisdom within the body, revealing aspects of one's physical, emotional, energetic, mental, and spiritual-self that otherwise remain a mystery.

Personally, the impact of what I refer to as Elemental Alchemy, has been so profound that I've devoted much of my time to teaching others how to use it as a process of personal transformation for strengthening intuition, and discovering the beauty and wisdom within nature, whilst simultaneously realising the same divine qualities reside within oneself.

People can spend their entire lives unwittingly trapped by limiting thoughts and beliefs, following the logical direction of the mind without any consideration for the wisdom within nature and the human body and its extraordinary potential for sensory perception.

They say the longest (and shortest) journey we ever make is from the head to the heart and Elemental Alchemy illuminates that pathway with practices and principals that will guide you towards unequivocally trusting the whispers of your soul and guidance of nature.

WHAT IS ELEMENTAL ALCHEMY?

Elemental Alchemy is an invitation to remember one's magic, beauty, grace, and deep connection to nature. Alchemy is the process of purification and it occurs when we deepen our relationship with nature by learning how to empower, inspire, and heal our relationships with ourselves, others, and our environment.

Weaving ancient earth wisdom and modern mysticism, the process explores how the five elements are teachers in the school of life, supporting our evolution with tangible and relevant teachings to strengthen intuition with confidence, grace, and ease.

The act of listening to our intuition indicates we have faith in divine guidance, wisdom beyond our own mind. In following subtle guidance from the universe, it shows that we are willing to open the cage of limiting beliefs, go beyond the illusion of individuality, and expand into the vastness of unity.

Placing our trust in intuitive guidance is having faith in what we cannot see and choosing the mystery and unseen over the limitations of what's presented with our eyes alone. This is the mindset of freedom.

If you feel you're ready to explore new ways of showing up in life each day, to discover new layers of beauty within and around you, and to effortlessly reinvent yourself, the first step is completely and wholeheartedly accepting yourself, exactly as you are, right here, right now, the very moment you're reading these words, without exception.

Once you enter a state of unconditional acceptance, you are ready to expand your perception of who you are, opening new pathways to dance through life, feeling supported by the world around and within, guided by your intuition.

Our senses are the filters through which we perceive and understand the world around and within us. As we practice making our senses acute and strengthen our intuition, we are deepening our individual comprehension of life, developing both a sense of clarity and unity, a true spiritual meaning to existence.

This is why the process is called awakening; we suddenly become aware of a new way of being, as if previously asleep or in a haze from the incessant cloud of thought and distraction.

Developing our relationship with the elements strengthens our intuition in an effective, simple, yet sophisticated manner by heightening our five senses. Each element governs one of our five senses and is also the vitalising force of our physical, emotional, energetic, mental, or spiritual bodies. When we balance, harmonise, and strengthen the subtle bodies and senses, our intuition is naturally enriched and enhanced.

RITUAL SPEAKS IN A LANGUAGE OLDER THAN WORDS

Words and knowledge can only teach us so much; they exist in the mind and on paper. So, in order to develop our elemental wisdom and intuitive prowess, we must personally experience how the elements exist and play within us, using the practice of meditation or ritual.

Ceremony and ritual have been used by indigenous cultures since the dawn of time to celebrate occasions, to conduct rites of passage, and to transcend thought into the subconscious, or an altered state. Try these simple ritual meditations to develop your relationship with each element, amplify the senses and develop intuitive wisdom.

EARTH RITUAL MEDITATION - FOR STABILITY, STRENGTH, & VITALISING THE PHYSICAL BODY

Use essential oils, flowers, and incense to activate the sense of smell whilst visualising roots connecting you to the Earth.

Take five deep breaths, focusing on the base of your spine, or your root chakra as you inhale to connect and ground to the earth.

WATER RITUAL MEDITATION - FOR TRUST, GRACE, ACCEPTANCE, & VITALISING THE EMOTIONAL BODY

Use cacao or tea to activate the sense of taste and take a bath or shower, or simply visualise yourself stepping under a cleansing, crystal clear waterfall.

As you connect to the water, allow all that is to flow through you: emotions, love, and fear, trusting that the art of allowance will ensure everything will fall into place. Use the exhale to release, renew, and let go.

FIRE RITUAL MEDITATION - FOR TRANSFORMATION, CONFIDENCE, & VITALISING THE ENERGETIC BODY

Light a candle or small fire to release into the flames what no longer serves you and create space for something new to be born, activating the sense of sight by visualising your transformed state.

See it in your mind's eye and be sure to hold the feeling of inspired transformation in your chest and solar plexus.

AIR RITUAL MEDITATION - FOR INSPIRATION, CLARITY, AND VITALISING THE MENTAL BODY

Outside, connect to the breeze, inside connect to your breath. Activate your sense of touch by becoming acutely aware of the air on your skin; is it warm, or cool?

Take 7 deep breaths, slowly inhaling, and exhaling completely, using breath to calm the body and bring clarity to the mind. Use the seven seed mantras for each chakra to amplify this ritual (Lam, Vam, Ram, Yam, Ham, Om, silence)

ETHER RITUAL MEDITATION - FOR DIVINE GUIDANCE, CONNECTION TO SOURCE, AND VITALISE THE SPIRITUAL BODY

Sitting with a straight spine, allow the energy to flow up from your root as you inhale to your crown, then as you exhale, flowing from the crown to the stars.

Visualise yourself as an energetic conduit between earth and sky, drawing wisdom from the earth to your heart and connecting to divine intelligence through your crown.

Activate your sense of hearing by becoming acutely aware of sounds around you and listen to life with your entire being.

The meaning of life is to grow, so your only purpose is to create a nourishing space within your mind, body, life, and heart to flourish, thrive and be of service to yourself, your loved ones, and this planet. You are one in eight billion, reclaim your sense of belonging, your exquisite and unique beauty, and return to wholeness.

ABOUT THE AUTHOR

Rache Moore is an empowerment coach and spiritual mentor, and founder of Rainbow Tribe and Online Elemental Academy.

She inspires conscious professionals and modern mystics to strengthen their intuitive wisdom, reclaim a sense of belonging, and effortlessly reinvent themselves so that they can return to wholeness and equanimity with confidence, grace, and ease.

Rache has worked with thousands of men and women for over twenty years as a global event producer and urban ceremonialist, using her expertise in healing arts, ancient earth wisdom, and modern mysticism, facilitating transformational events, contemporary rituals, and courses in self-discovery to enable them to experience deeply enriched and harmonious lives.

Her clients come to her to learn how to strengthen their intuitive wisdom so that they can reconnect with their joy, feel energized, create harmony and balance within, and celebrate the beauty of being human.

Website: www.rachemoore.com
and www.rainbowtribe.com
Facebook: www.facebook.com/rainbowtribeevents
Email: rache@rainbowtribe.com
Instagram: www.instagram.com/rainbowtribe_

SANDRA SUAREZ DOMINGUEZ

SOUL JOURNEYS: DEEPEN THE CONNECTION TO YOUR LUMINOUS INNER WISDOM

Why are soul journeys so important, and what can they provide for you? Actually, you might be thinking soul journey? What the heck is that? And why would I even want one?

Well to explain it to you in depth, it would be best if I tell you a little about me and my story in hopes that it will resonate with you in some way. It just might light a way for you and this journey we call life.

My whole entire life I have always been connected to my intuition. It's just I didn't have a name for it. Growing up in my family, one of the main things that we were taught was that you don't talk to your spirit!

Why? Because it's a terrible thing to do! Being in my Hispanic family, it was just not normal to listen to your spirit. But for some reason, not listening to my intuition just felt weird. I always felt like something was missing.

There were so many "deja vu" moments growing up that I couldn't explain. I've felt deep emotions and I always knew what people were thinking, but couldn't figure out why. This caused A LOT of conflicts for me and within me.

All I knew was that there was something wrong. Every time I didn't listen to the voice of my spirit, mayhem ensued. But when I did, things would just go smoothly. It was as if, magically, life was perfect.

It was becoming crystal clear that when I wasn't paying attention to my spirit, something was definitely off and chaos appeared. I needed to figure out what was happening. But how?

As time passed, I decided that I needed to make a decision. I left that decision within my heart and finally committed to myself and my growth. Then one day (8 years ago to be exact), I was at a craft store and I had a lovely woman helping me with my material order.

I took my time touching every cloth and its texture, asking myself "Does it feel good? Does it make my heart happy?" I was now in a place in my life where I was asking myself these types of questions, and this lovely young woman had so much patience.

Being in her presence made me feel calm and happy. Her boss asked her to come help someone else since he noticed she was spending way too much time with me.

A young man came closer to me and all of a sudden I felt a trembling movement within my body. I literally felt my entire body convulsing, but physically I was standing still. I looked around me and noticed everyone else looked okay. It was only me.

I finally realized that this energy that was causing me to shake internally was coming from the young man, who was helping me with my order. It was freaking me out, so I just left the store. As soon as I stepped outside my body started to go still. I instantly felt an inner calm and heard the words, "It's time to dive deeper."

As I looked around to see who said that, I realized that it was my spirit because there wasn't anyone there but me. So I just ran to my car and tried to recall everything that had just happened. What the heck was this? Was I dreaming? No, I was wide awake.

My intuition told me that I'd gotten the call to dive deeper and my spiritual awakening began to unfold.

As I began my journey, I realized I needed to find the answers to my questions. Like: What was all of this trying to show me? Who could I ask? Where should I even begin?

But I realized that my parents and family members were not going to be of any help to me. So I had to find other people who could. But who was going to help me?

And where was I going to find these people? Instantly I decided to ask the one person I grew up with because he knows everything: God. Who else could I talk to without being judged?

So I asked him: What on earth is happening to me and who can help me figure it all out? I asked Him to please send me the right people who can help me figure it out and guide me to what it is that I am meant to do next.

And because #godhasjokes, I kid you not, everything and everyone began to show up in my life.

I learned that what I was feeling, seeing, learning, and hearing was because I was an intuitive empath. Finally, a name for it. I was guided to a beautiful soul, who helped me dive deeper into my intuition, my purpose, and my gifts.

I learned that the more I dove into my stories, the more these invisible shackles would appear. These were shackles that I've *ALLOWED* consciously or unconsciously to be placed upon me or that were placed on my soul from other lifetimes.

The deeper I dove into these stories, the more I was peeling back the layers like an onion so my soul could be fully expressed to be who she is meant to be.

In one of my sessions I had with my mentor, it became abundantly clear that I needed to forgive and heal a specific story. This story was about my ex-husband, who had physically, sexually, and emotionally abused me. I was being asked to forgive him and myself for all that transpired between us.

The first thing I asked was: WHY? Why did I need to look at this story? I hadn't thought about this person in like a hundred years. But I was told it was necessary because it was hindering me in such a big way. It was affecting ALL of my relationships, my marriage, my work, and especially my prosperity.

So I took a deep breath and told myself that I could do this. But deep within my chest there was sharp pain that became present. Oof! My chest was killing me. I knew right then and there that this was a story I really needed to take a look at.

In my healing session, I was asked to bare my soul. To be vulnerable, honest, and raw. I asked for help from my higher self because I was scared of what was going to happen. Then all of a sudden, I saw a whole crew of my female ancestors come forward to support me through this process.

Row after row of women who were grateful for my bravery, thanking me for releasing and healing from this story that had been present lifetime after lifetime.

My River Goddess and my Grandmother (two beautiful guides who walk with me in this lifetime), showed up to help me heal this experience. This attachment, this story, has held me back from fully owning my spiritual gifts, from manifesting, from having healthy relationships and a happy life.

In my mind's eye I was taken into a huge sunflower, where my grandmother and my River Goddess went around and around my body, removing these invisible shackles that were placed upon me.

My heart chakra began to open up and poured out these old dark wounds and the healing began. They started removing these old chords, these roots that seem to be embedded within my chest.

Over and over again my ancestors held me in prayer, singing while my grandmother and my River Goddess would gently touch my heart, my back, my hands, and my feet, throwing everything into a violent fire. I was held within utter love and compassion.

When it was all complete and done, each one of my ancestors stood in front of me, gave me a hug and a gift, and touched my third eye. At the end of this session I could literally feel a tenderness in my chest. I was tired, exhausted, but felt a weight lifted off me.

I thanked each and every light being that helped me through this healing. It was such an intense session, but I was grateful for my mentor at the time, for her love and guidance through this process. I was emotionally and physically exhausted.

The next day I woke up feeling sick and achy. I had this pain in my chest. But I reminded myself that I had just had this huge healing session, so it was normal.

The following day, my chest pain continued. I just allowed myself to move through it, telling myself, "It's all part of the process." But the pain was getting worse, so I called my doctor, who told me to come in. I was diagnosed with pneumonia.

Checking in with my intuition, I was told that this was all part of the healing process, expressed in physical reality. Those attachments, those roots, that had lived within my heart space in all of my ancestors' lives, lifetime after lifetime, had finally been cleared.

Through all lifetimes, through my generational lineage, for all the women who are healing themselves. I was chosen to be the brave one to do this work in this lifetime. God had a bigger plan for me.

So exactly four months later, after all of the pneumonia, who reaches out to me of the blue and sends me a message? Who after 16+years?

Yup, that's right. My ex-husband. I knew it! This was now happening because #Godhasjokes. I couldn't stop laughing. Why? Because this is God's way of testing me to see if I had really healed this story.

Yes, he likes to see if you really healed that story, or if there is more healing that needs to take place. So I texted my ex back and I thanked him for everything that had transpired when we were married.

I wished him nothing but the best, and I blessed his new life and family. I forgave. But the greatest gift I received in return was that there was no attachment to him or this experience.

I was free. There was absolutely nothing. You see, when you no longer have an emotional attachment, there are no triggers. No emotional indicator within your body that something is wrong. It didn't affect me in any way. Nada.

Before, the mere mention of his name would cause my chest to hurt, my stomach to ache, and now, zilch. NADA! That's when you know my friend, that you have fully healed that story. There are NO ATTACHMENTS. #Winning!

God will always send you a lesson several times in your life and that is simply his way of saying: Hey, you see this thing? This thing that I keep showing you? It has shown up three times already. Are you noticing? Yeah, that is what I want you to take a look at. This beautiful soul is how God is asking you to grow.

So since #Godhasjokes, he just had to make sure that I really did heal that story. Two months later, my ex-husband texted me again. I just simply laughed and I thanked God for this gift of growth. I felt nothing and deleted the text message, sending him more blessings and wishing him the best.

I am free. My ancestors, my lineage, are free. I have opened myself to deepening into my purpose. After this healing, my relationships got better. I had solid boundaries. I stopped being a people pleaser and, most of all, I learned to have *RUTHLESS COMPASSION* for myself.

The more I allowed myself to own my purpose, the more my path became clear. I have helped so many beautiful souls to do the same. Healing their stories, guiding them through it, and showing them the way to allowing themselves to live the life that lives within their heart. It is filled with unconditional love, abundance, and prosperity, guided by their divine luminous wisdom.

The more you release these old stories, the more you amplify your gifts, the more you get to create the life you want.

These soul journeys are truly transformational. They give us a look at what we are holding onto, consciously or unconsciously.

They allow you to move through traumas you may have experienced and the self-limiting beliefs that you may be holding on to: the need to micromanage everything around you and the people pleasing tendency that drains you. The doubt you have within yourself.

The lack of self-love that causes you to keep over-giving to others in your life. For some of these reasons, it is necessary to open yourself up to allowing yourself to move through these energetic blocks that keep you stuck in these patterns.

We allow ourselves to take on other people's self-limiting beliefs. We allow other people's judgements to prevent us from moving forward.

My question to you, beautiful soul, is: Aren't you tired? Tired of feeling as if you can't achieve the life you want? Tired of not knowing what to do or where to go next? Tired of the doubt? Of not trusting the process? Trust, beautiful soul, that you will always be guided if you allow yourself to receive it.

To live in unconditional love, abundance, and prosperity, whatever it is that your soul is seeking. It is already yours. Open yourself up to it. You are worthy of the life you want.

You just have to make a decision.

It is your birthright to have a life filled with unconditional love, abundance, and prosperity. I want to take you through a process, a soul journey, that will connect you with your higher self, your inner wisdom.

In this process you will see your higher self and learn what is holding you back, what your next step is, and what your life can look like a year from now if you follow the guidance. So let's begin.

HERE'S what you will need:

- A sacred space. This is a place in your home or office where you can sit and be in silence for a little while. You can create this space with things that you are intuitively aware of or guided to bring into this space.
- Candles, crystals, essential oils, flowers, etc. Whatever it is you need to support you.
- A journal, a pen, and water to drink.

Give yourself a minimum of thirty minutes to go through this soul journey.
**When you are all set and ready let's begin, please know that you will always

receive the messages from your luminous inner wisdom, your higher self. Even if you don't notice anything, you are always receiving all of the messages.**

Go to the link below for your *Soul journey,* to connect with your higher self's luminous wisdom:

www.dropbox.com/s/m1lu1q58p2dfgvq/New%20Chapter% 20meditation%2052020.m4a

Thank you, beautiful soul, for allowing me to share this soul journey with you. I'll end this chapter with this small prayer:

May you always know that you are utterly and completely loved, supported, and protected in your journey in this lifetime.

May God bless you and your family with his unconditional love, health, and prosperity, as it is your birthright to have it.

May you shine your light brightly so that the beautiful souls who are waiting for you and your magic can find you. Be strong, have courage.

Sending you many blessings always.

And so it is. And so we allow it to be. Amen.

ABOUT THE AUTHOR

Share your magic!

Sandra Suarez Dominguez is the creator of Luminous Inner Wisdom: Activating the gateway to your soul. A certified Intuitive Empowerment Coach, Akashic Records Practitioner, Akashic Clearing Practitioner, Warrior Goddess Facilitator, Certified Crystal Healer, Certified Oracle Card Facilitator, Certified Reiki Healer, Shaman Practitioner, mother of two beautiful girls, a domestic violence survivor, ovarian cancer survivor, Sacred Guide, and overall badass spiritual healer.

She's been featured on the *Divine Download* podcast, participated as a speaker in the *Soul Seeker Summit: We're All in this together*, and *Activate your Inner Badass Summit*. She is a believer that everything has a purpose in your life, that God always has a bigger vision for you. She encourages you to trust the process and allow yourself to stay open to receive it — you and your divine guidance is unique to you.

Website: www.luminousinnerwisdom.com
Facebook: www.facebook.com/sradominguez
Email: Sandra@luminousinnerwisdom.com
Instagram: www.instagram.com/sradominguez

SARAH-JANE PERMAN

RECLAIMING YOUR SOVEREIGN FEMININE POWER

The day my womb called me home, the world as I knew it transformed.

Her summoning was urgent and commanding as if the time had come for me to take my position as a guide, to light the way through the chaos that was arriving on Earth. She cracked me open and pulled me into the dark vortex of her inner sanctum, walking me through many initiations of remembrance.

Our reunion was sublime. Heralded by divine feminine guides like Isis, Inanna, and Mary Magdalene, I was gifted with the keys that would awaken my abilities as sovereign woman and New Earth leader. A woman who knows the power of her transmission, the ways of energetic alchemy, and her ability to birth new worlds through the holy portal of her womb.

As I pen these words, my womb is alive and excited to be sharing my story, as a ray of diamond light from my womb to yours. Open your body to receive my words with your whole being and let this passage bring your energy to life. Perhaps you feel a tingle in your sex or a ripple up your spine, a rush of goosebumps as you let these words conjure a recollection of forgotten wisdom. Like a candle flame igniting in the darkness, illuminating truth and showing you the full spectrum of who you are... or at least what you are ready to receive.

* * *

My upbringing was not so "normal," which frustrated me a lot at the time, but now I honour my mystical mother for bringing me up with an eagle (or perhaps galactic) view of life on earth, where channelling the "off-planet frequencies" was the norm and travelling the world to anchor the light and receive the ancient wisdom through our bodies at specific grid points was a part of my education. As I reflect on my wild experiences, exploring Egypt, Israel, Greece, Turkey, and India from a young age, the bigger picture of my path as a living crystal has always been clear.

I have always believed in the infinite possibilities of creation and have easily magnetised my desires, giving me insight into my natural abilities as a master of the inner alchemy of manifestation before I knew it was a thing. However, such magnetism comes with a warning label and the need for responsibility, as whatever you hold in your awareness arrives fast, the good and the challenging.

I often felt like a magician with a new magic wand who had access to so much power, yet a lack of understanding of how to efficiently harness and direct it. This lead to all sorts of intense experiences, including a full short circuit of my being in the form of a kundalini awakening in my early twenties that left me depressed, anxious, and agoraphobic.

I turned to medication and other drugs to cope and suppress these electric waves of Shakti as it was too much to feel all at once in my body. This experience taught me the lesson of grounding. Just as an electrician would install a grounding wire to earth the current, I too had to remember how to plug myself in to stabilise the energy that ran through me.

This is where my womb awakening comes in.

Where so much meditation and spirituality refers to "ascension" and the light, the feminine path is a descent into the darkness of inner/underworld and the mystery school of the body. Connecting with our blood and sexuality, the kundalini serpent of creative life force and our primal nature as wild women of the earth.

Entering the void of the womb can feel ominous, a little like opening Pandora's Box, as we reveal the layers of stories and experiences (some traumatic) that we have gathered in this life and beyond. The residues that keep us locked into patterns of shame, guilt, and repression keeping us from experiencing the full spectrum of our aliveness. The accumulated dross of energetic imprints from memories that block our channel, our energy stagnating, body held in tension, reducing pleasure and the ecstasy that is our birth right.

As we summon the courage to dive in, free falling into her formless depths in full trust, we reconnect to the resonance of the earth womb in her deeply feminine, yin resonance. Beyond the fear, we find the nourishment, replenishment, and grounded safety we seek and the Divine Love of the Mother.

Over my life I had become very good at working with the solar light of the cosmic womb (more yang and masculine) but I had forgotten the depth of the feminine wisdom that lay within me and the Earth. In order to be an efficient New Earth priestess I had to remember how to balance and merge the two polarities, as it is when these two meet that we create high alchemy to birth our visions. So this has become my personal quest and my mission to support my sisters in reconnecting to the grounded, sovereign, self-sourcing power that we all have within us, amplified by the earth and Universal Love.

When I commune with my womb, it's not like they tell you in books; this is my own embodied transmission that is not shaped or distorted by anyone else's experience. And I would expect your process to be different than mine. Mystery school teachings are experiential by nature and only accessible by committing to the inner work that is required, to be embodied rather than intellectualised and over analysed.

My womb shows me truth in sound, sensation, and vision, the vibrational hum that anchors me into the inner sanctum of my body temple. She shows me her cauldron of magic, a dark well of energy to be cultivated and directed at will, growing brighter and stronger everyday with my dedication. Her awakening feels like walking through endless gateways, burning masks of false identities on the ritual fire to reveal my essence. As I soften into her darkness, allowing myself to be held and nurtured as my body so deeply craves, I remember how to receive and ride the waves of her natural cycles.

She smoulders as she comes alive, responding to my curiosity and yearning to be initiated in the mysteries that I have forgotten. To remember the ways of my lifetimes as Rose Priestess, reclaiming the codes that I am here to share through this body as an initiate of the lineage of Sophia. When I bask in the light of Sophia she is the balm to my wounds.

She calls me forth in the purest and fullest expression of who I am, the me who exists across all space time realities and dimensions. As she crowns me with a halo of light, the crown the the Shekinah, and I feel the sweetest recalibration and homecoming and the invitation is always clear; to embody and anchor this new and undistorted light in this now moment on Earth and to share the frequency through my transmission as my contribution to the birthing of the New Earth.

However, let this be my warning to you. This transformational path is not for the faint of heart, as it requires courage to walk the cycle of death and rebirth day in and out. Birthing my son three years ago was another step on the passage of initiation that required me to not only walk close to physical death but also painfully surrender my highly independent and stubborn maiden-self, who kicked and screamed throughout the whole process. But as with all initiations, I am grateful for the experience, as it has dropped me into a more grounded experience of the mature, feminine archetype of Mother.

Why is this so important to this time on planet Earth?

YOU are part of this great Womb Awakening. In this time of birthing the New Earth, we must return to the throne of our sovereign feminine power, the zero point where all life begins, sowing the seeds of our vision in the fertile womb as the weavers of a new reality, returning to the ways of our ancestors, when feminine wisdom was revered before it was hidden and forgotten.

Do not fear that we have deviated too far from our path or suppressed too much of our feminine nature, as she is always here. Like the rushing river of the Great Mystery, no matter how many times we deny her or how many barriers we place in her way, it is her nature to flow.

Every time a woman reconnects to her womb wisdom, she awakens her innate power, as creatrix and medicine woman. She ignites the womb spark of creation that makes everything possible, the only limits to her capacity are the ones constructed by her mind. It is through this reclamation that she is liberated.

This is where I like to play; in the infinite possibilities of creative potential and what we are capable of when we are fully activated, plugged in, and alive. If I can open your mind and facilitate an experience of your magic through your body, then my mission is fulfilled; you will know who you are and what you are capable of, letting go of the need to be so concerned about the micro-unfolding of your life as you have been gifted with the eagle view of the bigger picture.

This does not mean we do not feel emotions and experience upheaval in our lives... oh no! These initiations that make us feel so much are all part of the rich experience of being human; we get to relish in the highs and lows, the full spectrum of life on Earth that we are here to devour. Although, when you can become the observer of your experience without being so drawn into the stories, you maintain your sovereignty. You can be the grounded pillar of calm in the chaos of the storm.

And we are here to be fully expressed and alive!

How do those words feel in your body?

Perhaps you feel an awakening of your sexual energy, your life force that wishes to re-wild you or your inner animal-self that wants you to dance, make love, sweat, and growl, and sound with freedom.

We are here to live a life that is fully expressed in our own way. Does this mean you have to tear apart your "regular" life, dance naked in the forest, live in a tantric temple, and explore polyamory and sex magic rituals? Not at all… unless you want to. This energy can be subtle and expressed your way. It may be unseen yet completely felt as you ripple out into the field like a magnetic wild fire.

Your frequency is everything. This is your blue print, your energetic signature; this is your gift to share with the world. Beyond the identity and the doing, by simply coming alive into the full expression of you. You sexuality, your longing, your voice, your softness, your innocence, and your sovereign power.

It is my greatest wish for all beings to know the power that lies inside and to remember the body as the mystery school temple that holds the keys to experience the magic of what you are.

Your only job is to dive in, to peel back the layers, to remove the masks, to drop the armour that is so heavy to carry. To dissolve the tension you hold in your body, especially your pelvic bowl and your sex. To burn down the walls of our self-imposed cage and open our eyes to the bigger picture, which is so much more beautiful than we can comprehend.

HERE ARE THREE SIMPLE RITUALS TO ASSIST YOU IN YOUR RECLAMATION

Temple Body

Rediscover and honour your body as the temple she is. Lavish her with touch, awakening your earthy sensuality and pleasure. Anoint her with your favourite oils and feed her food that delight your senses. Stand naked in the mirror and see yourself, taking in all parts of your beautiful body and face, embracing your natural form and consciously smiling and sending waves of love to all parts of you: organs, flesh, bones, blood, genitals... every single cell.

Let her move intuitively and freely in her own dance, using somatic movement to release tension and stagnant energy. There are no rules to follow, only listen in and let your body be the guide as you follow the feelings that arise. Give yourself permission to feel and come alive, becoming receptive to your body's signals and sensations.

This practice could look like putting on your favourite music and giving yourself freedom to let yourself go. Exploring different levels of intensity from soft, sensual and flowing like the water, to grounded and earthy, and intense shaking in a fiery, wild woman dance.

Speak your name ("Sarah-Jane come home") out loud to call all parts of you back to your body, especially the parts of you that have been denied or suppressed. Let the movement be your homecoming.

Womb Connection

FIND a comfortable seated (or standing) position where you can feel a connection to the earth and take a deep breathe all the way down to your womb, softening into her warm darkness as you feel yourself begin to fully inhabit your pelvic bowl. Feel or visualise your roots spiralling down and connecting to the centre of the earth (earth womb). Let each inhale draw up the nourishment of the earth energy, filling and rejuvenating your pelvic bowl with life force.

Let your exhales be audible, allowing the primal sound of your womb to be heard and relaxing your jaw, genitals, and pelvic floor with each exhale. Feel each sound remove another layer of tension as you feel the connection between your vocal cords and your pelvic floor, softening and opening your channels in relation and receptivity.

Sense and observe what is alive for you in your womb space. Does she feel shut down and difficult to connect with? Do you feel pain? Or perhaps you can feel the infinite space of the multiverse swirling inside of you in the void of the zero point.

Speak to your womb space, even visualising the goddess of your womb appearing. Open up a conversation with her and ask her if she has a message for you. Feel her longing. Strengthen your connection with her and she will guide you to know your truth in a deeper way.

Creative Awakening

ONCE YOU FEEL CONNECTED to your womb, begin to feel or visualise a flame igniting in the centre of your womb space. It could be as subtle as a candle flame; you feel this flame filling your womb with golden light, noticing how you can amplify and condense the flame with each breath. Cultivate the energy.

Explore how you can rise this energy in your body, breathing it up your central channel with the assistance of a light contraction of the muscles of your genitals/pelvic floor on your inhale and relaxation on your exhale. Notice how you can call the energy up your spine or into specific organs that need to be rejuvenated. If you feel shaking or heat in your body as the energy moves, please know this is normal and that there are many specific techniques to raise your kundalini energy, should you wish to explore them.

Cultivating life force as part of your self-pleasure (or love making) rituals is also very powerful. Instead of making orgasm your goal, as the waves of pleasure begin to arrive, slow down, breathe, and relax. Breathe the orgasmic energy up your central channel to your heart, expanding like a fountain of light through your body.

As you begin to feel even more aroused, envision what it is you wish to create and feel the pleasure that having the desired outcome manifest in your life brings you. Let your orgasm wash through you as your vision is sent out to the cosmic womb to create the seed of new life as you "let go and let God," trusting the Universe to weave its magic. This is one way you can ecstatically birth the new earth.

I hope these rituals are useful for you.

* * *

WHEN I WAS GROWING up in Australia, there was this TV infomercial where this guy called "Tim" would sell all manner of things (like knives that are so sharp they can cut through leather shoes) and right when you thought the deal couldn't get any better, he would say, "But wait, there's more" and then proceed to throw in a set of steak knives. This has stuck with me through my whole life. It is the perfect analogy for the moments when we think we have a handle on who we are and what is going on in this life...

"But wait, there's more..."

And there always is. More pleasure, more abundance, more orgasms, more love, more joy, and more activation. Just when you think you have an idea of who you are, or the magic of this life, you reach a new level of the video game and you up-skill at a rapid rate to play in the new terrain. You tools upgrade along with your frequency as you listen in to receive the next part of the mission.

Now is the time to think and dream bigger, to trust in the sovereign power that lives within us and rise as the creator beings we are. Stepping up as visionaries and activists of love, activating our womb spaces as portals of transmutation to alchemise the distortions of the old paradigm into gold.

I have a crystal clear vision of all of the women of the world, wombs activated, plugged in, turned on and ready to share our unique frequency. Connecting heart to heart and womb to womb, weaving a golden web of light that wraps the world in love. Holding each other in full support as we ecstatically birth the New Earth.

Hold that picture in your mind's eye, and feel it in your body. Feel the powerful part you are playing in this unfolding, via the bounty of gifts and sacred transmission. We are doing it... and can be so proud of your progress.

Stay plugged in. Hold the frequency. This is why we came here.

ABOUT THE AUTHOR

Sarah-Jane Perman is a spiritual catalyst, transmissionary, and agent of awakening, serving women in the remembrance of who they are as sovereign creators of the New Earth. Through her work as Womb Alchemist and feminine embodiment guide, she supports women to reclaim the wisdom of their bodies and liberate their wild, sensual true nature.

A life-long dancer, yoga teacher and shamanic facilitator working with tantra, taoism, somatic embodiment and priestess arts, Sarah-Jane created *Sacred Wom(b)an Mystery School, Wild Goddess Retreats* and online womb initiations to serve as the safe container for women to access the powerful medicine they have to share.

She has facilitated in almost all continents of the world, appearing at festivals like *Wanderlust* and *Bali Spirit Festival*, where she holds powerful sacred space, weaving multidimensional journeys of somatic movement, womb awakening, goddess invocation and shamanic ritual. As a Rose Priestess of the Isis Sophia lineage, she also guides remembrance journeys in Egypt and Glastonbury.

In 2016 she birthed her son and began the humbling and heart expanding journey of becoming Mother + Priestess.

Website: www.sarahjaneperman.com
Facebook: www.facebook.com/yogawithsj
and www.facebook.com/sjperman
Email: jacqstar@sacredsignatures.com

SASHA MOSS

THE INVITATION: TO RECONNECT, REMEMBER & SHINE

Dear beautiful soul, you have journeyed far, and I am so glad to meet you here at this pivotal moment in our collective history!

Undoubtedly, if you have found this book, you too are a soul who is birthing our new earth, creating new systems and shifting consciousness in radical and beautiful ways, even if you don't yet know it!

Your journey is no doubt unique, full of key experiences and transformations that have brought you to this very moment in time and space.

Whether you are in search of something in particular, or drawn by an unknown force to read these words, you perhaps are ready for my invitation: an invitation to embark on a journey of return to yourself, to realign with your feminine essence, to remember and reconnect to your passions, purpose and gifts.

This is a journey which for me, began some twelve years ago and which has seen me embark on a major career shift from lawyer to psychotherapist and coach, facilitating over 200 women's circles and working individually with women across the globe, midwifing the whispers of their soul.

I remember so clearly the day I began this very journey myself. Standing in the lounge room, the wooden floors alive with squealing and frantic toddlers, the late afternoon light was streaming in as we celebrated my nephew's second birthday. Like those two-year-olds, I was bubbling with excitement. Earlier that week we had announced that we were pregnant with our second child.

Fun, love and happiness were rich in the air.

Then it happened.

Time slowed down, and amongst the chaotic din of exuberant toddlers, I became aware of the air around me shifting, enveloping me in a deep peace which took my breath away.

While I had never "heard voices," this was the only way to describe what happened next.

While the party frenzy carried on around me, it was as if a mute button had been pressed – I watched the celebrations carrying on, yet inside was quiet. I heard a gentle, clear, and very strong voice, prepare me with the news that my second baby was not going to make it, or if they did, they would be very unwell at birth. There was no "telling", but rather a transmission of knowing – what I have now grown to know as my own claircognisance. This transmission was so deeply loving, gentle and pure that I did not experience even a second of shock or fear.

I am highly anxious by nature, so this total peace was extraordinary, and for the first time in my life, I felt the difference between fear and intuition. This was an understanding that would alter my way of being in the world forever.

As is often the case, on this journey of awakening, that day in November 2007, I did not know it yet, but my invitation had arrived: an invitation to return to a sacred place in and of me, long buried and unknown. An invitation to acknowledge and open into something much greater than my current existence. But first, I returned to the 'real' world.

I still held within my being this pearl of peace and knowing. I knew it to be so true in my body that I took myself off to the emergency department multiple times. On each occasion, I was equally ecstatic and bewildered to learn that the baby was doing fine. I concluded, happily, that my big, deep experience was no more than a tell-tale sign of an anxious mother and, when we reached the second trimester, I breathed a sigh of relief.

Then, a few weeks later, I had minor spotting and, as any woman in this situation would know, my heart fell, and fear rose within me. I rang my midwife, who reassured me that all was most likely fine – to not worry and to come in the following week for my scheduled appointment. Despite her assurances, this time I knew that something was wrong. So I insisted on an appointment and the next morning my obstetrician confirmed that I was experiencing a miscarriage. The baby had passed

AWAKENING

away and I would need an immediate D&C or else it would become dangerous for my body.

I was numb and grieving, but also I felt so connected to this little soul and the powerful experience of that November evening. As devastated as I felt, I knew so clearly that this was always going to be my journey with this little being.

A very large part of me felt so grateful – I could not at all figure out why – but I knew this was a form of divine intervention, a soul contract fulfilled for a significant reason yet to be unveiled. I awoke from general anaesthetic, still with a gentle grief, but most noticeably I felt a true sense of having given birth and I felt my little one with me so very strongly.

It was one of the most beautiful experiences of my life. Never had I felt so deeply connected to my body, to my intuition and to a greater field of life.

Some weeks later, my obstetrician called to let me know that the baby had died from a non-genetic chromosomal abnormality called Turner's syndrome. He advised that these babies often die in utero and some survive but are very ill at birth – the exact words I had heard some eight weeks earlier.

Miscarriage is one of those things that is so little shared, so little discussed, and I was shocked by the number of women who came forward to tell me about their own, hidden miscarriage journeys.

On top of this, I was experiencing my loss alongside a massive awakening to joy, my soul, my intuition and everything that was happening brought to life within me such a deep sense of faith and grace in my journey, and such fulfillment in my connection to this little soul, that I was grieving in a very different way from the women I was talking to.

There was little space for words such as gift, grace, awe, and love – all of which were so crucial in my experience of this loss, birth and rebirth. As I pondered how to be in this space, I remembered a book I had read many years earlier – one which had changed me deeply – *"A Circle of Stones: A woman's journey to herself"* by Judith Duerk.

In this book Judith magically weaves a web of wonder, which enlivens the divine feminine spirit within every woman, as she asks "How would your life have been different if," you had grown up experiencing the monthly connection and nurturance of a sage women's circle? How would your life have been different if, each month in this circle, you were encouraged to explore who you are, *all* of who you are, and held firmly in the truth of your full power as a woman?

As I re-read her words, my deep yearning for my own women's circle erupted. I too wanted a place where I was held, where I could be supported and to return to myself. A place where I could share this deeply feminine experience of miscarriage that was so personal to me with women who could hold me in it all - the celebration as well as the devastation, the awakening as well as the loss of a dream.

I wanted a space to explore who this new woman was that I was birthing; the new gifts and abilities, the new yearnings for something more, something different, the new needs. What was all of this, what did it mean and where on earth did it fit in my life? I wanted to be connected to other women in this process. I wanted and needed to be witnessed by these yet unknown women, and to have the privilege of witnessing others walking this sacred feminine path also.

So, it was at this very point that I accepted the invitation which had been presented to me some months earlier on that November evening: the invitation to return to myself, to all of me, my forgotten gifts and new desires.

Back in 2008, in a city with relatively few women's circles, I could not find one that was the right fit for me, so I knew I had to create my own. In the years to come, as I completed my Masters in psychotherapy and became certified as women's coach and facilitator, as I deepened my skills as a teacher of meditation and mindfulness and allowed myself to open to my intuitive guidance system, it amazed me how many women responded to my call to join me in sacred space.

I have come to see and feel this, in myself and others, as the highly attuned modern woman's desire for the age old wisdom of the divine feminine, to be present, taught, cherished and nourished in a world system which has not yet allowed them to thrive in the deepest of ways.

I share with you my story, to open a space for you to take up the invitation that is before you now. You wouldn't be reading this book if you weren't ready to do so!

Whether you have arrived here after a very personal experience, like my own, or whether you have been impacted by the collective cracking open of our global consciousness through the #metoo or Black Lives Matter movements, or through the shattering of systems brought forth by COVID 19, here we all stand, together, birthing ourselves anew, in order to awaken the new earth.

Over these years of working with women individually and in sacred circle, what I know to be true, is that magic happens when a woman listens to the whispers of her soul and leans into her divine feminine essence. This is where women are amazed, affirmed, and freed as they hear their stories echoed in the voices of others. This is the place where we commit to seeing ourselves, each other, and the world differently in a way that gives us permission to be all of who we are, now and in the future.

While there are many elements within this powerful invitation to return to yourself, in this chapter I would love to ignite within you the most foundational of them all: creating and sustaining self-love and compassion as your new guidance system, as the basis for all you do and all you can be in this world.

A deep and abiding love for the self is well established across psychology, spirituality and even pop culture, as a foundation for a fulfilled life, yet too often we don't really know what this means beyond treating ourselves to a massage or manicure, indulging in a luxurious bath when the kids finally fall asleep, or making time for that cup of coffee with friends.

While each of these are nourishing and beautiful gifts to ourselves, the kind of self-love we need as revolutionary women birthing a new age flows much deeper. We need to commit to giving ourselves, the same levels of love, respect, gratitude, and compassion that we so easily lavish on our loved ones. We need to talk to ourselves and turn towards ourselves in the same way that we do our children, friends, and partners.

You would think these skills would be quite transferable, but as women, we have been conditioned for eons to be focussed on others, to sacrifice and compromise our wellbeing for theirs. Now, we must learn how to tap into this sacred well of love and compassion for ourselves – a well which provides safety and allows us to transform and grow. The love and compassion we are now called to cultivate within is the ingredient which gives us the freedom to be exactly who we came here to be.

The first question then is: what does self-love and compassion mean and what does it look like?

Over the years I have asked my clients what makes them feel most loved, and while it may have been expressed in different ways, the same theme arose without exception: "presence."

They all reported feeling most loved when someone was deeply present to them – when they were fully seen, heard, and received for all of who they are – the good and the not so good. In these places, they felt safe enough to express their deepest desires, emotions, needs and thoughts.

So, our second question then becomes, do you give this transformational gift of presence to yourself? How would it feel to sit with yourself, allowing, and being present to all your thoughts, needs, emotions and desires, without judgment, the way you offer this to your loved ones?

The journey to self-presence will look different for everyone.

I invite you to begin by intending to notice the feelings which arise in your body. This may seem simplistic, but we live in a society of busy schedules and disconnection from our physical and soul bodies. A simple intention will spark our minds to remember that this is a connection we wish to foster. Then, when an uncomfortable emotion arises, pause and acknowledge it - take a deep breath, possibly place your hand on your heart and ask yourself what you would say to a loved one who was experiencing this same feeling right now?

Take another deep breath and gently speak to yourself with that same level of support that you would offer another.

The intention here is to be deeply present to that part of you, which was brave enough to come forward, in the face of the many things which pull your attention daily, to call out for your care and acknowledgment. She is standing up, calling out to be heard – and that takes courage!

Imagine this feeling of discomfort is like a small child standing, nagging, waiting for your attention as you make dinner or finish a conversation. Yes, you're busy with all this other stuff that needs to get done but notice how she calms as soon as you turn towards her, acknowledge her presence and ask her what she needs.

She wants to be seen, heard, and acknowledged without judgment for who she is and what she is expressing; just as we all want to be! As we develop this practice of inner awareness, care, and support, we transform pieces of our heart which then frees us to live more and more deeply into our truest self, and ultimately give more of our gifts to the planet.

I encourage you to take a moment to sit quietly and reflect on these practices for yourself. Ask yourself what the greatest gift of love is anyone has ever (or could ever) give to you and contemplate how you could give yourself the same gift.

Then, commit to gently growing your awareness around the power of being deeply present and compassionate to yourself. While this needs to be done by you alone, I also encourage you to find a trusted coach or counsellor or a women's circle that is right for you, who can walk alongside you on this transformational journey. More than ever, women need to return to community to become who they are meant to be; to be witnessed and celebrated in their breakthroughs, supported and held in their breakdowns.

Finding the space that works for you will exponentially amplify your journey in the most profound and beautiful ways. The Feminine holds so many gifts for the world, and in committing to a path of knowing and honouring ourselves as women, we are making a conscious choice to bring into the world a powerful and sacred energy which will carry humanity into a beautiful new phase.

My greatest professional joy is connecting women back to their power, their knowing, and their greater field of life. This is something I like to refer to as "midwifing the soul." This begins with the journey of self-care and compassion. I walk alongside and hold their hand through this journey. I remind them of the purpose of their contractions and the promises they made to themselves to fully be who they came to this planet to be, and to share the gifts they came here to offer.

I ASK:

How might your life have been different if there had been a place for you?
A place for you to go ... a place of women, to help you learn the ways of woman ... a place where you were nurtured from an ancient flow sustaining you and steadying you as you sought to become yourself. A place of women to help you find and trust the ancient flow already there within yourself ... waiting to be released ... A place of women ...
How might your life have been different?
(Duerk, 1989, p. 104)

I INVITE you to journey with me, either individually or in circle, in person or online, to discover how different your life may be, when you have a midwife or perhaps an entire circle of women walking beside you, speaking your story, filling you with the love and compassion that you may not always draw forth for yourself.

I invite you to discover for yourself the power and beauty of a space for you to find the ancient flow from within, and to become, in a place of women.

ABOUT THE AUTHOR

Sasha Moss is the founder of *From the Feminine*, a practice providing psychotherapy and counselling, coaching and facilitation to brilliant, highly attuned women across the globe. With compassion and ferocity, Sasha invites women on a deep journey of return to themselves -- to realign with their feminine essence and reconnect to their passions, purpose and gifts.

After practicing law for close to a decade, through a journey of loss she unexpectedly found her true calling as a voice for the Divine Feminine rising on our planet. Through her Women's Circles, individual counselling and coaching, intuitive guidance, writing and group facilitation, Sasha is a passionate advocate for the beauty, strength and wisdom which flows *from the feminine* and how it is now poised to transform our world.

Website: *www.fromthefeminine.com*
Facebook: *www.facebook.com/fromthefeminine*
LinkedIn: *www.linkedin.com/in/sasha-moss-233839178*
Email: *sasha@fromthefeminine.com*

SASKIA ESSLINGER

GROW YOUR OWN FOOD

"All of the world's problems can be solved in a garden."
– Geoff Lawton

Homer, Alaska, where I live, is a quaint fishing town with great coffee shops, art galleries, and a few small farms. It sits on the shores of Kachemak Bay at the very end of the road and the supply chain.

Food is either trucked thousands of miles up the Alaska Highway, or barged into Anchorage and then transported 4.5 hours down to Homer.

When the news of the quarantine hit, the two grocery stores were completely wiped out. Everyone panicked.

But not me.

I still had plenty of food in my pantry, freezers, and root cellar. It was spring and things would soon be growing in my garden. The chickens were laying eggs again. I have strong local connections already in place for meat, dairy, honey, and fruit that I don't produce myself. I know how to harvest and preserve and prepare many of our wild foods as well.

This is a lifestyle I've been working towards for many years. In college I studied

Environmental Science and decided that the industrial food system was incongruent with healthy people or a healthy planet and, if we could change the way we produced our food, we would be a lot happier, healthier, and more sustainable.

This is the path I chose to walk. I wanted to make the change not only for myself, but on a cultural level. I wanted growing food to become a normal thing that most people did.

After college I worked on organic farms, taught gardening to children, and traveled the world learning about permaculture and how other people produced their food.

In 2007, my partner and I bought a run-down home in Anchorage and got busy turning it into an urban homestead. I started teaching gardening in 2008, while I was getting my Master's in Regenerative Entrepreneurship.

We pushed ourselves to grow more and more of our own food, and in 2011, while I was pregnant with our first child, we undertook the Alaska Food Challenge, where we ate only Alaskan food for one year. We grew over 1600 pounds of food that year on our normal city lot. And there was still room to grow much more.

When my husband and I sold our urban homestead to go traveling with our two boys, I realized how spoiled I had become with all the good quality food. Going back to grocery store food was a huge letdown. Sure, I could buy just about anything, but I had no connection to it, didn't trust the quality, and it really didn't taste the same. It tasted... empty.

We returned to Alaska and moved to Homer, choosing a rental that had an overgrown, fenced garden. The one thing I knew was that I had to get back to growing my own food.

But what I didn't realize was how much my garden provided me beside food. During a very stressful separation and divorce last summer, my garden was my grounding and my solace. It helped me step outside the insanity of the situation and find something solid to grab onto.

When I was frustrated, I would go pull weeds. When I was drained, I would nourish my body with food bursting with flavor and nutrition. When I got lost in fear, the song of the birds would bring me back to the present, reminding me that there is sweetness to be found in the hardest situations.

The garden also offered peace of mind as my life situation changed. I suddenly had full responsibility for my 6 and 8-year-old homeschooled boys. Money was tight as I transitioned my business online, but I knew I would always be able to feed them amazing organic food.

So, here I am. A full-time, single, homeschooling mom, growing a garden revolution. I found one of the most simple and satisfying ways to nourish my body, soul, and mind. It is not a coincidence that it also provides one of my most basic needs.

I have a vision of gardens growing everywhere, overflowing with food right where people need it. I see fruit, berries, vegetables, edible flowers, and herbal medicine growing where grass and ornamental plants used to be. I see people learning to value and nurture the earth, connecting to the cycles of the seasons and life.

I see people getting stronger and healthier with their clean, fresh food and natural remedies. I see people empowered to take charge of their own health instead of relying on doctors and products.

I see people getting to know their neighbors as they spend more time outdoors. Sharing their knowledge and their extra produce, and helping each other in a myriad of ways. I see communities becoming stronger and more interdependent.

And I clearly see that right now is the perfect opportunity for us to make this shift.

GARDENING IN THE TIME OF COVID

The pandemic is already affecting the global food supply and showing us where the weaknesses of our food system are.

The movement of workers, seeds, and produce has been impaired, preventing farmers from planting crops, or getting their food to market. Suppliers are having a hard time redistributing food that was supposed to go to restaurants and institutions and are having to destroy huge quantities of perishables. Virus outbreaks have closed meat-packing plants and food-processing factories.

All of these issues are compounding the effects of unprecedented flooding, freezing, fires and drought caused by climate change. And the industrial food system is actually a huge contributor to climate change. It is using fossil fuels to mine the earth's soil to produce highly processed food that is making us sick.

We were taught that the "green revolution" is the most efficient way to feed the world. We were "relieved" of our labor on the land, and in many cases, denied access to land.

But this is a lie. We can actually grow much more food per square foot of intensively hand-cultivated land than we can with a tractor in a field. And we can cut out the chemicals, the petroleum to drive the tractors, the packaging, the manufacturing, the waste, the pollution, and the transportation.

It does require more human time and effort, it is true. But it is not back-breaking, callous-causing effort. It is a soul-nurturing, life-giving effort.

In fact, it is the very connection to our earth that we crave.

The women… we feel it the most. The connection to our Mother Earth. It is like a coming-home. In connecting to the earth, we connect to ourselves. When we nourish the earth, we are nourishing ourselves.

This grounding is exactly what we need right now in these uncertain times, when everything we know has been turned upside down and we are not sure what the future holds. The garden gives us something very tangible to put our energy into.

We put effort in and reap the reward of healthy, nourishing food and reduced anxiety and stress. The fresh air and exercise is wonderful for our bodies and soothing for our souls.

The garden encourages us to not be perfectionists. Nature is ultimately in charge. Plants die, things get eaten. It's all ok. It's part of the great cycle of life.

And we can trust in it. We can trust that the sun will rise tomorrow. We can trust that spring will come. We can trust that things will grow. Growth is natural. And so is death. And rest, and rebirth.

We can work with these natural cycles to find deeper meaning in our lives. We can use our gardens as a place to ground our energy when things feel unsafe, stressful, or out of control. And we can nourish our bodies and souls with this life-giving food we have grown with our own loving care.

Mother Nature is asking us all to slow down and reconsider our priorities. She is asking us to stay at home, spend more time with our families, and focus on what we can control.

To me, this is the perfect invitation to begin or expand a garden. If you don't know how, this is the time to learn. And if you have children, this is a great time for them to learn a valuable skill that will serve them for the rest of their lives.

RE-IMAGINING FOOD PRODUCTION

So let's take a moment to imagine the alternative to the industrial food system.

What if when you look out your window instead of seeing a lawn, you see an apple tree, loaded with fruit ready to be picked? Underneath are some sweet, tart gooseberries, black currants, and a riot of flowers.

Climbing up your fence is a kiwi vine, and nestled in its shade are giant garden mushrooms. In the sunny spot in front of the sweet little greenhouse, there are green beans, broccoli, kale, zucchini, and many other veggies, along with herbs, and edible flowers, alive with visiting bees and butterflies.

You see children checking out an insect they found, until they spot some peas to munch on. They are happy to explore the garden for hours. Work is done for the day so you wander out into the soft afternoon light to harvest some veggies for dinner. You pull a few errant weeds while you are at it.

From behind the greenhouse comes the gentle sounds of your chickens. They are happily digging in the mulch in their straw yard and delight in the weeds you toss them.

You notice the raspberries are falling off the canes again. You pop a few in your mouth and can't wait to come back outside after dinner to pick them. A friend will be stopping by to help and you will laugh and chat as you harvest the delicious, sun-warmed berries.

You inhale the warm, earthy air, and breathe out a deep sigh of relaxation. You remember how you used to spend this time after work in your car, stressed out and ragged. You are proud of this life-giving food you grew to nourish your family, and now you can't imagine life without it.

This garden is not a fantasy. If I can create this in Alaska, you can do it wherever you are. The specific things you grow may be different, but the feeling of being in a life-nurturing space can be created anywhere.

THE HEART OF REGENERATIVE GARDENING

This is not a garden with long, dusty rows of cabbages and back-breaking weeding. It's not a few raised beds neglected in the back corner of the yard. This garden is an oasis that provides refuge, solace, entertainment, and learning. This garden is based on permaculture, which uses natural principles to design regenerative systems.

Regenerative. That is, restoring to a higher or improved state. This method of gardening heals the earth. It builds soil instead of degrading it. It stores water and carbon and neutralizes toxins. This type of gardening makes the world a better place, both for the environment and the people who live here.

We can heal the earth one yard, one alley, one vacant lot at a time. And we can heal ourselves and our communities in the process.

So how does a regenerative garden actually work?

Picture yourself in a forest. You walk among the trees, crunching through a thick mat of dried leaves on the ground. There are berry bushes, nutritious nettles, and wild roses growing in the dappled shade of the canopy.

You notice a hollow that is collecting water and leaves from which a riot of new plants are growing. Vines climb up the trees and mushrooms are popping out of the ground. You hear the sounds of birds chirping, bees buzzing by, and the scurrying of a forest creature.

The forest is teeming with life. Yet nobody comes to tend it. Nobody waters it, weeds it, or fertilizes it.

This is what we seek to recreate in our regenerative garden. We aim for an ecosystem that self-waters, self-fertilizes, and mostly takes care of itself while also giving us food, drink, medicine, fiber, and beauty.

Mother Nature is the guide. Everything we do in the garden must take care of the earth and all its inhabitants.

THE UNFOLDING

It's possible for many of us to grow 10% of our own food. This is a great goal to start with.

That's about 200 pounds of food per person. A typical breakdown might be 50 pounds of apples or other fruit and berries, 50 pounds of potatoes, 25 pounds of winter squash, 25 pounds of tomatoes, and 50 pounds of other mixed vegetables. Multiply that by the number of people in your family.

One apple tree will produce over 100 pounds of apples each year. One 10-pound bag of seed potatoes will produce 100 pounds of potatoes. One winter squash plant will yield 10-25 pounds. One tomato plant will produce 10-15 pounds. You can buy everything you need to get started for less than $50, including the apple tree.

It takes about 100 square feet, or 10 square meters to grow this amount of food for one person. The typical American lawn is about 5,000 square feet, so this is only a tiny fraction of the lawn. But once you get growing, you might decide you have no need for a lawn anymore. The garden is way more interesting for adults and children alike.

After a while, you might also think about having chickens for eggs or other small animals that can provide meat for your table and fertility for your garden, and perform work such as pest control and tilling. This is one key for creating a natural system that doesn't rely as much on outside inputs. In cities you will be able to rely on the abundance of organic waste for your fertility instead.

You will want to find ways to hold water in your soil, in rain barrels or ponds to make watering easier. You may even find a way to utilize gray water from your sink and washer. You will come to truly appreciate every drop of this life-giving substance.

You will become well acquainted with the life in your garden. You will learn how to work with the birds, the animals, the worms, and the microorganisms that live in the soil and feed your plants.

You will learn how to preserve your produce for the off-season with drying, fermenting, canning, freezing, and cold storage. You may start saving your own seeds because it is fun and interesting and it will help you become even more resilient.

You will tune into the energy of the moon cycles and how that affects your seeds and plants. You will understand the purpose of each season and give thanks for the death and rest just as much as the growth and life.

This type of gardening encourages us to become co-creators with nature. It encourages us to sink our roots in deep and form a profound bond with our land. We become a part of nature instead of separate from it.

START WHERE YOU ARE AT

A regenerative garden does not grow overnight. It takes patience and persistence. It takes a willingness to learn new things, ask for help, and make mistakes. It takes an investment of time and money.

Whether you are a beginner gardener or have been growing for many years, the important thing is to take one more step forward on your journey. Plant one seed in a pot, build a bed, expand your garden, learn to preserve your produce, or start to incorporate elements such as animals. You cannot do this all at once. You must take one step forward at a time.

Perhaps you are traveling, live in an apartment, or rent and don't have land of your own. Do not let this stop you. Bring seeds on your journey and plant them for the next traveler. Find a plot in a community garden, an elderly neighbor who has space but lacks energy, or an unused alleyway. Garden on your balcony, on your roof, at your workplace, or in a sunny window.

There is always an opportunity to grow something. The yield is only limited by your knowledge and imagination.

What is the next step on your garden path?

If you are just starting out, I urge you to find a bit of space outside or get a pot. If you don't have a pot, find an empty milk carton and cut a few holes in the bottom for drainage. Find some soil. It can be from a bag or from the ground outside. Mix in some coffee grounds for fertilizer.

Find some seeds for something that sounds tasty. Basil or other herbs are a great place to start. Plant the herb seeds 1/8" deep and one inch apart. Give them a good drink of water and keep them moist until they emerge. Give them lots of sunshine and love and watch them grow. Breathe in their intoxicating fragrance and use their leaves for your dinner.

And then, take one more step towards your regenerative garden.

Congratulations! You are now a part of the garden revolution!

ABOUT THE AUTHOR

Saskia Esslinger is growing a garden revolution by teaching people how to nurture their soil, bodies, and soul.

She is a certified permaculture designer and teacher, and a mentor with the Women's Permaculture Guild. She holds a B.S. in Environmental Science and a M.S. in Regenerative Entrepreneurship. A lifelong gardener, she has worked on organic farms in upstate New York, developed a children's gardening program in Austin, Texas, and volunteered with Permaculture projects around the world.

Saskia is a full-time single homeschooling mama to two adventurous boys who help her grow, forage, and process a significant portion of their own food in Homer, Alaska. She once went an entire year eating only Alaskan food, much of which she grew herself.

Website: www.teachgardening.com
Facebook: www.facebook.com/groups/thegardenrevolution
Instagram: www.instagram.com/teachgardening

SIERRA MELCHER

CONSCIOUS PARENTING: PROFOUND IMPLICATIONS FROM MICRO-SHIFTS & MICRO-ADJUSTMENTS

I recognize the impossibility of capturing the essence of conscious parenting in a single chapter. Yet here I will offer some key elements to consider as you delve into the life-long spiritual and practical work of raising a human (or several).

In the scope of this chapter I offer three principles, the *HOW* of conscious parenting, with tangible, practical tools you can apply today to support yourself and your family. Being a conscious parent means meeting your kids where they are, being present in what they are experiencing and expressing. We can only do this when we, too, are centered and present.

My approach, as you will see, is three pronged, attending to our: thoughts, words, and actions.

I have come by my insights honestly, both through academic and practical means. I have a master's degree in education and worked as an international educator for over fifteen years, teaching in the United States, China, and Colombia at every level from pre-school to postgrad, but spent the bulk of my teaching career working with adolescents. (I love the hormonal, angsty potential of this age.) I was raised by two Tibetan Buddhists and grew up with meditation and mindfulness deeply rooted in my daily life. Additionally, I am a student of neuroscience, psychology, and human development, as well as being a parent myself. My daughter has taught me as much about parenting and living as any study.

My philosophy emerged through my study to become a Reiki master, Yoga teacher, resilience mentor, and leadership coach. Furthermore, I trained as a doula, supporting women to become mothers and facilitating the transcendent power of birth, which can bring a woman fully into herself and her power.

* * *

PARENTHOOD IS SO MUDDLED with expectations (our own and those of others). We, the individual souls, can get lost in it. I advocate conscious parenting for men and women but must recognize, regardless of culture, a bulk of the responsibility still falls on mothers. You are familiar with *"the cult of motherhood"* whether you have heard the term before or not.

Simply put, it expects women to put the role of motherhood above all else, caring for others at the expense of herself, and assumes that beyond motherhood a woman needs no further identity or quality. While this is a dated term, the insidious nature of the underlying belief still holds. Modern parenting is a gauntlet of paradoxes. I write as a mother, and a single mother at that, so know that without dedicating serious attention, we can lose ourselves.

* * *

EVEN WHEN WE don't mean to be, we are models for our kids. They are always watching and learning from our actions and words. They are very observant sponges. As such, the best teaching is by example. It's millions of times better than "do as I say, not as I do," which may be how you were raised to some degree. If we are practicing nurturing ourselves, then that is what we are teaching our children, to be whole human beings and responsible for themselves and the lives they live. It is easy to fall into patterns of familiar routine rather than staying in the present with intentional devotion to the moment.

You can't teach what you don't know, which is why when asked, "What is the best preparation to become a parent?" or "How can I be a more conscious parent?" I always respond with something that surprises my clients: I say, "Do your own inner work, heal your own trauma, tend to your own mess, and break the cycle of inherited unconscious-relating to one another."

We come into this world open and pure. Through living, we are inevitably injured, either emotionally or, in the worst cases, physically abused. Life's wounds cut us off from ourselves and one another until we can learn to nurture ourselves.

We can revise our story to heal enough from our own traumas so as not to pass them down. Conscious parenting, therefore, requires that before we care for another, we care deeply for ourselves. Self-love is a prerequisite for generous, infinite love of another.

FIERCE IMPERFECTION

Don't let the struggle deter you. It will remain undone if we don't acknowledge the importance of putting ourselves first.

The thing about authenticity, lauded as the new gold-standard, is that our authentic, true selves are far messier and more "flawed" than most of us would wish. If you aspire for *authentic*, please also make room for *imperfect*.

I, especially these days, have been practicing what I call *Fierce Imperfection*. I am dedicated to doing things as best I can (in one go, and then letting that be good enough). It is the only way for me to sanely create, contribute, and be a single parent in 24/7 quarantine with a 5 year old, while being a momprenuer as well.

I can't afford perfection. Not now, not ever. My commitment to my physical and emotional health surpasses my desire to get it 100% right, whatever *IT* may be: a podcast, an article, a creative project with my daughter. We are normalizing making messes, as an intentional process for both of us, to learn and grow into imperfection.

My art teacher in high school used to say, "If you aren't making a mess, you aren't doing it right." The same holds true for parenting. It is an inherently messy business, parenting/living. Our willingness to allow conscious messes, both physically and emotionally speaking, as well as our ability to clean up said messes, teaches us and our children so many valuable lessons about resilience and being human. It is well worth the discomfort and the temporary disasters along the way, be they covered in paint or tears.

MINDFULNESS PRACTICE: THOUGHTS

We start with our thoughts for two reasons: 1) because they are the building blocks for our reality and 2) because we have influence over our own thoughts.

How a mother practices mindfulness may be unique. Since most of the spiritual leaders over time have been men, traditional mindfulness practice neglects some realities of motherhood. If sitting on a cushion for 30 undisturbed minutes or a week-long retreat is not feasible, because someone has to feed your kids, know that mindfulness is still completely available to you!

It all comes down to thought, words, and action, again. Mindfulness, at its core, is breathing and developing body awareness as a way of accessing the full awareness of the present moment. Learn to listen to your thoughts and recognize them as just thoughts, not reality.

The other day I described myself as a mindful mess. Mindfulness does not imply constant calm or bliss. Learn to be present in the thick of it and notice your reactions and sensations rather than letting them rule you.

One can be mindful in any situation. Here are some simple ideas to play with.

- *Breathe.* Notice your thoughts as they come and go, without attachment to or judgement of them. Feel your body. Listen to your mind and feel your emotions as they arise. Let things come and go. For further assistance, listen to my *mindful momma podcast practice.* [*www.anchor.fm/integral-women*]
- *It is a practice* to gain skill it needs to be regularly repeated. Intentional mindfulness can make a significant difference in your day, but if you only practice once a month, the influence will be much diminished. Think of regular, otherwise mundane tasks; bring mindfulness while doing the dishes, bathing a child, singing a lullaby, and doing other daily chores, even non-mom activities.
- Consider committing to *mini-mindfulness (4 minutes a day)* for the next 30 days. (Keep a mindfulness journal - Download a free one here [*www.integral-women.com/mindfulness-journal*]) — let me know how it goes.
- *Reminder:* Starting a mindfulness practice is like a *consciousness detox* of sorts. When you start, you are likely to feel *worse* rather than feeling immediately better. Don't let this common illusion deter you. Like a physical detox, you need to clear away the clutter before you can feel light, fresh, and connected.
- We practice mindfulness intentionally so that we can build *mental muscle memory* to remain mindful in other moments, to interact with

our children and partners from a mindful place rather than allowing a temper tantrum or an innocuous comment to unleash ages of rage and become a problem of its own.

SELF-TENDING: WORDS

Internal v. External

In my work with clients, I teach a lot about identity and the distinction between the external aspects (our career, persona, relationships, and roles) and our internal aspects (our deep self, the relationship we have with ourselves, our guiding narrative, etc).

Many clients are stunned at the outset, having never paid much attention to the internal realms. Dedicating all of their attention and energy to their external aspect (physical appearance, romantic relationship, their career, and life goals) comes at the cost of developing an internal world.

Self-tending is the development of an internal world, a relationship with the self.

This comes down to the story you tell about who you are and what inherent value you hold: the words you use in your mind as you think about yourself and your life, and the words you speak out loud that tell others who you are and how you deserve to be treated.

SELF-PARENTING

How do we tend to our own needs, and heal our own trauma? How do we raise ourselves?

Self-parenting is offering ourselves the support, love, and patient guidance we would ideally offer our children and craved when we were young. Undoing our past is not an option, yet we still can choose to learn from it and heal.

Let me share a story of my own to illustrate:

I set aside the month of May to dedicate to my own inner life and promised to take on no new projects or commitments (beyond my writing, parenting and business commitments); that is full enough. I have been uncovering a childhood sexual trauma that has left a tangle of implications across my life.

In my weekly women's circle today, I noticed my false assumption that I could resolve this past trauma in a month. (Laughing out loud at my bravado... and foolishness!) That is not how healing occurs. I share this to illuminate an important point.

You do not have to put your life on hold or dedicate yourself 100% to "fixing yourself" before you are ready to be a parent. None of us would ever qualify if that were the expectation. Nor am I saying you have to have "all your shit together" in order to be a conscious parent. On the contrary.

This morning I allowed a new idea: if I attended to healing myself with support of professionals as needed, over the next year, I could give enough space for it to naturally evolve. This is the loving kindness I deserve, the patience I offer others. That is self-parenting. Healing, like living, is cyclical, not linear.

Here I offer some questions I am asking myself to heal and tend to my inner life:

- What did you want/need at the time?
- How can you provide that to yourself now?
- What needs went unmet in the past?
- How can you come to peace with the past in order to have a different experience in the future?

While contemplating these things, I am drawn to consider who I want to be as a parent. May these questions serve you:

- What do you want to offer/teach your kids (lessons/experiences) that you didn't have?
- What did you have that you want to pass on?
- How do you want to characterize your relationship with your own kids

CULTIVATE AN INNER AUTHORITY

A strong inner self serves us in our role as parents because we are grounded and aligned with our deep nature. When we take responsibility for having our own needs met, we can communicate from a place of centered self-assuredness. We want that for our kids, right?

We can't teach what we don't know!

Most women, myself included, have given our power away by depending on an external authority. This propagated shame, mom-guilt, and feeling of never being enough. No one knows better than you how to do this loving, devotional work of parenting your child(ren).

Reclaim your power/authority. Imagine living with loving boundaries, for yourself and others, rather than exhausted resentment and bitterness from having given too much of ourselves. Discovering and listening to your inner guidance is a process in and of itself. This is what I support people in creating for themselves. (I have written a book called, *Date Yourself*, (to be published soon) that delineates the steps to reassert primacy of your inner nature.)

My self-work is solely for me, yet, it has residual effects on my daughter and my life. What I am able to resolve will determine what she inherits from me. Now the stakes and motivation are double.

Giving birth to my daughter awakened something in me; in honor of that, I am willing to go into some difficult places within that I previously avoided. I am continually untangling a childhood sexual trauma, as well as body issues, a history of bulimia and emotional eating, and emotionally shutting down. This, as you can see, is a life's work, not a season.

My daughter will, inevitably, have her own struggles and challenges. This is part of living and growing. I want to be able to support her as best I can in that process, but won't unwittingly burden her further because I was unwilling to give myself the nurturing and healing I deserve.

The best thing you can do as a parent is tend to yourself first. Heal your own wounds, so that you can devote an eternal wellspring of love and energy to your children. When we run dry, when we are empty, we have little to offer. It is essential that your oxygen mask is on first. This flight reminder used to make me so angry. I thought in order to be a good mother, a valuable woman, I had to give first.

That mindset had me giving from an empty well, seething with resentment and gorging on bitterness for years. It took a series of realizations to bring me back to the simple wisdom I had been hearing all along and finally understood the truth in it and saw the need to practice it myself. Let your thoughts and words support a world where you matter and come first, so you all can thrive.

LESS IS SO MUCH MORE: ACTIONS

The words we say matter. I say, "I love you" often. But more importantly, your actions must align with your words to mean anything.

In the 21st century, there is an insidious overdoing. To quote a dear friend, Dr. Stacy Berman, "we are human doings, not human beings." We have given way to the ever-increasing demands and expectations of highly competitive environments.

When I taught in China, my 9th grade students were so worried about getting into college that they were giving themselves ulcers. Piling on extra-curricular and studying things, not because they were passionate, but rather because they hoped it would look good on an application.

As parents, we want the best for our children, obviously. But what is that really? Being swept away in the compulsive drive for more activities and more stimulus may not be in anyone's best interest.

Innovative thought and creative problem solving happens in the wide open unstructured moments. In highly regimented days we can be efficient and productive, yes, but at what cost? These are culturally imposed and assumed goals of life, but at the expense of having a deep and abiding inner life. There is no time for us to *be*; to be with ourselves, or to be together. Notice if you are trying to avoid yourself by over-scheduling your life.

Generation by generation, we have been losing our capacity to *be*, without the harried *doing*. We teach our children how to live. As we fill their schedules and place higher demands on them, we are driving ourselves crazy. When we are always distracted, multitasking, and juggling an ever-increasing number of action-items, mindfulness is even harder.

Be Intentional. *Cultivate a life that supports your deepest values. Sit down with the stakeholders, so to speak, of your family and come up with a list of values.*

- *What are your guiding values? What needs are elemental?*
- *How can you assure that your values are honored in your lives?*
- *What brings you joy?*
- *Where do you want to strive and where do you want to play?*
- *What can be reduced or eliminated?*

NEVER TOO LATE TO TRY

Whether you are not yet a parent or a parent of a toddler or a teenager, it is never too late to become a conscious parent. Even when your children are grown, you are still their parent. At our core we are adaptable, more so when we are young, but we hold this capacity deep within.

Neuroplasticity is the name for our brain's ability to adapt and change. Even after a debilitating stroke, the brain can form new connections and relearn. We ourselves, regardless of age, can learn new habits and thought patterns, physically changing the structure of our brains. Our organism wants to heal and grow. We can overcome unspeakable trauma, so know that we can improve and transform our lives and the lives of our families. It starts within, and it starts with us.

Reach out to me with questions, struggles, and celebrations; I would be honored to hear from you.

TAKEAWAYS:

- Meet your kids where they are.
- By attending to our thoughts, words, and actions, we can cultivate a higher degree of conscious parenting. Try a 30 day mini-mindfulness practice.
- Devote attention to your inner self.
- Self-parenting heals old wounds and resolves an energy imbalance.
- Practice Fierce Imperfection.
- Align and simplify your life.

ABOUT THE AUTHOR

Sierra Melcher is a Personal Fulfillment Advisor, best-selling author, and international speaker. She supports leaders and change-makers to flourish so that the powerful impact they have on the world fuels them -- heart and soul -- by providing fundamentally life-changing personal guidance to discover the ultimate authority that resides within. As a sought-after thought leader, she uses humor and empathy as essential tools, because transformation doesn't have to be hard.

Sierra has a Master's degree in education and has taught around the world. As the founder of *Integral Women*, Sierra offers game-changing insight to individuals and the global conversation around purpose and fulfillment. She is a regular guest on various podcasts and hosts her own, *Integral Women Soundbites*, where women from around the world share insight and wisdom in the time it takes to drink a cup of coffee. Originally from the United States, Sierra currently lives in Medellin, Colombia with her young daughter.

Website: *www.integral-women.com*
Podcast: *www.anchor.fm/integral-women*

TAMALA RIDGE

THE SACRED ART OF DETOXING

For Ian Bland and Anthony Bourne
2 of my greatest teachers

Growing up in a household that was enmeshed in domestic violence, alcoholism and infidelity, taught me a lot about how to stuff down my feelings, run away from conflict, blame everyone around me and give up when it all got too hard.

I spent my childhood feeling unsure, unsafe and unheard. I spent my adolescence desperately searching for love in all the wrong places and then my 20's and 30's partying like there was no tomorrow and for most of my life, I really didn't care if tomorrow came or not. In fact I used to dread the sun coming up at all.

Coming home in taxis after pulling an all-nighter and looking out the window, hating on all those happy joggers out for their morning run, I used to say to myself "Surely it's not possible to be that happy and healthy. They must be suffering on the inside — just like me." The sun would be peaking up from the horizon and I would feel the terror of having to face another day start to consume me and all I could do to ease the pain was to think about and plan my next opportunity to numb it all out, the next party, the next drink, the next nightclub.

Those years seemed to go on and on. I was in and out of consciousness as regularly as I brushed my teeth. Preferring only the unconscious, the high, the alcohol, the drugs, the dancing, the boys, the laughter, the tribe and the thumping beats. This was my idea of Heaven. This was the life that I had created to escape the other and yet, I was still dying on the inside.

I was raised Catholic and so the concepts of Heaven and hell were ingrained in my conscious and subconscious. I was rebelling against these traditional ideas and I was trying to create my own version of Heaven but little did I realize, I was actually creating more hell.

I would turn up to work with a smile on my face, dressed to impress and would do a full days work to my best capacity. I was what you would call a "functioning drug user." Looking back on those days I still surprise myself at how well I managed to keep it all together, suffering in silence whilst no-one knew. I was the master of disguises and kept up the illusion that I was invincible.

Years later in my 40's, after having established myself a career as a Drug and alcohol Counselor for 15 years and now, after creating my own Institute for Spiritual Companioning, I realise that what saved me from going down the big black tunnel of suicide, self harm or some other mental health diagnosis, was because, from a very young age, I stepped into the role of being of service.

It began in my own family as a child. When my mother and father would fight, I would fight fiercely to break them up. I would try to save my mum and fight off my dad. I knew he would never hurt me and I learnt how to conjure up my courage through a sense of Justice and a deep need to create safety. I became emotionally strong and brave. He didn't frighten me, I was used to his outbursts and violent behavior and to this day, one of my many special talents is the ability to hold space in a crisis. I go into a type of organised frenzy, the world seems to slow down and I can see EXACTLY what needs to be done, who needs support, what support needs to be called in and what everyone needs to do in order to create a safe space again.

SUPER POWER number 1 was born out of the need to create safety for myself and those around me, when there was none as a child. I became the peace-maker, you may be able to relate; the child in the family who tries to get every one to kiss and make up. The one that spends hours and hours trying to get each person to listen to other one, holding space to hear and console those who are hurting, yearning desperately for that happy ending.

As an adolescent and into my young adult hood, I became the rescuer, the one who's shoulder everyone cried on, the one who dragged friends out of the gutter and into a warm bed, the one who sat up until dawn talking my friend out of a suicidal depression. I know to this day that the only thing that saved me from going down the big black hole with many of my friends was that I was the one standing at the top pulling them out.

Being of service to others has been my greatest lesson in life, my greatest challenge and my greatest joy and I thank my parents for this sacred opportunity. Everything is perfect, not that I knew that then, but I know it now.

When I became a drug and alcohol counsellor, I tried to "Save" everyone. I wanted to rescue every lost soul, wrap them up in a nice warm blanket and take them home. I saw their pain and suffering and I desperately wanted to fix them and take it all away. Needless to say I burnt out.

I met two men in that time that changed my life, two mentors, father figures, father energy that I never had before. Men who held space for me in a way that was so foreign at first but felt so good. Men that asked me questions and refused to give me the answers, no matter how hard I stamped my foot.

Men that made me think and go deep within to find and eventually learn to trust my own inner wisdom. Men that loved me not for my external beauty but for my internal courage, strength and passionate heart. Men that taught me that no one could rescue me except myself and they would be damned before they would try to do that for me.

This is how my *Super Power number 2* was born, the ability to hold space for someone else the way I had been denied as a child. When I felt it from someone else, I felt as though I had come home, to a place of safety and divine connection. This was to become my most potent medicine. The Sacred Art of Spiritual Companioning. How to empower someone else, to introduce them to their own innate intuition and wisdom by asking the right questions, holding them in their place of discomfort and offering tools to transmute their fear. BOOM! This is what I had been searching for, for all those years.

So I now had super power number two but I wanted more. I wanted it all, the happy high's the powerful space holding capacity and I wanted to dive more deeply into my connection to Spirit. For I knew that I couldn't possibly become the introduction agency for others to meet their divine self unless I was intimately familiar with her myself.

I knew I had to clean myself up in a way that went far beyond stopping drinking.

In order to re-connect with the Divine, I had to remove all the veils that kept me separate. I had heard that there were many ways to experience natural high's and I was on a mission to discover these for myself. I desperately wanted to experience the Heaven that I knew was all around me yet I couldn't quite reach it. I knew in the depth of my Soul that it was entirely possible to feel high without drugs and I was determined to discover how.

I truly believe it is an innate desire in all humans to want to alter our consciousness. Drugs these days are so easily accessible and we have lost all respect and reverence for the reason we used to take drugs (or earth medicine in our indigenous cultures). The way we consume drugs now is destroying our souls. I wanted to find ways to reach higher realms of altered states of consciousness in order to uncover the truth of who I was. I was a happy high seeker after all.

Here's what I discovered along the way:

1.) In order to get high, I had to clear all that which was bringing me down, everything that was making my vibration low and slow. I had to go deeper into my addictions and get real damn honest about what they were.

I dove into caffeine, sugar, TV, shopping, spending money, sex, relationships, procrastination, self-sabotage, anger, and stress. All different types of addictive substances and behaviours. We all have them, let's be honest, we have become a planet of zombies, blindly following our internal craving to stuff things down and numb out any uncomfortable emotion. I watched my parents do it for years with alcohol and food.

One of the most powerful things that I discovered when I was working in the addiction industry is that we were focusing on the wrong thing, we were trying to get our clients to stop the one thing that gave them any reprieve from their agonising self-loathing and expected them to be successful at this. But they weren't. We can all experience spaces of sobriety from - any addiction but we all know that sooner rather than later, they will be back with a vengeance.

Here is what I also discovered:

2.) Addiction is the opposite of connection.

In order to break any cycle of addiction, we need to flood it out with our connections to self, others, earth and to spirit. All addictive behaviour triggers the stress response particularly during the come down, the hangover, the sugar crash, the debt on the credit card; all produce feelings of anxiety shame and self-loathing. We need to crowd out the adrenalin and cortisol with our happy hormone; Oxytocin – the love drug.

Addiction is not a dirty word, in fact we are hard wired to become addicted to things, have you ever tried to wean a baby off the breast? That little boob and milk addict is a hard-core love junkie. Flooding your system with oxytocin producing connection activities will eventually crowd out the stress hormones of adrenalin and cortisol. There is no come down from deep intimate love-inducing connections baby!

I invite you to get yourself into a deeply relaxed and present state, close your eyes and asked yourself each of these questions one at a time — "What are the ways that I connect most deeply with myself, with others, with earth and with spirit?" You now have your sacred and devotional to-do-list right in the palm of your hand.

I invite you to put these strategies into your diary as a priority over any other activity. It's the way your soul yearns to be fed on a daily basis. It took me years to pop my self-care into my diary first and then all of my work simply had to fit in around it. Filling your cup has to come first, otherwise you will be on the fast train to stress-ville and self-loathing again.

These are the activities that your soul is truly craving and yet we are all mistaking them for sugar and Netflix cravings.

I can stand in front of the fridge now when I am blindly searching for something sweet and I can catch myself using mindful awareness. I stop, breath deeply and ask myself – "Why am I about to create self-loathing?" Because that is exactly where I am heading after consuming that block of chocolate. I celebrate the noticing of these cravings and thoughts and I can actually separate myself from them and observe them like clouds floating past in the sky. The next question I ask myself is, "What is my soul really craving right now"?" I can then go deeper, beyond my physical body to the energetic. I close my eyes and ask, I breathe, I connect to my heart, I close the fridge door, I listen and an answer will ALWAYS come.

I need a bath, I need to go outside and stand barefoot on the earth, I need to laugh and giggle with my children, I need to lie in bed with a herbal tea, I need to do some yoga, I need to call a friend, I need a hug from my partner, I need to pray.

No longer am I seeing amphetamine and opiate addicts. The type of clients I see now are Spiritual Leaders, Lightworkers and Coaches wishing to ascend at a more accelerated pace. Wishing to make the medicine that they have to offer the world much more potent and effective because they are committed to doing their own internal work to clear any addictions that are preventing them from turning up as their most potent selves.

3.) You can't take anyone past where you are at energetically.

If you are committed to walking your own talk, clearing all that which stands in the way of you serving with a greater level of spiritual integrity in order to gift your own medicine to a more powerful and potent capacity to your clients – then I am speaking directly to you.

In order to stand up, speak up and truly step into the role of lightwork, you must have a clear and aligned vessel. In order to connect more deeply with the divine and for her energy and wisdom to flow through you, you must be deeply committed to an ongoing cleansing process.

The world is desperate for more light workers such as yourself to spread your sacred tools in order to raise the vibration of the planet – but you can only take others closer to Source if you are constantly in divine service to yourself.

4.) Super power number 3 was born when I discovered the Sacred Art of Detoxing.

It was the second time I had discovered how to get high without drugs (the first was meditation) and I was literally hooked, after roughly 30 detoxes myself, I decided to start teaching this to my clients. I was pleasantly surprised at how eagerly others took this on and fell in love with the outcomes; the high, the clarity, the conscious awareness, the vitality, the deep communion with spirit that ultimately occurred simply by stripping away our physical, mental and emotional toxicity.

I'm not talking about fasting or juice cleanses here (although they are also potent medicine). The way I teach detoxing is all a out adding in and there is no deprivation in sight.

A simple vegan diet, with all fresh (preferably organic) fruits, vegetables, nuts and seeds will take your entire being into a higher realm of consciousness. It is a process of unveiling the truth of who you are by removing all physical, mental and emotional toxins. The most important additions are the connection strategies of self, others, earth and spirit that I mentioned earlier. You must add these in before anything is removed. They nurture and feed the soul, which will ultimately support you to overcome the cravings for the physical addictions.

So here I am, a total #DetoxJunkie, Spiritual Companioning Mentor and lightworker – all born from my 3 super powers.

Detoxing has been the final piece of the puzzle for me. It has supported me to go to places I never knew existed. It has provided me with the opportunity to discover my shadow and bring it out into the light. It has been another incredible tool for me to discover all of the answers within myself, rather than continually searching for them externally. I now have my hot line straight to God, to Divine Infinite Universal Consciousness. And I am passionate about teaching this to the world. How to create more Heaven in our lives, is simply a choice and entirely possible.

HERE ARE MY TOP TIPS TO SUPPORT YOU TO GET MORE ADDICTED TO LOVE AND LESS TO YOUR FEAR

1. Add in before you take out. Use the questions I have laid out above to discover your own sacred connection strategies that will ultimately produce a flood of the oxytocin love drug throughout your system. Make this a priority if you ever want to get high on life.
2. When you go to the fridge next time and you are craving that sugar or wine, ask yourself: "Why am I craving self-loathing?" Because that is exactly how you will be feeling afterwards. The shame, the guilt, the inner critic will have a field day and this is exactly what you are addicted to, way more than the wine or chocolate. We are addicted to the come down because we spend a much longer time in this space. The high may only last a few minute or hours yet that inner critic will beat you up for days, weeks, or months. This is the true addiction that we are all trying to recover form, our addiction to fear. Ask yourself: "What is missing in my life right now?", "What is my soul really craving?", "Which connection strategy would feed my deep desire for love?" And do that instead. Easier said that done sometimes I know, which is why it is also so important to learn mindfulness.
3. Take a mindfulness class, download some Mindful Meditations, not just

guided meditations that take you to a nice place, but actual mindfulness where you begin to notice your thoughts from a distance, to observe them, so that you are no longer blindly led by them. It's all about separating from the ego. Then you can go back to the fridge and watch that sneaky sucker do its work, notice and make a loving choice instead of one that will ultimately feed your fear.

4. Consider the art of detoxing. If you are looking to ascend at an accelerated pace. If you want to increase the potency of the medicine that you bring to the world. If you are committed to increasing your own spiritual integrity and you want to enter into a Rite of Passage that will change your life forever, then research and find a reputable program that DOES NOT DEPRIVE YOU. The way I teach detoxing is full of healthy nutritious vegan food and it is literally impossible to feel hungry. For more details, stalk me on FB or go to my website to download my free Ebook on How Detoxing will Increase you Income.

You now have the perfect opportunity to awaken, everyday you have a choice, will you choose love or fear? It's as simple as that. The media, the government and the health system are all perpetuating a state of fear on a global scale and even though you may feel as though some of your choices have been taken away, you still have a choice that will change the direction of your life.

Heaven is already here, it is not a place that we go to when we die, everything is in the now. It's just that we are constantly distracted by our fear in the form of temptation, addictions, the inner critic, our ego etc and the only way to feel, see and experience more heaven is to change our perception and detoxing is one of the most powerful ways to do this at an accelerated pace.

Your mind is craving fear
Your body is craving sugar and Netflix
Your soul is craving loving connection
Which one will you feed?

ABOUT THE AUTHOR

Tamala Ridge is the Founder and Director of the Institute for Spiritual Companioning. She is an International Number 1 Best Selling Author, Addictions Specialist and Spiritual Mentor. She empowers divine feminine healers and coaches to release their own limiting and self-sabotaging habits so they can hold space for themselves and their clients with a greater degree of integrity. She supports other Space Holders to clear their own path to success, abundance and divine sovereignty.

Her mission is to inspire others to experience Heaven on earth through the sacred art of detoxing. After her own battle with addiction she is now a self - confessed #detoxjunkie and gets off on the sobriety of her untainted soul.

She is the coach's coach, working with, challenging and inspiring spiritual entrepreneurs to become more clear, conscious and magnetic in order to increase the potency of the medicine that they bring to the world -- thereby increasing their income, impact, and influence.

Website: www.tamalaridge.com
Facebook: www.facebook.com/tamalaridge1
Email: tamala@tamalaridge.com

TARSH ASHWIN

SELLING YOUR SOUL WORK IN THE NEW EARTH ECONOMY

We are living in a pivotal time in history. We are at a crossroads of two potential timelines. One that is fed by fear and one that is fed by love.

One that heralds control and one that heralds freedom.

This is the time you've been training for. Every single modality you have studied, workshop you have attended, and personal development book you have read has prepped you for this.

Many of us have felt The New Earth calling for a long time.

If you have ever stopped to question the tradition of blindly following the status quo and instead decided to carve your own path, you have helped call in The New Earth timeline.

She is birthed by people like you. People who have cultivated the courage to live life on their own terms. People who take action on the intuitive nudges of their own heart, even in the face of societal backlash. People who yearn to live life in a more conscious and tender way.

I believe that at the forefront of this paradigm shift are the conscious and holistic entrepreneurs.

The trailblazers and visionaries who are actively challenging traditional norms. The business owners who understand that it's one thing to have an idea, and quite another to bring that idea to fruition.

Importantly, the healers, therapists, coaches, and mentors who are working on the front line, facilitating life-changing transformation as they help their clients to process old traumas, fears, and limiting beliefs so that they can release the shackles of the past and lean into love. If we are to effectively transition into The New Earth timeline, our planetary healing is an essential first step and it begins with our personal healing.

If the work you do in your business helps to facilitate this life-changing transformation, you are being called right now to step up into empowered leadership so you can share your medicine with the world.

You've probably felt this, the feeling that there's no time left to dwell in fear or to stay small and silent. Your soul mission is being activated by these world events and now is your time to step into your role as a missionary for The New Earth Timeline.

If you're feeling resonance with this, then I'd love to introduce myself. My name is Tarsh Ashwin and I guide female healers and coaches to realise the bigness of their soul mission, align their energetics and mindset with powerful strategy to grow their business, and make amazing money by sharing their medicine with the world.

I've been steadily building my business for nearly 10 years now and have had the pleasure of working with hundreds of incredibly talented female leaders and entrepreneurs who facilitate life-changing work. These women are soulful entrepreneurs. The work they do in their business is their *soul work*.

For many of these women, facilitating their transformational work comes very naturally to them. It is the marketing and sales where they struggle. This was my journey as well. I had to learn how to do business in a way that was aligned with my values and how to *soulfully* sell my services. There were old patterns, beliefs, and fears that I had to let go of before I started seeing tangible results.

I believe that we all have our unique ways of doing business and sales and that it's our responsibility to discover these ways that come naturally to us. If you want your transformative work to reach the ears and eyes of your soulmate clients, you owe it to *them* to learn how to sell your soul work. As a missionary of The New Earth timeline, this is a top priority.

THERE ARE 3 pillars that I'm going to unpack for you that have tremendously helped my clients learn how to sell their soul work:

1. *Mission:* Understand your Soul Mission + how you facilitate this in your business
2. *Model:* Learn how to map out your highest-level business model
3. *Mindset:* Cultivate a robust + resilient mindset to fortify your business in uncertain times

These 3 pillars act as powerful foundations that will help to keep you grounded as we make the transition into The New Earth. Without them, you may start to feel like a helium balloon cast adrift with nothing to anchor it.

Without them, it can be easy to let fear of the unknown and other resistance patterns kick in and keep you small. When these 3 pillars are effectively implemented, your ability to grow your business becomes easy and joyous.

1. MISSION: UNDERSTAND YOUR SOUL MISSION + HOW YOU FACILITATE THIS IN YOUR BUSINESS

If you're a soulful entrepreneur, then your business is the vehicle for your soul to express its mission and purpose.

Can you see that all of your life's experiences, negative and positive, has guided you to the transformational work you currently facilitate?

If you answered yes to the above question, then I want to invite you to witness your business through the eyes of your soul, who understands inherently the blueprint for your life. Your soul mission propels you to continue moving forward in the face of adversity. It is the overarching reason *why* you do what you do.

So - *why do you do what you do?* What compels you to get up in the morning and put effort into growing your business and serving your clients? What encourages you to speak up when you want to stay small? Be seen when you want to hide? Continue to nourish your business with your love, time, and energy, even when people tell you it's a crazy idea?

It's your soul mission and potentially it's one of the reasons why you signed up for this crazy, rollercoaster ride here on Earth. You've come here to fulfil this mission.

Articulating your soul mission and incorporating it into your messaging and marketing is a powerful way to begin the process of magnetically drawing your soulmate clients toward you. It adds depth to your content and helps to give context to your audience. It is the thing that connects your personal story with your business message.

My soul mission is to be a catalyst for planetary transformation. It is my mission to help channel some of the $80 trillion dollars that is currently circulating in the economy into the hands of conscious entrepreneurs and leaders who are spearheading this paradigm shift and who can effect change at a global level. I help my clients to understand that the more money they make, the more transformation they are facilitating. It is their responsibility to use that money wisely.

Every single time I talk about this, people reach out to me, wanting to know more about my work. It is very powerful to have a vision and enrol people in that vision.

If you're uncertain about the overarching reason *why* you do what you do, it is a top priority to uncover the answer. Answering the following questions will help you:

- What is the change you deeply desire to see in the world?
- *Why* are you so passionate about that?
- What is your highest-level vision about what's possible for your clients?
- What is the ripple effect that's possible from your transformative work?

Distilling your soul mission into a couple of sentences or paragraphs is tricky and can sometimes feel contrived; how can I put in so little words the reasons why I am here, on the planet? But I encourage you to try. It will act as your north star and be the thing that you return to when you need encouragement to keep striding forward.

2. MODEL: LEARN HOW TO MAP OUT YOUR HIGHEST-LEVEL BUSINESS + SALES MODEL

Are you aware of the highest-level transformation that you facilitate for your clients? Are you claiming it?

When it comes to the essential art of articulating the outcomes of our work, many soulful entrepreneurs sell themselves short. We can get into the habit of talking our work down and holding ourselves back from *truly claiming* our highest-level results. As a result, we may stay stuck, working in the single session model, which means that our clients don't get the full experience of our work and often don't get the best results possible.

Shifting your business model from single sessions to high-end packages has the potential to change your client's lives *and* your financial destiny. When you understand how to create transformational packages that bring the gap for your clients between problem and solution, you are effecting change at a high level. The bigger the gap, the more you can charge.

It can help to understand the Pain/Pleasure paradigm.

Your clients will generally be coming to you in some state of discomfort or pain. You'll want to understand deeply this state of pain or discomfort. What is the trigger point for them to realise they need support? How does this state of pain impact their life? What do they deeply desire to solve? What are the things keeping them awake at 3am in the morning?

On the other side of your transformative work, your clients will experience pleasure and possibility in their life. What is the vision they are working toward? What are their goals and aspirations? If you could wave a magic wand, how would they *love* their life/business/health/relationships (insert your areas of speciality here) to be? How can you help them facilitate that?

The gap between pain and pleasure is your transformational methodology. Learning how to distil your brilliance into your own unique methodology is a game changer for your business. This becomes your Intellectual Property and instantly gives you credibility, a framework to move your clients through and ample ideas for content and offers.

I've found that a transition to a higher-end package model can actually facilitate deeper transformational results. You will attract a certain calibre of client who is willing to go all in on themselves and invest at a higher level. You can be intentional about calling forth true soulmate clients (the people who are the absolute best fit for your deep work). I believe that you have a sacred contract to work with soulmate clients. When you come together to work, you are both left transformed. They are a joy to work with. They are empowered to effect change in their lives and get amazing results because of it.

3. MINDSET: CULTIVATE A ROBUST + RESILIENT MINDSET TO FORTIFY YOUR BUSINESS IN UNCERTAIN TIMES

It doesn't matter how amazing your strategy is, if your mindset isn't aligned, it means nothing. It is an essential component to growing a soulful business with ease and grace. That doesn't mean that it is *always* going to feel easy and graceful, but your ability to be resilient in the face of uncertainty is very powerful.

Business is the best personal development course you will ever take. It requires you to face and process you inner 'stuff' on an almost day-to-day basis. The process of ramping up your visibility, sales systems, and pricing *will* bring you face-to-face with your shadow, your fears, your anxieties, and your resistance patterns. It's normal; expect it to happen.

Your ability to navigate the peaks and troughs of entrepreneurialism, combined with the fear and uncertainty that is brewing in the current times, comes back to how easily you can adopt an 'evolving mindset' versus a 'survival mindset.'

Put simply: are you allowing yourself to evolve and thrive in these current times? Are you solution-oriented? Or are you getting caught up in fear and survival energy? Are you problem-oriented? This is the one difference between entrepreneurs who will make it through these times, and those who won't.

Your ability to *lead* your tribe is essential right now. True leaders show up and allow themselves to be seen. They have a mission and are a stand for effecting change. They actively cultivate *courage*, the most essential quality in business. They build community and call their tribe forward to rise into their next, great version of themselves.

This begins with your mindset.

Do you see yourself as a leader? As your tribe's most trusted advisor and go-to mentor? Are you willing to claim your genius and be the expert in your field? At the end of the day, your community is buying your confidence to deliver the outcomes you state you can facilitate. Whatever you need to do to build confidence in your work, it is essential.

You can work on cultivating a robust and resilient mindset by incorporating simple practices into your day, such as intention setting and reflective journaling, using release tools, such as EFT or the Sedona method, and being willing to have a coach that has your back, can support you through the rocky times, and be an essential sounding board for you.

Birthing The New Earth is not going to be a walk in the park. You will be challenged and tested on a weekly basis. The old patriarchal and political structures need to be released and with that we will witness the final throes of the dying political beast. Now, more than any other time in history, we need conscious leaders, healers, and coaches to step forward and guide humanity through the process.

If you would like a community of soulful women in business to support you through this process of birthing The New Earth, I'd love to extend a sacred invitation to join my free Facebook group - The Business Alchemy Collective (*www.facebook.com/groups/businessalchemycollective*)

We have regular #realife discussions about what it takes to be a soulful entrepreneur in these times. I also post weekly strategy sessions and hot-seat coaching to help you continue moving the needle forward in your business.

You are a being of infinite light and wisdom who is here for a very important reason. Your story matters. Your message matters. Your transformational work *matters*. Hold fast to your mission and continue to show up and share your medicine with the world.

Finally, remember your role as a Lightworker. In the words of Matt Kahn, '*a Lightworker is one who knows themselves as light and intentionally and purposefully shines that light for the betterment of others.*'

Don't be afraid to be the lighthouse for your soulmate clients so they can find you in these times. They're seeking your medicine.

Are you willing to be seen so they can find you?

ABOUT THE AUTHOR

Tarsh Ashwin is an International Best-Selling Author, Business Strategist, and Kinesiologist. She is also the creator of *'Business Alchemy Mastermind,'* a business ascension program for female entrepreneurs.

Tarsh specializes in guiding soulful women to grow their impact-driven business, skyrocket their income, and step into empowered leadership.

Her work is a bespoke fusion of inner mindset work, energetic transformation, and outer strategy implementation that paves the way to purposeful profit.

Tarsh's passion is to help women monetize their soul work and experience maximum impact through their deepest level service, with maximum results.

She lives in Newcastle, Australia with her partner and son.

Website: www.tarshashwin.com
Facebook: www.facebook.com/tarshashwin
and www.facebook.com/groups/405667426825846
Email: tarsh@tarshashwin.com

ABOUT AMA PUBLISHING
& ADRIANA MONIQUE ALVAREZ

"Writing a book is sacred. It's not easy, nor is it difficult. It is a holy act."
~Adriana Monique Alvarez

Being a life path number 3 means I have deep reverence for a clear vision, imagination and the joy of living. Creativity and self expression are my right and left hand.

So it makes sense that my soul thrives when I am assisting others in communicating the stories that matter to them.

As entrepreneurs, there's an added layer — our stories literally call in the people who we are meant to work with.

I am the first woman in my family to put my knowledge, experience, and wisdom in books that can be passed down through generations.

I suspect you might be a first as well.

This is a sacred calling.

It's been said that 85% of the population have the desire to write a book, but only 1% actually write and publish it.

THE MAYANS WERE A MESOAMERICAN CIVILIZATION, noted for Maya script, the only known fully developed writing system of the pre-Columbian Americas, as well as for its art, architecture, mathematical and astronomical systems.

Their writing system was made up of 800 glyphs. Some of the glyphs were pictures and others represented sounds. They chiseled the glyphs into stone and inside codices.

Codices were books that were folded like an accordion. The pages were fig bark covered in white lime and bound in jaguar skins. The Mayans wrote hundreds of these books. They contained information on history, medicine, astronomy, and their religion. The Spanish missionaries burned all but four of these books.

The Ancient Mayans were a very religious people. Mayan actions were based on rituals and ceremonies.

I HAVE BEEN ASKED to return to the rituals and ceremonies that activate and invoke the writer within those who are being asked to write and release their stories in the world right now.

The first step is leaving the distractions that keep us busy, occupied, and convinced we don't have the resources — be it time, money, or energy — to write a book.

The second step is to connect to ourselves, the book that is calling us, and those who will read it.

The third step is action that is surrounded by support.

You don't need to know how to write and publish your book.

You don't need to know how to market your book.

You don't need to know how to make money from your book.

You simply must know YOU MUST DO IT.

You must know this is not a "someday" thing.

It's a "right now, sense of urgency, surrendering to the call" thing.

JUST THREE YEARS ago I published my first book, "*Success Re-defined: Travel, Motherhood and Being the Boss.*"

That book is what launched my online business. I had been offline before that and it allowed me to get 35 wonderful clients, right off the bat. It then led to me getting featured in publications like Forbes, International Living, and The Huffington Post, and I then went on to run a program just six months later that had over 100 clients in it.

Right after that I really felt this strong urge to help women write their own book and figure out how to get featured in publications just like I had done, so I ran a program called "Instant Authority" and it was magical... it was all clicking and coming together and I had plans of running and transitioning my business to where the focus would be on books and helping women communicate in a really powerful way.

However, just a few months later I found out there were major complications with my third pregnancy and I would later go on to lose that baby.

From that point on, all I have done is put one foot in front of the other. I've done my best to show up every single day to live this life in her honor, remembering to really be present with the two children that I do have with me, to having a wonderful relationship with my husband, and to pouring my heart into my clients and my business.

It was in April, 2019 that I felt like it was time to take the stream that had went dormant and bring it back, and it was an interesting thing because I had hired a new coach at that time, and she said, "I think you should move in the direction of books, and that you should make this part of your business model."

I ran with her idea because it was the confirmation that I needed, and since that time I have sold over 50 spots in these book collaborations.

This has been an amazing journey and what I want you to know is that this is what happens when you keep following your heart and keep putting one foot in front of the other.

There are times when entrepreneurship and business and dreams in life can be all over the place, but the key is is that we stay on the path.

Sometimes I think, "Why was this two-year detour part of my journey? What was that all about?"

And what I hear is that the people who were meant to be in the books with me, they weren't in my life yet, and I was not yet the woman who was going to lead them through those difficult times.

I was forced to dig deep, I was forced to find my most authentic voice, and now it's that much sweeter.

Since I've been announcing the books, I've had a lot of men approach me who want to be in books as well.

When I was doing business consulting I was really honoring the unique differences between men and women and how I could help women through both motherhood and business and navigating that and now I'm so excited to be opening the books up to have male contributors as well.

Adriana Monique Alvarez (AMA) Publishing would love to help you tell your story too. We have helped to publish authors through our course, through our multi-author books, and as solo authors.

Here's the thing... **Your story, it's ready to be told**.

Website: *www.adrianamoniquealvarez.com*
Facebook: *www.facebook.com/AdrianaMoniqueAlvarez*
Youtube: *www.youtube.com/c/AdrianaMoniqueAlvarez*